WITHDRAWN
HARVARD LIBRARY
WITHDRAWN

This study examines the capacity of traditional Judaism to renew itself in response to the challenge of modernity. Concentrating as it does on the major Jewish Orthodox movements of the nineteenth and twentieth centuries, the book focuses especially on the Religious Kibbutz Federation in Israel, whose pioneering settlements attained a sophisticated synthesis of modern, and traditional Jewish, culture at the community level. Professor Fishman provides the first sociological study of the formation of modern Orthodox Judaism, as well as the first scholarly study of the religious kibbutz.

JUDAISM AND MODERNIZATION ON THE RELIGIOUS KIBBUTZ

JUDAISM AND MODERNIZATION ON THE RELIGIOUS KIBBUTZ

ARYEI FISHMAN

*Associate Professor of Sociology,
Bar-Ilan University*

Published by the Press Syndicate of the University of Cambridge
The Pitt Building, Trumpington Street, Cambridge CB2 1RP
40 West 20th Street, New York, NY 10011-4211, USA
10 Stamford Road, Oakleigh, Victoria 3166, Australia

© Cambridge University Press 1992

First published 1992

Printed in Great Britain at the University Press, Cambridge

A catalogue record for this book is available from the British Library

Library of Congress cataloguing in publication data

Fishman, Aryei.
[Beyn dat le-id yologiyah. English]
Judaism and modernization on the religious kibbutz/Aryei Fishman.
p. cm.
Expanded English version of: Beyn dat le-id yologiyah.
Includes bibliographical references and index.
ISBN 0 521 40388 X
1. Orthodox Judaism – Israel. 2. Orthodox Judaism – History.
3. Kibbutz ha-dati (Israel) 4. Kibbutzim – Religion. 5. Religious Zionism.
I. Title.
BM390.F57 1992
296.6′7′0956940904 – dc20   91-2135 CIP

ISBN 0 521 40388 X hardback

In memory of my beloved parents,
Leah and Shmuel Fishman

Contents

Preface	*page* xi
Introduction	1
PART ONE PROLOGUE	7
1 Conceptual and historical background	9
PART TWO THE PARENT ORTHODOX MODERNIZING MOVEMENTS	29
2 Torah-im-Derekh Eretz	31
3 Religious Zionism	46
PART THREE THE RELIGIOUS KIBBUTZ MOVEMENT	67
4 The foundations of the Religious Kibbutz Movement	69
5 Charisma and rationalization	81
6 The halakhic–socialist collective	101
7 The confrontation between *halakhah* and external reality	115
8 Between heteronomous and autonomous authority	141

Afterword	158
Appendix A The Religious Kibbutz Federation settlements	160
Appendix B About the religious kibbutz members quoted in this book	161
Appendix C Ideological periodicals referred to in book	164
Notes	165
Index	194

Preface

This is a study in the transformative capacity of traditional Jewish religious culture. I shall examine the ability of the historic Jewish religion structured around *halakhah* – Torah law – to sustain a modernizing thrust and systematically to design rational life-patterns toward the achievement of religious goals; in other words, to undergo rationalization in regard to modernization. I intend to show that within the bounds of Orthodox Judaism, traditional Jewish religion can provide vigorous mechanisms for legitimate innovation in response to modernity, as well as limit change.

The study's historical point of departure is the traditional Jewish society that preceded Jewish Emancipation. Its social agents are the major nineteenth- and twentieth-century Orthodox modernizing movements. And its main focus is a fairly small subsection of the Jewish national community of Israel: the Religious Kibbutz Federation, or RKF. In 1990 the RKF comprised seventeen kibbutzim, about six percent of the total number of collective settlements in Israel, with a population of about 8,000 souls. Yet despite their small numbers, the members of the religious kibbutzim play a significant role in Israeli society: they have enacted, and continue to enact in their daily lives, the creative tension between twentieth-century ideologies and a time-honored religious culture.

The Religious Kibbutz Federation formally came into being in 1935. The founders of the RKF were Orthodox pioneering youth, mostly of German origin, who opted for the kibbutz form of settlement as the pre-eminent route to Zionist self-realization. Drawing upon what Max Weber would have termed the "rationalizing thrust" of the major Orthodox Jewish religious modernizing movements that preceded it, but adding a new impetus, the RKF appears to have achieved the most far-reaching degree of rationalization *vis-à-vis* modern life attained by any sector of Orthodox Jewish society to date. In this process it has gone beyond its parent modernizing movements in successfully integrating universal with particular Jewish values.

The uniqueness of the RKF lies in its having formed a modern religious community patterned after the secular kibbutz, which had spearheaded modernization in the national community under the joint influences of nationalism and socialism. Born as an intentional community before World War I, the kibbutz had become institutionalized in Jewish national life in the 1920s; it had proved itself as the vanguard of Zionist pioneering in settling barren regions of Eretz Israel* and in establishing and defending the political boundaries of Jewish national society. The secular kibbutz had also developed a distinctive socialist mode of life through collective production and consumption in an egalitarian and democratic system of shared living.

The RKF, in the process of building its own self-contained settlements, developed and actualized within the Orthodox framework a religious subculture that incorporated the central values and norms of both Jewish nationalism and socialism. The efforts of the RKF pioneers to integrate a modern secular kibbutz culture grounded on ideology with a religious culture rooted in tradition, all within the virtually closed system of their communities, provide almost "laboratory" conditions for an assessment of the ability of a traditional religious culture to assimilate modern secularism. At the micro-social level, then, I see the religious kibbutz as a test case for the measure of Judaism's capacity to evolve a coherent modern religious life.

The study's theoretical framework is linked to the classical studies of Max Weber and Werner Sombart on the relationship between Judaism and modernization. Its core conceptual framework draws upon Edward Shils' theory of the "center." The religious innovators of the RKF, and of its antecedent Orthodox modernizing movements, invoked the sacred in what Shils calls the "transcendent center of the universe" to legitimate their religious thrust. In other words, they invoked Torah as religious charismatic authority. I shall show how the perception of Torah as charisma, flowing from Jewish religious tradition, enabled the Orthodox innovators to invalidate

---

* This book employs the historic Hebrew name for Palestine, *Eretz Israel* (the Land of Israel), because the name links the pre-state Jewish national community to the State of Israel and because it is a cultural as well as a geographical term in Jewish religious life.

accepted religious elements and create new ones in their stead, thereby rendering Torah a constituent element of institution building. And I shall analyze the interplay between religion and ideology in these innovators' invocation of the sacred, and in their building of new religious systems.

In writing about these systems I have drawn chiefly upon primary sources. In the case of the RKF these sources include: publications of the religious–pioneering youth movements in Germany, eastern Europe, and Eretz Israel; the central periodicals of the RKF; the bulletins of the individual religious kibbutzim; and pamphlets and books written by leading ideologues of the religious kibbutz movement.

The span of years to which I have given closest attention extends from the RKF's embryonic phase in the 1920s to about 1960, when the rationalizing thrust of the RKF had leveled off, and to the spillover of that thrust. Viewed from the perspective of the early 1990s – a time of resurgent traditionalism within Israel's Orthodox Jewry – those pioneering decades stand out in bold relief for their innovative religious endeavor.

Part I of this volume explores the nature of Torah as religious charisma, and the relationship between religion and ideology. Against the background of traditional Jewish society, this section also introduces the Jewish modernizing movements that set the scene for our discussion. Part II presents the RKF's parent Orthodox modernizing movements that helped inform its religious ideology. Part III discusses the formation of the RKF and the relationship between charisma and rationalization in the RKF experience; it then considers religious rationalization at the symbolic ideational level, the motivational–commitment level, and the normative level. This section concludes with a discussion of the conflict between the major reference groups of the religious kibbutz movement, as reflected in the tension in the movement's identity between its charismatic and traditional authority.

In its first incarnation this book was a doctoral dissertation that was submitted to The Hebrew University in Jerusalem in 1976. In its second, it was published in Hebrew by Yad Yitzhak Ben-Zvi in Israel, in 1990, under the title of *Beyn Dat Le-Idyologiyah*. The English edition constitutes an expanded version of the Hebrew; it was given its basic shape when I was on sabbatical leave at Harvard University in 1988, within the framework of the Center for Jewish Studies and the Department of Sociology. I deeply thank Professor Isadore Twersky, Director of the Center for Jewish Studies, for his warm interest in the work.

I wish to express my gratitude to my teachers and mentors who contributed directly and indirectly to the development of this study: Professors Ozer Schild and R. J. Zwi Werblowsky, under whose encouraging guidance I wrote my dissertation; Professor Shmuel N. Eisenstadt, whose teachings are widely reflected in the work and who kindly commented on its final version; Professor Jacob Katz, whose writings on pre- and post-Emancipation Judaism constitute a social–historical backdrop for this study; and the late Professor Yonina Talmon, who first introduced me to the sociology of religion and of the kibbutz.

In the various stages of its preparation the book benefited from the advice and critical remarks of Professors Mordechai Breuer, Eric Cohen, Moshe Greenberg, Charles Liebman, Ezra Mendelsohn and Ann Swidler. It has also profited from the incisive comments of several anonymous readers for Cambridge University Press. Tzvi Tzameret, Director of Yad Yitzhak Ben-Zvi, took a personal interest in the work and was helpful in various ways. The Secretariat of the Religious Kibbutz Federation extended all the assistance that I requested from it. Eliezer Goldman, of Sdei Eliyahu, with whom I discussed various sociological aspects of religious kibbutz life over the years, joined Dov Rappel, of Yavne, in contributing "oral history" to Chapter 7. Yaakov Tzur of Ein Ha-Natziv, Lippah Aharoni, Yehudah Barth and Mikhah Rosenthaler of Saad and, especially, Efrayim Ya'ir of Tirat Tzvi, were also generous in their co-operation. I am very grateful to one and all.

It is a pleasure to acknowledge the editorial assistance which enriched the English manuscript in various stages of its preparation. I was fortunate in obtaining the editorial services of Jay Howland, who conscientiously devoted herself to improving the fluency and organization of the basic version. Priscilla B. Fishman, who has been a faithful partner in my academic endeavors, unstintingly worked to improve a later draft. I also wish to acknowledge the contribution of Naomi Schneider to the enhancement of the text. For secretarial assistance I am thankful to Hadassah R. Raab and Esther Herskowitz, and for practical assistance to Nurit Fishman.

I owe special thanks to Alex Wright, my editor at Cambridge

University Press, for his helpful guidance in the preparation of the final version of the manuscript, and for seeing it through to production. I am further grateful to G. E. Turner for her meticulous copy-editing.

My thanks go as well to the librarians and archivists of the following research institutions: the Jewish National and University Library, the Religious Zionist Archives at Mosad HaRav Kook, and the Central Zionist Archives – all in Jerusalem. I am especially grateful for the invaluable assistance of the archivists of the Central RKF Archives at Yavne, as well as of the individual kibbutz archives of Yavne, Tirat Tzvi, Sdei Eliyahu, and the Sons of the Etzion Bloc Association.

Finally, I wish to record my thanks to The Lucius L. Littauer Foundation for funding the preparation of the English edition, and to The Memorial Foundation for Jewish Culture for supporting the writing of the first version of this study.

Jerusalem,
Israel

Introduction

> Rational religion is religion whose beliefs and rituals have been reorganized with the aim of making it the central element in a coherent ordering of life – an ordering which shall be coherent both in respect to the elucidation of thought and in respect to the direction of conduct towards a unified purpose commanding ethical approval...
>
> Rational religion appeals to the direct intuition of special occasions, and to the elucidatory power of its concepts for all occasions. It arises from that which is special, but extends to what is general.
>
> Alfred North Whitehead, *Religion in the Making*

RELIGION AND MODERNIZATION

Rationalization is immanent in man's intellectual urge to understand the world as a meaningful cosmos through symbolic ideational patterns, and to take a unified stance toward it through patterns of norms and value-orientations.[1] According to Talcott Parsons, "Every sharp break with traditionalism involves rationalization, for the breaker of tradition is by his very act forced to define his attitudes towards that with which he has broken."[2]

The need to rationalize Judaism in relation to modernization arose in Orthodox Jewry in response to Jewish Enlightenment and Emancipation of the nineteenth century. For it was when these two movements opened the world at large to the Jewish people that Judaism was pressured to justify participation in the general cultural and social life, after being turned inward toward its traditional past for many generations.[3] This is when Orthodox Jews broke partially, but consciously, with the traditional world and sought to extend the range of their religious values by reappraising the Jewish place and duties within the modern world.

Ideologues of the Orthodox modernizing movements sought to reconcile modern culture with tradition by drawing upon mechanisms of change within traditional religious culture; in other words, upon Torah in the sense of religious charisma.[4] The charismatic breakthroughs that they precipitated – under such slogans as "Torah and civic life" and "Torah and labor" – had to be rationalized before they could be consolidated into new symbolic patterns to legitimate cultural and social change.[5] By integrating their view of the world within the perspective of Torah, these ideologues were able to crystallize a modern Orthodox identity.

The classic case of religious rationalization in relation to modernization – which may be defined as the process of systematic social change whereby people continually increase their knowledge of, and control over, their environment through rational means – is that of the Protestant ethic, as expounded by Max Weber.[6] According to Weber, the Calvinist stream of Protestantism played a crucial role in the breakthrough of European society to modernity, by replacing the medieval perception of God as demanding that humankind adapt itself to the existing world, with the idea that it was God's will that man should labor in the world so as to establish the Kingdom of God. By redefining the sacred, Calvinism fostered a religious ethic of world transformation based on self-control, rationalism, self-awareness, and an impulse toward activism. This, in turn, created a new channel of salvation divested of spiritual and mystical dimensions.

Although Weber focused his investigation on the nascent rational capitalist system that underwent consolidation in the seventeenth and eighteenth centuries, his overall intention was to show how the Protestant ethic promoted the rational aspects of modernization – science, technology, and the bureaucratic systems that were also becoming established in that period – and reinforced their transformative thrust.

While Weber's study of the Protestant ethic was concerned with religion as a driving force behind modernization, later study – which has greatly expanded since the 1950s – examines the ability of traditional religions both to sustain and to advance it.[7] It is within these parameters that we shall examine Judaism.

Shmuel Eisenstadt expanded upon Weber's thesis in relation to traditional religious cultures. In his analysis of the linkage between the development of Protestantism and the consolidation of modern institutions, Eisenstadt identified four elements that can be seen as enhancing the ability of religious culture to undergo rationalization in respect to modern life. These elements, which Eisenstadt calls "transformative capacities,"[8] enable cultures to undergo inner change and then to legitimate modern symbols, roles, and institutions. The first two elements are implied in the Protestant ethic: (1) the culture must be capable of cultivating individuals with a developed self-awareness and sense of personal responsibility; (2) these individuals must be able to act in the world under the inspiration of a transcendent religious worldview where the religion is divested of mystical and ritual elements; then (3), the religion must be one that grants its adherents freedom to redefine the sacred without relying on institutions that mediate between the individuals and the divine; and (4) it must consider openness to the greater social world as legitimate. Eisenstadt implies that the more a traditional religious culture possesses these four qualities, the greater will be its ability to sustain modern life.

How these transformative capacities can be applied to modern ideological systems is of special interest to the potential of Judaism to undergo rationalization. Nationalism, socialism, and liberalism constitute the principal vehicles of modernization.[9] The combination of nationalism and socialism – which occurs in the kibbutz – is one of the most powerful motivational forces for directed social change; socialism and liberalism are important elements in the traditional culture's capacity to absorb the Western ethos of progress as a source of both motivation and legitimation of social change.[10]

JUDAISM AND MODERNIZATION

The capacity of traditional Jewish culture to sustain modernization has not yet been systematically assessed by sociologists. While classic studies by Werner Sombart (1911) and Max Weber (in the second decade of this century) hint at the close connection between historical Jewish religious culture and the rise of modern capitalism, these studies deal with the pre-Emancipation period, and their conclusions have not been examined in the light of modern Jewish reality.

In his analysis of rabbinic culture, Sombart concludes that the Jewish ethic, thanks to its central legal component, is strikingly similar to, and fosters the same value-orientations as, the Protestant ethic. He views the commandments of the Torah – or *mitzvot* (divine precepts) – as leading the Jew to subdue and control his natural feelings in order to rationalize the world through a religious perspective. According to Sombart, it was Judaism rather than Protestantism which provided the religious impulse for rational capitalism that paved the way for the evolution of the modern world.[11] Indeed, Weber viewed biblical Judaism (which preceded rabbinic Judaism) as having made the cultural breakthrough that eventually led to modernization.[12] According to him, this arose from two characteristics of the Jewish world view: (1) the perception that the world was created *ex nihilo* and would be transformed in the messianic era, and (2) the view that the relationship to God and His world is grounded in man's duty to observe religious precepts in his everyday life. By differentiating between man and the world and conceiving the world historically, the first perception allowed for the possibility that the world can be changed, and by focusing on the divine precepts to be performed in the mundane world, the religious perception of the world was divested of magic. The concept that religious salvation can be attained through everyday activity was specifically expressed in the Sinaitic revelation and was enlarged upon by the prophets, who presented God as a deity who demands moral activity in the world, in order to perfect the world in accordance with a universal legal order. The prophets thereby created the world-rationalizing mode of salvation.

Although Weber accepted the general thrust of Sombart's thesis – that rabbinic Judaism fosters a rational ethic – he rejected Sombart's contention that the Jews created modern capitalism. He denied that rabbinic Judaism implied the systematic self-control capable of supporting a religious ethic that could lead to the creation of capitalism, and "above all," he argued, rabbinic Judaism lacked the motivation to create a new economic system.[13] The Jewish people, according to Weber, were a "pariah people" who segregated themselves from the rest of the world during the rise of capitalism; they shifted the biblical focus of salvation from the human action that might transform the world, to the meticulous observance of the commandments, through which the world would be transformed by a divinely ordained miraculous act: the advent of the Messiah. According to Weber, then, rabbinic Judaism repressed the ethos of world transformation.

This book will demonstrate the reopening of Judaism's world-rationalizing path of salvation. For, by carrying the Weberian theoretical perspective a step further, it can be argued that when Emancipation dissolved the segregation of Jewish society from universal society, it enabled Judaism to re-establish its link with the world and thereby revive its biblical transformative ethos. And once this ethos was restored, Judaism proved eminently capable of assimilating the idea of progress. Following the analyses of both Sombart and Weber, modern Jewish Orthodoxy can be shown to nurture an autonomous, self-aware person who is motivated to transform the world through everyday activity, governed by self-discipline and a rational orientation. Indeed, in regard to Judaism's ability to foster a systematic ethic through self-control, Sombart's view seems to be borne out.

I further intend to demonstrate how Orthodox Jewish culture allows for individuals and groups to develop new religious symbols and reinterpret the religious culture according to the values of the present, without the need for institutionalized religious authority. Indeed, we shall see how the central position of *halakhah*, or Torah law, in the religious culture allows Judaism to undergo far-reaching rationalization. We shall also see, however, how the ritual aspect of religious law curbs the momentum of modernization.

Judaism's potential for modernization, as pre-eminently manifest in the RKF, will be analyzed at the three levels, or spheres, of rationalization that Talcott Parsons enumerates.[14] These levels, that were central to the breakthrough of Orthodox Judaism into modern life as they were to the breakthrough of the Protestant ethic, are:

1. The symbolic–ideational level, at which rationalization involves creating a systematic, lucid, and coherent worldview.
2. The motivational–commitment level, which involves cultivating religious value-orientations that co-ordinate with the orientations of modern – particularly economic – activities and thereby link the ethos of world mastery with a life based on methodical conduct.
3. The normative level, which involves establishing a hierarchical pattern for both religious and secular norms that is directed towards systematizing all behavior into one unified ethical pattern in the service of God.

A second theme in this study relates to the religious ideologies created by the Orthodox modernizing movements. Both religion and ideology endow human life with meaning and identity; the boundaries between the two, however, tend to become blurred.[15] Characteristics that differentiate religion and ideology, and their general relationship as they integrate into a unified meaningful system, will also be considered.

To sum up: an underlying theme of this study is the impulse of the Orthodox Jew to co-ordinate his religious consciousness and his rationalizing drive as a result of traditional Judaism's opening up to the modern world. Each of these components thrusts towards existential unity from a different direction. Religious consciousness, inspired by transcendent reality, seeks to encompass all realms of value-bearing existence within its orbit, in terms of charismatically-inspired Torah. The rationalizing drive, deriving from the immediate intellectual urge of the Orthodox Jew to order reality meaningfully, seeks to objectify the values of the renewed religious consciousness and build a modern life under their guidance; this involves elaborating Torah in accordance with the three levels of rationalization enumerated above.

The existential–phenomenological perspective which regards human consciousness as its field of research is the method of inquiry best suited to our inquiry.[16] Since the data most relevant to us are the thoughts of people who expressed their religious responses to their experiential situations in writing, we use their own words to learn about the ways their consciousness traversed in their quest for existential order.

PART ONE

Prologue

CHAPTER I

Conceptual and historical background

The goal of the pioneering communities established by the Religious Kibbutz Federation – to give "rebirth" to the Torah on a community level – involved a confrontation between two modes of religious charisma: an innovative religious consciousness, and institutionalized religious elements, especially elements of *halakhah*. In the words of a participant in the RKF experience, this was a confrontation between

> two main aspirations latent in the premise of a pioneering religious movement: a dynamic, which impels towards active creation through a revolt against the accepted and the sacred, and spiritual submission, which demands the preservation of the extant, of the sacred in religious tradition.[1]

By integrating modern ideological elements and traditional religion operationally, in the process of building its pioneering communities, the RKF sought to outstrip the rationalization of religion attained by the modernizing Orthodox movements that preceded it. And, indeed, the RKF kibbutzim seem to have reached the farthest inner limit of the rationalization process.

In this chapter, I shall explore the nature of religious charisma in general and the spontaneous charisma that was used in the RKF; survey traditional Jewish society and the changes that followed Emancipation; and set the scene for discussing the modern religious–ideological Orthodox movements that culminated in the RKF.

THE TRANSCENDENT CENTER AND CHARISMA

According to Edward Shils, the "vital layer of reality" in the transcendent sphere of human experience derives its vitality from the "center of the universe." He perceives this transcendent center as the "locus of the sacred," the source of order in all existence, human as well as cosmic, and the bearer of ultimate authority.[2] Man, in his effort to fulfill his natural aspiration for a meaningful life, turns to a transcendent order for inspiration and guidance; he draws upon the vitality of the transcendent center, in its manifestation as charisma, to order his existence.[3] But the charisma that orders human existence may be either spontaneous and intensive, or institutionalized and regulated by routine.

Spontaneous or primeval charisma manifests itself in situations of extreme cultural change and social disintegration, when accepted symbols and norms are no longer sufficient to sustain human existence from either the cognitive–meaningful or the practical standpoint. It is at such times of tension, chaos, blurring of identity, and even anomy, that those who are disoriented by the upheaval are attracted by the message of charismatic personalities, who are animated with a sense of power and mission by the sacred vitality that emanates from transcendent reality to reorder existence.

On an individual level, the innovative ideology presented by the charismatic personality provides the disoriented with a new symbolic order, that reintegrates their worldview and builds a bridge between transcendent and earthly reality. As individuals experience and express transcendence unitedly by their common use of the new ideological symbols, the value-content of these symbols becomes part of their conscious "objective" reality.[4]

On the collective level, the charismatic personality strives to order experience by directing the building of a new social order in accordance with, and under the inspiration of, the vision of the transcendent order. By casting primeval charisma into new social norms and roles that allow the individuals to fulfill themselves through a new social dimension, the charisma is transferred to social institutions. The new social order then strengthens the "objective" validity of the symbolic order by establishing what Berger and Luckmann call a "plausibility structure"[5] for it. In other words, the charismatic message recrystallizes the identity of the disoriented in accordance with their place in the new worldview, and their social role within the realization of the transcendent vision.

Whereas spontaneous activity characterizes the personality infused with primeval charisma, institutionalized charisma stabilizes the new social order by routinizing the activity of those who occupy the roles in which the charisma has been cast. When the new social norms become institutionalized, they compress activity that bears the stamp of the primeval charismatic message into defined, fixed patterns. Just as pure charisma may express spontaneous sacredness, so institutionalized charisma may express a sacredness that has crystallized in cultural and social elements or even in an independent social order. But these elements may also become sanctified as they become the contents of tradition, and thus directly connected with the sacred, at the center of the universe.[6]

Once charisma has been institutionalized, existence is ordered by a social center, consisting pre-eminently of cultural and political elites who are imbued with authority by public recognition of the legitimacy of their central roles.[7] The cultural elite or center is then perceived as interpreting the sacred to the rest of society, enabling them to partake of it, usually through institutionalized patterns. The political elite or center leads and regulates the social order in a defined geographical territory under the general guidance of the ultimate values.

However, charisma has a dialectical nature in that its force can both build and destroy. In the words of Shmuel Eisenstadt:

> This charismatic fervor is rooted in the attempt to come into contact with the very essence of being, to go to the very roots of existence, of cosmic, social and cultural order, to what is seen as sacred and fundamental. But this attempt may also contain a strong disposition to sacrilege: to the denial of the validity of the sacred, and what is accepted in any given society as sacred.[8]

Thus, when the validity of a society's accepted symbols and norms weakens, charismatic groups may serve as new cultural centers by creating a fresh, direct channel to the sacred, through which they claim authority to redefine sacredness. The enthusiasm of such groups melts down the institutions in which crystallized sacredness has resided and inspires values for building new institutions, and even a new social order, that are perceived as more valid and true than the routinized institutions or order. Those who are attracted to the charismatic message then become committed to the new cultural center, which presents a fresh path to salvation.

TORAH AS CHARISMA

The transcendent center of Jewish religious existence is identified with God, the giver of the Torah at Mount Sinai. It is through

Torah that Jews seek to know and worship God, according to the two coexistent modes of Sinaitic revelation: Written and Oral Torah. The former was given explicitly at Sinai and is embodied in the Pentateuch; Oral Torah, implicitly given at Sinai, is enfolded within the Written Torah. The succinct Midrashic statement, "Whatever a veteran scholar is destined to innovate was revealed to Moses at Sinai" (*Midrash Rabbah*, Leviticus 22:1), patently indicates the Sinaitic ethos in relation to new formulations of Torah. Oral Torah is extensively manifest in talmudic literature, the broad base for the elaboration of the Torah as a religious culture.[9]

The solid core of Torah is *halakhah*, a body of legal precepts, *mitzvot*, that both regulate the conduct between man and man – in the ethical, civil and criminal domains – and define man's ritualistic relations toward God. "The sages of *halakhah* in every generation" authoritatively interpret the Pentateuch's precepts in the form of Oral Law – the legal component of Oral Torah – according to logical hermeneutical rules.[10] Both the rules and the authoritative interpretation of the Law derive from Sinai. The Torah also comprises *aggadah*, a body of parables, homilies and other types of symbolic systems that amplify the non-legal portions of Scripture and order the Jewish worldview. While the precepts of *halakhah* possess absolute validity, and their interpretation is subject to specific rules and institutionalized authority, the symbolic systems of *aggadah* are not normatively binding, and their development is not subject to defined rules. These two spheres influence each other; not only may new symbols be created to provide a perspective for the defined norms of *halakhah*, as in the search for "the rationale behind the *mitzvot*,"[11] but new religious symbols may also influence the establishment of new religious laws.[12]

But Torah in Jewish religious life also assumes the character of charisma, that is, Torah as a synonym for God who is the root of the world order and the source of primeval power. Early expressions of these meanings are found in the *aggadah* and were expanded in the mystical literature of *kabbalah*, where Torah is conceived as primordial "divine vitality," or the metaphysical essence that sustains the cosmic order; as primordial "creative power" deriving from God.[13] In the language of midrashic commentary, Torah is "the working tool of the Holy One." The sixteenth-century Rabbi Judah Loew of Prague called Torah "the order of God."[14] In short, Torah, the master plan according to which the world was created when it was removed from chaos, delineates the true existential order of Jewish society.

Within this conceptual framework, Sinaitic revelation constitutes the most distinctively charismatic experience of the Jewish people. For it was at Sinai that divine vitality was bestowed upon the people, absorbed into its consciousness, and captured in the symbolic and normative patterns that direct a religious ordering of life. Thus the precepts of Written Torah are the religious patterns in which primeval charisma crystallized as an expressed imprint of God's order in the world. And within the perception of Sinai the formulation of precepts within the framework of Oral Torah constitutes an expression of primeval religious charisma. In fact, in Jewish religious thought, expressions of the relevance of Torah to changing social reality imply the institutionalization of spontaneous human creation in the development of religious culture.[15]

Indeed, talmudic literature delineates the invocation of Torah as the source of order and authority when a religious order breaks down. In such a case, Torah can even activate the authority to impugn the validity of crystallized religious elements, including institutionalized precepts, and to create new religious norms and institutions. This dialectical character of Torah is poignantly expressed with regard to the breaking of the tablets at Mount Sinai: "There are times that the suppression of Torah is its foundation ... The Holy One ... said to Moses, 'Thou didst well to break the tablets.' "[16]

In our discussion of the RKF, we shall encounter the verse, "there are times when the suppression of Torah is its foundation," along with others that express the same radical meaning: "It is time to act for the Lord, for they have violated your Torah"; "And you shall live by them"; "The court may make a provision uprooting a matter in the Torah by way of direction to 'sit and do not act' and 'arise and act.' "[17] Indeed, latent hints concerning this aspect of Torah were embedded in some of the Orthodox modernizing movements that preceded the RKF, for example, the phrase "the holy rebellion," or allusions to "the sacred" as a source of religious innovation. In situations of crisis in the Jewish religious existential order, then, this two-edged charismatic meaning of Torah finds expression in the redefinition of sacredness.

The builders of the cultural system of the RKF were explicitly aware of the first two of the following three meanings of Torah:[18]

(1) Torah as a religious transcendent order that is charged with primeval charisma, as in the expression "the intention of the Torah"; (2) Torah as institutionalized charisma residing in the symbols and norms of institutionalized religious culture, but also, as we shall see, in established social roles and institutions; (3) Torah as primeval charisma invoked when ordering a disrupted Jewish existence. It follows that religious consciousness – the consciousness that perceives itself as knowing the will of God – can view Torah as charisma either innovatively or conservatively,[19] depending upon which of the two meanings of Torah is accepted.

A final manifestation of Torah as charisma that concerns our discussion is in the socio–religious order based on *halakhah*, which was designated at Sinai as a sacred community and as a vehicle for action in history.[20] In this respect, every *kehillah* (local community) is regarded as embodying the Jewish people. Through the interlocking in social roles of its members, the Jewish community creates a *sui generis* religious–cultural reality that could not be created by individual experience. In other words, the community embodies Torah by virtue of the religious charisma that resides in its institutions.

TRADITIONAL JEWISH SOCIETY

Traditional Jewish society that existed until nineteenth-century Emancipation[21] dissociated itself from universal society and its institutions and confined its meaningful world within particularistic boundaries. It was organized within self-governing local Jewish communities, restricted to ghettos, which embraced almost every facet of their members' lives. Jews were distinguished by their language and dress, and while the general society regarded them as strangers in their midst and limited their occupations to trade and money-lending, the Jews saw themselves as mere sojourners in their countries of residence, waiting for God to send the Messiah to return them to their land.

This segregation from the peoples of the world was justified from an internal Jewish standpoint by the status of the Jews as a chosen people, the bearers of the Torah. The symbols of the Torah, the source of Judaism's worldview and its ethos, saturated Jewish society and gave it its identity in the world as well as an internal unity, despite the fact that it was dispersed among the nations of the world and lacked central political institutions. The Torah symbols were nurtured by the Talmud-centered educational system in particular.

Halakhah played a crucial role in maintaining this unity. For *halakhah*, spanning all geo-political boundaries, was "the backbone of Jewish life in its entirety,"[22] the focus around which the institutions of the social order had to organize. To be sure, *halakhah* did not remain static. In every generation, rabbinical authority produced new formulations to manage new situations. But since the traditionalism of the society discouraged change, Jewish society's awareness of this change was slight.

Traditionalism engulfed awareness of the present in its awareness of the past; the present derived the essence of its religious meaning from its continuity with the immediate past. Traditionalism also gave customs that became institutionalized, a status of sacredness, of "Torah."[23] In short, the whole Jewish social order bore the imprint of Torah by virtue of its traditionalism. This traditionalistic orientation indicates the integrative strength of the conservative component of the religious consciousness, which perceives God as the conserver and maintainer of values. The conception of the will of God as fixed strengthened the validity of the social order in its entirety.[24]

The cultural center of the traditional order was embodied in the Rabbinate. The authority of the Rabbinate as an institution for interpreting the Torah was anchored in tradition, and expressed the charisma of revelation in its routinized form in defined roles.[25]

Despite the pre-eminently religious character of the traditional order, however, Jews perceived their existence as defective. In fact, the consciousness of *galut* (exile) that marred their sense of belonging to the world intensified in the wake of the messianic ferment of the Sabbatean movement in the latter half of the seventeenth century.[26] This sense of *galut* was to serve as a fulcrum for transforming the Jewish existential order.

Indeed, beneath the surface of the institutionalized social order within the framework of *halakhah*, as well as in the interstices between institutions, mystical religious currents flowed from cultural sub-centers that could serve as catalysts for wide cultural and social change.[27] These kabbalistic subcenters, which stressed Torah as primeval divine vitality, gained heightened status in the sixteenth century from the Lurianic Kabbalah, whose symbols presented the cosmic order in terms of a tension between exile and redemption. Lurianic Kabbalah interpreted the thirteenth-century *Zohar*'s pronouncement that "there is no awakening above unless there is awakening below" to mean that man can hasten redemption by means of his own actions, by perfecting his inner life.

Kabbalistic symbols did not disappear from the consciousness of traditional society after the Sabbatean outburst had subsided. Instead, they began to spread, taking root in the mid-eighteenth century in large groups of traditional East European Jews in the form of the Hassidic movement. Thus, just as the traditional order was about to disintegrate in Western Europe, religious mysticism in Eastern Europe was fostering new social patterns for quickening the individual- and group-affinity with God. If awareness of exile was the fulcrum for the transformation of the Jewish existential order, then the strengthening of mystical symbolism prepared the ground for legitimating this transformation within the framework of traditional Judaism. Indeed, according to Gershom Scholem, the Sabbatean movement was the origin of the changed perception of the traditional existential order that eventually brought about the rise of Jewish Enlightenment.[28]

This brief survey of the traditional Jewish order concludes with a note on the religious nature of Jewish solidarity. This solidarity originated primarily from the Jews' mutual responsibility in observing the divine precepts "as those who were ordered when standing at Mount Sinai, to observe the commandments,"[29] and secondarily, it derived from the divine sacredness with which the entire Jewish people was endowed at Mount Sinai, solidarity that was expressed in the belief that the Jewish people bears a collective responsibility *vis-à-vis* the nations of the world. Halakhic authorities throughout the ages were divided over the question whether those who divested themselves of the authority of the divine precepts were still to be considered Jewish; insofar as such people were awarded Jewish solidarity, it was on the basis of the second derivation.[30]

EMANCIPATION AND THE ZIONIST MOVEMENT

The traditional Jewish order crumbled in the wake of Emancipation, with the opening of the boundaries of traditional society in Western Europe and the invalidation of Jewish communities' halakhic infrastructure by the state.[31] Jews entered the life of general society as citizens of their states, and cultivated a self-awareness guided by new, mainly secular–ideological, cultural centers, each of which inspired its own charismatic message.

Two principal new secular cultural centers, the Jewish Enlightenment and Zionism, are relevant to our discussion. Each sought to reorder Jewish existence and Jewish identity by encouraging participation in a "full and complete life" within the political order of a modern national state.

The Jewish Enlightenment originated in western Europe toward the end of the eighteenth century under the direct influence of West European Enlightenment. Without attempting to define the transcendent center of the new movement, we note that it contained a strong deist component that spurred the radical transformation of Jewish culture by divesting Torah of its fundamental status in Jewish life, invalidating the central status of the religious precepts, and encouraging a selective approach to their observance; at the same time the Jewish Enlightenment's transcendent center inspired secular values that tended to integrate the newly emancipated Jew into the life of general society.

Jewish Enlightenment regarded the ghetto Jew as deficient in the human component of his being, and encouraged the development of the universal dimension of the Jew's new identity. It accordingly fostered the view that Jews were citizens with equal rights in a humanistic, rational society, participating fully in the occupational structure and, under the inspiration of shared ultimate values, enjoying solidarity with the non-Jewish population in the progression towards an enlightened future. The fraternal and egalitarian ideals of the French Revolution further nurtured this view. The Reform Movement newly emerging in Judaism, which annulled the religious validity of *halakhah* and the halakhically ordered community that had undergirded Jewish life in favor of beliefs and opinions borne by individuals,[32] gave religious legitimation to the new Jewish existential order.

Zionism originated at the end of the nineteenth century under the influence of European nationalism and of the Enlightenment. Created, however, as a counter-reaction to the latter, Zionism's premise was that the continuity of the Jewish people could not be maintained within the institutional framework of the European national state, once universal society was open to them.[33] To ensure that continuity, it sought to restore the collective dimension to

Jewish life through the establishment of a sovereign, modern Jewish society. Such a society would restore the unity of Jewish life by developing a national culture infused with universal values. Although Zionism drew its national symbols from traditional Jewish religious culture, it cast them into secular European patterns. Zionism expressed a secular transmutation of the religious messianic ideal by seeking an immediate realization of national redemption, and it articulated the Jewish people's conscious link with history by perceiving the national collective as a vehicle for shaping Jewish destiny. But this collective was also perceived in terms of the universal dimension of the Jewish messianic vision, that is, as an instrument for world transformation within the perspective of West European progress.

THE NATIONAL PIONEERING MOVEMENT AND ITS KIBBUTZ CENTER

The dialectical power of the charisma of the Zionist movement found its most distinctive expression in its secular stream, which displaced the traditional transcendent center of God primarily with a national entity,[34] but also with a universal–humanistic one. This new source of charisma kindled the national pioneering movement, which crystallized in Eretz Israel within Socialist Zionism in the decade preceding the First World War.

From the beginning, the "ideological primary groups" of the pioneering movement possessed a direct affinity with the transcendent center of the secular Zionist universe – as Me'ir Yaari put it, an affinity with "the God of Jewish history and the God of mankind."[35] Fired by revolutionary fervor, these groups redefined the sacred "out of the conflagration of the former values."[36] And coining the pejorative term *"galuti"* (exilic) to denote ghetto mentality and proscribed behavior, they rejected the traditional Jewish order as degraded by servitude and "abnormality" in its economic structure, and expressed "rebirth" by divesting themselves of their *galut* identity in favor of a new Jewish–human identity, forged in physical labor and rooted in the soil. "Self-labor" constituted a watchword of the pioneering groups. Indeed, they perceived their role as being fraught with the transcendent vitality of charisma; by establishing the infrastructure of a renascent Jewish society, they were fulfilling a mission of "the God of Jewish history."[37] And, insofar as they aimed to establish a model of a perfected human society, they also viewed themselves as fulfilling a mission of "the God of mankind."

The heart of the pioneer movement was the kibbutz movement, whose society expressed realization of transcendent reality in both the national and socialist spheres. For before the national community won political sovereignty, kibbutz society had developed a micro-cosmic, national social order. In this micro-society, the means of production were centrally concentrated, equality was established, members were able to participate intensively in political institutions, women were "liberated," and technological innovation was institutionalized. As kibbutz movement leader, Kaddish Luz, put it: "Socialist Zionism is a blend of nationalist messianism and social messianism. If there is any hope for the establishment of the vision of the millennium, then it is possible to realize it in our lifetime."[38]

By integrating its socialist structure with the national vision the kibbutz acquired a charisma of its own. For by systematically organizing members' roles in practical rational patterns, the central authority of the kibbutz effectively placed an entire pioneering community in the service of national revival. This was markedly evident in the central economic sphere of pioneering activity, wherein the kibbutz constituted the spearhead in the transformation of Jewish reality. The kibbutz became an efficient production unit thanks to the high degree of political rationalization of its socialist collectivity; the centralized authority controlled and systematically organized the means of production, including the economic roles of the members. And in accordance with a value-orientation pattern of self-control, rationalism, and a drive to practical action,[39] the kibbutz fostered a dynamic ethos with regard to nature on both the national and socialist levels: "to subjugate it, to enslave it to our wills, to our ends." It was through the readiness of the individual member to exercise self-discipline and place himself in his pioneering role at the disposal of the collective – that is, to rationalize his life in the service of national revival – that he could "realize" himself on the path to salvation.[40]

When the Orthodox pioneers sought to establish their own religious kibbutz movement in the early 1930s, they related to the secular pioneering movement, particularly its kibbutz component, as a cultural center and reference group – from which they derived their standards of conduct. Communal life, self-labor, settlement of the land, self-defense, technological progress, intensive economic activity, a new Jewish–human identity, and cultural renewal – all these values that were central to the secular kibbutzim – became central in the religious kibbutz movement as well, and called for realization in national micro-societies.

However, in the case of the RKF, Orthodox Jewry was also a reference group for the founders of the movement, and the traditional Rabbinate also constituted a cultural center. Although the traditional Jewish order in Europe had largely disintegrated by the early 1930s, there was a large subsociety that remained faithful to the traditional culture. A considerable sector of West European Jewry continued to observe personal religious precepts, to recognize the traditional religious authority of the Rabbinate, and even to maintain a religious community revolving around the synagogue, the family, and to some extent the school.[41] In Eastern Europe, where the majority of Orthodox Jewry (and of Jewish society as a whole) lived, and Emancipation had arrived later than in the West, religious Jewry continued to maintain – albeit tenuously – the broad institutional frame of the traditional order. And although most of the founders of the RKF came from Germany, the great majority of religious Jews living in Eretz Israel in the 1930s and 1940s had come from Eastern Europe, and the country's Rabbinate was largely embedded in the symbolic order of traditional society.

Hence the problem of the RKF in building its pioneering communities: it had to work out the operational integration of a radical, rational, secular ideology into a traditional religion. While the RKF drew upon new religious values of earlier Orthodox modernizing movements (Torah-im-Derekh Eretz and Religious Zionism), the fact that, since the end of the eighteenth century, halakhic adjudication had hardly recognized the institutional changes in Jewish life and, what is more, that the Rabbinate in Eretz Israel showed little sensitivity to these changes, made integration highly problematic.

THE ENCOUNTER BETWEEN RELIGION AND IDEOLOGY

While the Torah-im-Derekh Eretz (literally "Torah and civic life") movement arose in Germany in the middle of the nineteenth century, when the social–institutional structure of traditional Jewish life had all but decomposed, Religious Zionism took shape within East European Jewry at the end of the nineteenth and beginning of the twentieth centuries, when the disintegration of the traditional structure was still actively underway. Although the *raison d'être* of both movements was the search for rational means to ensure the continuity of traditional religious culture and of Orthodox Jewry faithful to that culture, the underlying rationale for their formation was an internal, religious one: the desire to sustain meaningfully post-Emancipation Jewish reality. Thus both movements, under the stimulus of modern ideologies, strove to develop a renewed religious self-awareness that would expand religious culture to the point where it would be capable of sustaining this reality.

As scholars have not yet agreed on the definitions of "religion" and "ideology,"[42] we shall confine ourselves to pin-pointing the structural elements by which the two may be integrated, and attempt to clarify distinctions and boundaries that separate them.

In our discussion of the Jewish religion and of the secular ideologies that arose within post-Emancipation Jewish society, we have seen that both religion and ideology find expression in symbolic systems that embody values originating in "the locus of the sacred" that resides in the transcendent center of existence. These symbolic systems tend to order the cognitive–meaningful aspect of human existence; they motivate individuals to behave according to defined norms that help realize the "true" social order, and to implant in them a defined identity in the universe. It is these common structural characteristics that suggest the possibility of integrating the two systems into a "religious ideology."

But, as Talcott Parsons elaborates, religion and ideology differ in their central spheres of reference.[43] Whereas religion focuses on transcendent reality, ideology focuses on empirical, particularly social, reality. Conservative ideology seeks to legitimate the central values of an existing social order; our interest, however, is in innovative ideology which is created under conditions of existential strain resulting from a disruption in the socio–cultural order.[44]

Torah-im-Derekh Eretz and Religious Zionism came into being as a result of the existential strain experienced by traditional Jewry precisely when its identification with, and participation in, modern universal reality were growing. Although both movements viewed positively the fundamental change in the status of the Jewish people that followed Emancipation, traditional Jewish culture proved unreliable in the new socio–cultural reality, and the ideological symbols of the larger society were not qualified to maintain traditional Jewish existence. When this sharp conflict of values brought about an identity crisis that led to a mass abandonment of the traditional culture, both Torah-im-Derekh Eretz and Religious Zionism came forward and sought to fill the gap by guiding the disoriented Jew to a new identity crystallized in modern reality. Torah-im-Derekh Eretz attempted to do this by recasting traditional religious culture in such a way that it could identify with the universal social order. Religious Zionism directed its efforts toward creating a religiously legitimate, modern Jewish social order. This goal was furthered particularly by the labor movement faction of Religious Zionism, ha-Po'el ha-Mizraḥi (the Mizraḥi Worker) – with which the Religious Kibbutz Federation was to affiliate – whose innovative religious–cultural movement "Torah va-Avodah" (Torah and Labor), awarded religious valence to Socialist Zionist values. Thus Torah-im-Derekh Eretz and Torah va-Avodah may be considered new religious subcultures in Orthodox Judaism.

The point of departure for the creation of these new subcultures – the view that the transformed Jewish status was a correction in the cosmic order – led to a redefinition of attitudes toward God and the world. The world was opened up as a field of activity for the religious Jew and he was given a new role in it: to be God's partner in the realization of messianic redemption through rational activity in the world. While Torah-im-Derekh Eretz saw this activity in the context of the universal dimension of the Jewish messianic vision, Religious Zionism saw it in the context of the particular dimension.

The creators of the new religious subcultures turned to primary religious sources for legitimating their messages. The "shocks" created by Emancipation (in the case of Torah-im-Derekh Eretz and Religious Zionism) and of national revival (in the latter case) disengaged their religious consciousness from the traditional order and its institutionalized contents, and turned it back to its primary religious sources. According to Victor Turner, a loosely structured social reality may be charged with vast creative power.[45] Here one may suggest that the decomposition of the Jewish traditional order may have released the religious charisma that was crystallized in its institutions, and the religious innovators, swept by this charisma in its pure and spontaneous mode, sought a renewed link with the transcendent center for guidance in ordering a new, "truer," religious social order. In any event, the intensive affinity of the religious innovators to primary religious sources inspired religious experiences that charged the here-and-now with divine vitality –

charisma. Whereas, in the traditional order, the present was perceived as a segment of time whose religious valence derived from continuity with the insular Jewish past, thanks to the religious experience kindled by Emancipation – and national revival in the case of Religious Zionism – the present was perceived as having an autonomous religious meaning and was open to the universal world.

Two distinct sources nurtured the autonomous religious dimension. One was a present-oriented transcendent center similar to that which nurtured the innovative ideologies of Enlightenment and secular Zionism. But the new values deriving from the well-springs of each of these two movements were perceived by their adherents as secular. For the new religious movements, however, whose transcendent center continued to coincide with God, the innovative ideologies were imbued with religious valence.

A second source that nurtured the independent religious valence of the present was the distant past. The religious experience aroused by the Jews' return to the world – and Jewish national revival – induced the religious consciousness of the initiators of the new religious movements to shift the focus of religious reality from the disintegrating social traditional order, to the "golden ages" of the distant past – mostly historical, but also mythical. Guided by the ideological symbols of the present, the new religious consciousness drew upon the religious symbols embedded in these vital layers of reality for associated symbols that were expressed in Scripture, either explicitly or implicitly.[46] As we shall see below, the transcendent religious orders coalesced around the religious symbols of the past as interpreted in the light of the ideological symbols of the present, and bridged the gap between the distant past and the present. Through these two channels, then, divine reality, radiating Torah values, penetrated the present, and rendered it a more compelling religious period than the immediate past.

It was significant that the concept of Torah was embedded in the slogans of the innovative religious movements; the movements' creators perceived this concept as, *inter alia*, having both a destructive and a constructive religious force. Torah imparted authority to impugn the validity of the traditional order and establish a new religious order in its stead; indeed, "rebirth of the Torah" was a key concept in Torah-im-Derekh Eretz and later in Religious Zionism, most prominently in the latter's Torah va-Avodah submovement. In their view, Torah could not achieve its essential manifestation in the traditional order, for the true realization of the Torah was conditional upon the "full and complete life" in accordance with the pattern of universal society. The interpretation of Torah according to false religious consciousness in the traditional order diminished its power as the guiding force in determining religious culture. The return to a "full and complete life" in modern times created the existential conditions for the revival of the Torah according to its "true" interpretation. In other words, the religious validity of the traditional order was impugned for internal religious reasons. And, to the extent that this radical perception of Torah was largely derived from the mystical stream of traditional culture, the creators of the new religious subcultures were nourished by that stream both consciously and subconsciously.

We have indicated that, in a stable social reality such as the traditional order, God is perceived as a meaningful, integrative focus of existence, in accordance with the conservative component of religious consciousness. However, in an unstable social reality, that same perception of God may be associated with the innovative component of the religious consciousness. In the latter case, He is perceived as One who possesses the power to weave seemingly exclusive value-systems into a unified order.

In sum, in the context of the radical modification of the messianic perspective, the transformation of traditional religious culture found expression in three interlinked ways: in a positive attitude to the world at large; in the recognition of the present as a religiously autonomous temporal dimension; and in rational Jewish activity in the world for the purpose of reshaping it.

PAST AND PRESENT IN RELIGION AND IDEOLOGY

Nineteenth- and twentieth-century Orthodox innovators introduced their transformed religious patterns into Orthodox Jewish life in face of the censure of traditionalist rabbinic authority. The latter's view was epitomized in a slogan coined in the first half of the nineteenth century as a negative response to the Enlightenment and Emancipation: "The new is forbidden by the Torah."[47] While the innovators negated this slogan, they did not disrupt continuity with the immediate past; they continued to recognize *halakhah* as the core of Jewish culture and reaffirmed the final authority of its norms.

The uniquely important status of the past in religion may be illuminated by considering a second distinction (in addition to that of Parsons cited above) between ideology and religion. I suggest that the transcendent center of the universe can be differentiated into an ideological center and a religious center. The point of departure for the former is the present, a segment of time in a given "historical space." To be sure, ideology tends to ground its symbols in the past, but in such cases it operates like a cutting from a tree that takes root after planting. The religious transcendent center, on the other hand, is located in the past, in a charismatic event through which a society was created, its identity determined, and the meaning of its existence elucidated.[48] Those who address themselves to the religious transcendent center are influenced by a consciousness that flows from the past to the present; in other words, religion influences the present from out of the past, just as the tree's roots nourish the crown.

Sinaitic revelation, the pre-eminent charismatic event of the Jewish people, constitutes the religious transcendent center of Judaism. To be sure, Jewish traditional culture recognizes other vital events that preceded Sinaitic revelation, such as Creation and the Exodus. However, Sinaitic revelation is the central meaningful focus of Jewish existence, from which the life of the Jewish people proceeds on its religious and historical course.[49] Sinaitic revelation, therefore, contained the potential elements of the religious order of every future Jewish society. What is more, the authority of Sinai has even been imprinted upon customs that have no basis in Scripture.[50]

Indeed, as we shall see below, when the new cultural–religious subcenters with which we are concerned sought to reorder the disrupted reality of the present, they turned to Sinai, the "eternal present of revelation,"[51] for creative religious power and authority to revamp the structure of the new reality from the religious standpoint. Thus, while the values of the new religious ideologies were created with reference to the transcendent center of the present, these values derived their legitimation from the transcendent center of the past.

Ritual – which links every generation of a society – is also connected with the religious transcendent center. If, indeed, the fundamental role of culture in human life is to create fixed patterns that cannot be provided by biology,[52] it is ritual which endows the culture with stability over time and nurtures what is permanent in the identity of man and society; if religion inspires the sense of eternity,[53] ritual constitutes the means for rendering this sense in concrete form.

In the Jewish religion, ritual is expressed in the observance of the precepts that maintain the mutual historical–religious identity of the Jewish people and its God. Around the precepts, Jewish religious ideologies may be transformed according to the existential situation of the society in different periods, without impairing the traditional continuity of the religious culture.

Whereas, in secular ideological movements, the transcendent center comprises a supreme entity or entities, such as the Jewish people or humankind, that have an empirical ground, the God of Sinaitic revelation is the supreme transcendent entity for the religious ideologists. The identity of this God, then, who exists in the transcendent center of the past as well as the present, is preserved through the institutionalized patterns – or rituals – of *halakhah*. It is through this identity that the Torah legitimates the values of the present in the innovative religious ideological doctrines. Just as the symbols of the distant past created the meaningful framework for sanctioning the ideological symbols of the present, the continuity of *halakhah* played a crucial role in their religious validation. Indeed, by virtue of the absolute validity of its heteronomous norms, *halakhah* renders the past ascendant over the present in the innovative religious cultures.

At the same time, the ideological symbols that originate in the present can impart a new religious meaning to the halakhic precepts. Thus Torah-im-Derekh Eretz viewed the precepts through a universal lens, while in Torah va-Avodah and the RKF the lens was mainly social. The religious ideology of Religious Zionism, and particularly that of the RKF, also viewed the halakhic precepts as compatible with the norms of a modern Jewish national society. In fact, this ideology actively sought the renewal of halakhic legislation, so that *halakhah* could accommodate modern national norms. Thus, while observance of the precepts indirectly ensured the basic religious legitimation of the ideological values of the present, the latter enabled the creators of the religious ideologies to view the precepts within the framework of a modern worldview.

To sum up: each of the Orthodox modernizing movements emerged out of a rebellion against institutionalized spheres of sacredness, and a sense of mission to reorder Jewish culture and life in accordance with a redefinition of the sacred. Stimulated by the secular symbols of the present, and invoking God as the ultimate authority, the religious consciousness of the creators of the modernizing movements sought associated religious symbols, embedded within vital layers of Jewish existence, to legitimate the rebellion and delineate the true religious order. In Torah-im-Derekh Eretz the religious consciousness was moved by the symbols of the Enlightenment, in the Torah va-Avodah subculture of Religious Zionism it was moved by the symbols of Socialist Zionism, and in the RKF subsection of Torah va-Avodah, the religious consciousness was moved primarily by symbols of the secular kibbutz movement.

PART TWO

The parent orthodox modernizing movements

CHAPTER 2

Torah-im-Derekh Eretz

Torah-im-Derekh Eretz manifests the rationalization of Jewish traditional culture within the perspective of the West European liberalism that stemmed from the Enlightenment.[1] In this respect, Torah-im-Derekh Eretz marked Orthodox Judaism's breakthrough into the modern world. The religious–ideological portals that this movement opened to general life made it possible for observant German Jews to integrate into that life by cultivating new awareness as both Jews and human beings. The father of Torah-im-Derekh Eretz was Samson Raphael Hirsch (1808–88).

Hirsch belonged to the third generation of observant German Jewish modernizers of traditional culture. I shall briefly address the systems of Hirsch's predecessors, upon which he was to draw.

Moses Mendelssohn and Hartwig Wessely, both of Berlin, were the significant figures of the first generation; they laid the groundwork for Jewish Enlightenment in the final days of the ghetto. Mendelssohn (1729–86) constituted the pivotal figure in the Jewish transition to the modern world.[2] A highly esteemed philosopher and literary critic within the West European intellectual circles of his day, Mendelssohn presented Judaism as a rational religion that is highly consonant with the values of the Enlightenment. The key to his modernizing thrust lay in his singling out the *mitzvot* as the sole prescriptive feature of Judaism. By distinguishing between the universal sphere of this religion at the level of beliefs and views, and the particular sphere at the level of the *mitzvot*, he implied that Jews could share a common religious life with non-Jews in all matters outside the observance of *halakhah*. He thereby set up a new axis for ordering the Jewish symbolic and normative world. But Mendelssohn made no less a contribution to the formation of modern Jewish Orthodoxy by the personal example that he set; he demonstrated that an observant Jew could be thoroughly at home in the modern cultural world, and accepted as an equal by his fellow non-Jewish intellectuals.

Hartwig Wessely (1725–1805), Hebrew philologist and poet, translated Mendelssohn's doctrine into practical terms and thereby gave Jewish Enlightenment its initial ideological frame. Focusing his modernizing thrust on the traditional Talmud-permeated Jewish educational system, Wessely employed two sets of terms that Hirsch was later to cultivate in defining the relationship between Torah and universal life. Wessely distinguished between the "Torah of man," consisting of secular theoretical and practical knowledge acquired through human reason and experience, and the "Torah of God," anchored in revelation and epitomized in *halakhah*.[3] He regarded the first type of Torah as a prerequisite for the study and practice of the second type. In a parallel vein Wessely capitalized upon the germane relationship between Torah and the equivocal concept *Derekh Eretz* that appears in talmudic and midrashic sources. (Derekh Eretz in these sources implies, *inter alia*, occupation and proper manners.[4]) Elaborating upon midrashic passages that indicate that Derekh Eretz anteceded Torah, Wessely argued that secular knowledge and practice constitute a necessary precondition for cultivating Torah.[5]

The second generation of Orthodox modernizers introduced their innovations against the background of the ghetto's formal dissolution. The Napoleonic reforms in Germany, which incarnated the values of 1789, opened Jewish life to the world-at-large: Jews were free to choose their occupations and place of residence; they changed their dress and language; they fostered a new type of school that taught secular studies in addition to Bible and Hebrew grammar. And although the physical ghetto completely disappeared in many German cities only after several generations, the old, secluded Jewish world no longer existed. It was in this fluid setting that religious reforms were introduced into Jewish life – at first in the synagogue. A modern type of rabbi emerged to replace the traditional religious leader; possessing an academic background, this new rabbi preached and wrote in fluent German in an attempt to provide a meaningful reorientation for the emancipated Jew in his new existence. The reforming thrust of most of these rabbis reached as far as halakhic observance. However, several of them remained faithfully obedient to the commandments.

The outstanding member of this latter, small, group of observant "enlightened" rabbis was Isaac Bernays (1792–1849), the religious leader of Hirsch's home community in Hamburg. Bernays modernized the synagogue service, making it more aesthetic, and introduced secular studies into his community's Hebrew school curriculum. The first Orthodox rabbi to preach in German, Bernays sought to interpret Jewish tradition through a universal lens. His views on the role of Judaism in realizing the universal values of the Enlightenment and on the specific role of the *mitzvot* in furthering this goal were to echo in Hirsch's writings.[6]

HIRSCH REACTS TO REFORM JUDAISM

It was Hirsch's charismatic approach to traditional Judaism and the overarching worldview that he delineated that laid the ground for a new coherent religious cultural system.[7] Ordained at the age of twenty-two, Hirsch held several rabbinical positions in towns in Germany and Moravia before assuming the Orthodox rabbinical office in Frankfort am Main in 1851, where he officiated until his death.[8] His religious ideology was forged largely as a reaction to the religious Reform movement in Judaism.

What both laymen and rabbis had been building up unwittingly since the turn of the century as a trend toward reform in traditional Jewish practices had turned into a self-conscious ideological movement by the 1830s.[9] Maintaining that the "deghettoization of the Jewish community must be accompanied by the deghettoization of Judaism,"[10] Reform Jewish thinkers focused on *halakhah* as the chief impediment to Jewish integration into the modern world. The major reference group of nineteenth-century German Jewry in its effort to integrate into the general society was the newly formed German bourgeoisie. The central values of this class – individualism, humanism, science, and technology, joined within the ideological perspective of progress – were acclaimed by the Reform movement as central Jewish religious values. In terms of Mendelssohn's delineation of two spheres within Judaism, the Reform movement hailed the universal component of Judaism as its quintessence, and depreciated its particularistic component; at first it modified *halakhah* and later repudiated it altogether. By mid-century, the Reform movement was to make deep inroads into German Jewry.

Hirsch's innovative disposition led him to empathize at first with the religious reformers (see below, page 37). Only in the 1840s, when it became clear that the new religious movement was bent on overturning the historic structure of Judaism, did he strongly denounce Reform Judaism. Hirsch saw his self-proclaimed mission to portray a revitalized Orthodox Judaism as no less resonant with the modern world than Reform, without its having to compromise the continuity of *halakhah*.[11]

The key to Hirsch's rationalization of traditional religious culture lay in the distinct status that he awarded *halakhah*. By reaffirming Mendelssohn's position that *halakhah* is the essential obligatory component of Judaism, he unequivocally differentiated between Orthodoxy and the growing Reform movement. In Hirsch's words: "*La loi* and not *la foi* is Judaism's catchword; it is obedience, not faith, or hope or prayer, that makes a Jew a Jew."[12] But by delimiting traditional culture to specific behavioral patterns defined by *halakhah*, Hirsch's system also led to the development of a new religious self-consciousness that accommodated modern culture. One person raised in an Orthodox environment at the end of the nineteenth century elucidated the pivotal role of the *mitzvot* in forming the new order as follows:

> There in Halberstadt, I was deeply conscious of the cognitive aspects of the *mitzvot*, the burden of the *mitzvot*, while in the village where I was born [Messingwerk], I felt the joy in the performance of *mitzvot*. The feature common to both was that the *mitzvot* served as the predominant, perhaps central part of our lives ... When we were taught the values of Judaism as opposed to Christianity, they never failed to mention that Judaism has no dogmas, since its values do not contradict common sense, or Heaven forfend, authentic science. In general, Judaism demands so little of us in the theoretical realm. Only a smattering of religiosity, since what matters is the practical performance of *mitzvot* ... [13]

And if observance of the *mitzvot* set Orthodox Jews apart from other members of general society and limited interaction with them – which Hirsch advocated – not only were the barriers that it created partial, but, as we shall see, they were intended to serve humanity.

THE JEWISH MISSION

Hirsch's point of departure in delineating a new symbolic order was the unique status of the Jewish people in creation, from the universal standpoint. According to Hirsch, there is an all-encompassing divine law undergirding the structure of creation, and this law breaks down into three components, each of which governs a specific sphere: (1) universal natural law, (2) universal moral law, and (3) Jewish law or *halakhah*. The Jew can contribute to the perfection of creation by applying himself to each of these spheres. This formulation enabled Hirsch to provide a rational theodicy for the imperfection of the world. For, he explained, God intentionally created the world imperfectly, according to a "plan in history," that would enable man to become His partner in creation by perfecting it. This plan, which originated in the Torah, will be realized when mankind establishes the Kingdom of God on earth through controlling the world in His service.

In Hirsch's scheme, the sequence of the three spheres of law represents a progression toward perfection in accordance with the divine plan. By behaving according to universal moral law humankind differentiated from nature to become "improved nature." And because of their particular law – *halakhah* – that differentiated them from the rest of mankind, the Jewish people constitute the highest stage of humanity or "pure humanity."[14] In other words, by observing the *mitzvot*, the Jew actualizes the unique aspects of his humanness. The term *Mensch–Jisroel*, man–Israel, which Hirsch coined to characterize the metaphysical entity of the Jew, indicated the structure of religious–existential unity of the post-Emancipation traditional Jew. For, while "man" – who preceded Israel chronologically – constitutes a necessary condition for realizing "Israel," "Israel" – which emerged from "man" – constitutes a sufficient condition for perfecting the human dimension of the Jew.

According to Hirsch, the Jewish people's special status justifies its separation from the rest of mankind. For the *mitzvot* were vouchsafed to the Jewish people so that it could learn how to fulfill its cosmic role in the light of such universal values as love, equality, and righteousness. And as the Jewish people constitutes "a unique nation among nations, one that does not exist for its own fame ... but for the foundation and glorification of the Kingdom of God on earth," it serves as "a lever for the advancement of mankind's education" "until all mankind will turn, united, to God."[15]

In the introduction to his commentary on the book of Psalms, Hirsch summarizes the unique role of the Jewish people in the cosmic master-plan:

The Books of the Law have revealed to us our destiny as men and as Jews, and have taught us the tasks through the execution of which we may fulfill that destiny ... Even as the Torah has taught us to acquire the proper thoughtful appreciation of nature through God, and of the place of man in nature, so it also demonstrates to us that the founding and destiny of our people are most intimately linked with the course of history of mankind as a whole, which is no less guided by God than is our own. It teaches us to recognize that the purpose of our founding and our introduction in the midst of nations was that we might teach mankind ... the knowledge and recognition of God, and of its own destiny and task assigned it by Him.[16]

THE SACRED REDEFINED

It was the breaking down of the traditional barriers around the Jewish people that accompanied Emancipation that awakened the innovative component in Hirsch's religious consciousness, and led him to perceive transformed Jewish life in a Torah perspective. Whereas he saw the French Revolution as "one of the hours when God entered history,"[17] and the Revolution of 1848 as "the divine light permeating the human breast,"[18] Hirsch viewed Emancipation as a movement that could inaugurate a religious reordering of the world from both the universal and particular Jewish standpoints.

According to Hirsch, Emancipation represented an act of universal cosmic betterment, one that could return mankind to the historic beginnings from which it had departed and thereby caused creation to deviate from its destined path to the perfect world. And by enabling the Jewish people to participate in the world more vigorously, Emancipation allowed them to fulfill their role in creation according to the guidelines of Torah. For, in the traditional order, the Jewish people "had been banished from life, estranged from the world and its life ... and no longer considered them in comprehending the Torah." Emancipation made it possible for the Jewish people to open "a new phase ... in its historic role," through its return to life and the world.[19]

Hirsch therefore viewed the disarray in Jewish religious life that resulted from the disintegration of the traditional order as having a positive side. Although it was a time when "two generations [of traditionalists and reformers] confront each other, and when truth is on neither side"; when "we have no governing body no authority ... when almost every rabbi must strike out his own path," a situation of disarray can also signify the "birth pangs" of a state in which the free flow of existence promotes a creative drive toward its reordering.[20] For such a situation can arouse the emancipated Jew's religious consciousness to the point where it differentiates itself from the traditional order and returns to "the ancient source of Judaism, the Bible and Talmud" whose symbols reflect Judaism in its "purity and truth."[21]

Furthermore, the "spirit of the Torah" charged in these symbols inspires the authority to remove "the dust of centuries covering the edifice of Judaism" and "to forget the ... perverse views concerning Judaism that were bequeathed to us." "Emancipation could provide the spirit of Judaism with a wider track to fulfill its destiny."[22] Fundamentally, however, Hirsch's religious consciousness drew upon its divine source to legitimate the new cultural elements, for "[the] novel ... is grounded in the sacred."[23] Indeed, according to Hirsch, "all that is noble and good ... and true in European culture ... is for its greater part ... an offshoot of the divine sacredness."[24]

To sum up, in creating the Torah-im-Derekh Eretz movement Samson Raphael Hirsch used the disarray in Jewish religious life in the first decades of the nineteenth century as fertile soil for a charismatic message that drew Torah vitality from the religious symbols embedded in the ideal past,[25] and directly from God. He then used the charismatic authority deriving from these sources to impugn the sacredness of the traditional order – including customs lacking roots in *halakhah*[26] – and to endow the overall human order and its specific cultural and social components with sacredness.

RECIPROCAL RELATIONSHIP BETWEEN TORAH AND DEREKH ERETZ

In the Torah-im-Derekh Eretz formula, Hirsch aimed to delineate the structure of an authentic religious life within the general human framework. Torah-im-Derekh Eretz is translated as "Torah and civic life," but Hirsch gives several connotations to these two components in his writings without clarifying them. In this regard, however, Derekh Eretz fares better than Torah:

The term Derekh Eretz includes all the situations arising from and dependent on the circumstances that the earth is the place where the individual must live, fulfill his destiny, and dwell together with others and that he must utilize resources and conditions provided on earth in order to live and to accomplish his purpose. Accordingly, the term Derekh Eretz is used primarily to refer to ways of earning a living, to the social order that prevails on earth, as well as to the mores and considerations of courtesy and propriety arising from social living and to things pertinent to good breeding and general education.[27]

In other words, Derekh Eretz constitutes political and economic knowledge and interpersonal moral relationships, particularly in the political and social domains, as well as academic and vocational education. As such, it involves the universal norms through which the Jew can fulfill himself as man, particularly through his social life.

While he gives no similar summary for Torah, Hirsch's interpretation of this component would seem to fit the model we employ in this book: the creative divine vitality that evokes a transcendent order,[28] through which it motivates the impression of a worldly order upon existence, according to symbols and norms that interrelate to form cultural and social systems. In his article "Jewish communal life," Hirsch writes:

What is Torah? ... It is *esh dat* [the fire of law], that invisible fire which is present in every being and every atom of the created world ... the source ... flowing from God, of all being, all existence ... all power, all activity, all life ... that law of God that fashions and rules worlds, that *esh* rejuvenated into *dat* ... the principles for shaping human life in all its relations through the thought of God.[29]

In portraying the transcendent values of Torah that are to be realized in general life, Hirsch took the radical step of highlighting universal – as opposed to specifically Jewish – values. For these values receive their basic grounding "from the Torah that was handed down to Israel *and the rest of mankind* on Mount Sinai."[30]

But this universal connotation of Torah implies two types of revelation: (1) the internal revelation that is implanted in man by virtue of his having been created in God's image, which achieves expression in autonomous creative ability and in sensitivity to the moral and true, i.e. the revelation that is enacted in Derekh Eretz; and (2) the external revelation that was consummated at Mount Sinai, which is expressed in the heteronomous directive that man cultivate the divine traits implanted in him, through conscious recognition of their divine source and validity.

By positing, then, that the secular disciplines which fall upon the Jew as man are potential expressions of divine service, Hirsch was able to legitimate science, technology, and art, as well as humanistic values in terms of Torah.

Further, the Jew cannot completely realize his human dimension if he does not become involved in a social order that embraces a "full and complete life";[31] in effect, all social roles contributing to such a life were perceived by Hirsch as charged with religious meaning. "Judaism ... considers everything as religion: the seamstress at her needlework, the ploughman in the field ... the judge on his bench ... the priest at the altar – they are all engaged in divine worship of equal sanctity."[32] However, the social order can be viewed in light of Torah only when its members deem it to be an instrument for serving God; "when science ... industry and commerce ... agriculture and statecraft ... in short, all aspects of human power and greatness join forces solely for the glorification of God."[33] The polity in particular bears religious significance inasmuch as it administers the divine moral law and, as such, constitutes the social vehicle for religious activity in history. The Jew is, therefore, called upon to identify with the state in which he lives and to fulfill the civil norms incumbent on him.

Let us summarize the relationship of interdependence between Torah and Derekh Eretz in terms of the distinction between "man" and "Israel." Just as man constitutes a necessary condition for actualizing Israel, so Derekh Eretz constitutes a necessary condition for realizing Torah. By the same token, just as Israel constitutes a sufficient condition for the actualization of man in the Jew, so Torah constitutes a sufficient condition for Derekh Eretz. Hence, if general life constitutes the raw material to be worked over by Torah, the latter, as a transcendent order, constitutes "the essence and revelation of the purpose of His kingdom on earth, which it is man's task to translate into reality."[34] And, since God not only created man in His image, but also endowed him with the freedom of choice to harness his creative abilities to His service and participate in the improvement of creation as His partner,[35] the Jew fulfills his role and destiny as man by acting on the world for the purpose of reshaping it and establishing the Kingdom of God. All this meant that the post-Emancipation Orthodox Jew now had a new, universal channel for achieving salvation: the realization of history through universal law.

VALUE-ORIENTATIONS OF JUDAISM

Hirsch's presentation of the Jewish ethos of the post-Emancipation era tends to corroborate both Werner Sombart's attribution of a world-rationalizing ethic to rabbinic Judaism, and Max Weber's contention that this ethic – which he acknowledged in general terms – was in abeyance in the Jewish "pariah" state. Particularly noteworthy to us is Hirsch's corroboration of Weber's analysis of pre-Emancipation Jewry at the motivational level: according to Hirsch, the ghetto Jew was constrained from reforming the world in his search for salvation, because he was "estranged" from the world and its life. With emancipation having opened the path for Jews to engage in reshaping the world, Hirsch proceeds to delineate the value-orientations inherent in an encompassing, world-rationalizing ethos that fall upon the Jew as "man"; in this, Hirsch anticipates Weber's demarcation of the value-orientations of the Protestant ethic.

Thus the Jew is enjoined to submit his "whole life . . . his thoughts and feelings, speech and action, his transactions and pleasures to the service of God." Although the Torah "lays down the world at man's feet to possess and enjoy," it seeks to subdue "the idols of acquisition and pleasure" within the pattern of divine law. Just as the natural order exists in accordance with its own law, so it is incumbent upon man in general and the Jew in particular to obey their divine laws. But, while nature obeys its law unknowingly, man attains "his highest wisdom, his true freedom" by obeying the law "consciously and of his own free will." It is man's conquest of himself in the service of God that is the key to the perfection of the world.[36]

Proceeding from the premise of a self-disciplined personality, Hirsch demarcates the structural traits of the Jew cast in the role of *imitatio dei*. Just as the created world is the product of God's rationality and activism, the Jew is enjoined to help complete creation; first by employing his distinctive rationality to reveal the different modes of divine law and their technological applications, and then by reshaping the world through technology.

Thus Judaism cultivates a type of person who approaches his role in the world "fully aware of himself,"[37] and who "looks at everything objectively . . . The true Jewish mind forms no visionary fanatics who . . . wildly go beyond all bounds of reality . . . While Judaism does teach us the most intimate nearness of God to man, it wants to keep us to the clearest . . . sober, way of contemplating it."[38] This type of person, furthermore, is called upon to investigate the law "in nature and history . . . and to these the Jew adds Torah."[39] Indeed, Hirsch posits that Torah law can be investigated by its hermeneutical rules, by the same method as natural law:

> Two revelations are open before us, nature – and Torah. In nature all phenomena stand before us as indisputable facts, and we can only endeavor *a posteriori* to ascertain the law of each and the connection of all ... The same principles must be applied to the investigation of Torah. Its ordinances must be accepted in their entirety as undeniable phenomena, and must be studied in accordance with their connection with each other and the subject to which they relate.[40]

But, since "the Torah regards no speculation which does not lead to active, productive life as its goal,"[41] ghetto Judaism deviated from the spirit of the Torah when it minimized the importance of action and awarded primacy to cogitation.[42] For it is through the technological application of divine law that man rules as God's "representative and deputy" on earth,[43] and perfects creation.

On the level of nature, man takes part in perfecting creation by "the mastering ... and transforming of the earth and its products for human purposes,"[44] and on the social level he imposes moral law on interpersonal relationships in the framework of the polity, just as God imposed law on nature. But the Jew's pre-eminent means of perfecting the world is on the halakhic level, in which he is involved as "Israel." And, just as reason is enjoined to reveal the technological application of the law in the natural and general human domains, so it is in the halakhic order. Yitzhak Breuer, one of Hirsch's successors and his foremost interpreter, formulated this notion succinctly: "It is the function of reason to utilize the data of the Oral Law, so as to convert the precepts of *halakhah* into practical behavior. For is science not divisible into two: theoretical and applied? Hence, the role of reason in Oral Law is the same as its role in science."[45] Thus, just as the Jew as man reshapes reality through the first two modes of the law, so the Jew as Israel reshapes it through *halakhah*. The *mitzvot* sanctify the sectors of reality that they address by ordering them in time and space in accordance with the patterns of conduct that express God's will.

Based on the above explication of Torah-im-Derekh Eretz, one may conclude that Hirsch successfully rationalized Jewish religion at the symbolic and value-orientation levels by developing a religious–humanistic worldview and method of world transformation that corresponded to those of the secular ideology of progress. But, whereas secular ideology regarded science, technology, and morality as autonomous human goals, Hirsch regarded them as means of serving God.[46]

THE RELIGIOUS COMMUNITY IN HIRSCH'S DOCTRINE

In Hirsch's system, the halakhically ordered community constituted the "Israel" parallel of the general polity. For, although Emancipation had severely narrowed the Jewish religious community, confining it almost entirely to ritualistic institutions, Orthodox Jewry continued to regard this community in the light of its independent religious–political status. Thus, while Hirsch saw the general polity as bearing an independent value for man's moral–religious fulfillment,[47] "Judaism reaches the summit of its fulfillment only in and through communal living."[48]

> The task of each individual community is none other than the task of the Jewish body politic as a whole. The Jewish people as a whole has been entrusted with the task of carrying out the divine law ... and each single community is called upon to join with it in working for the same goal in its own smaller and locally restricted sphere. Where Jews live together in one place ... they have to unite for the practical fulfillment of their divine law and with their joint resources to call into being and maintain those institutions which this fulfillment requires or which at any rate each individual cannot provide for himself.[49]

German law reinforced Jewish communal existence in the post-Emancipation era in that it obliged every Jew to belong to his local religious community. New legislation in 1876 acknowledged the right to secede from such a body on conscientious grounds. The strong valence that German Orthodox Jewry continued to attribute to the religious community was highlighted when, following this legislation, Hirsch led a section of Orthodox Jewry to secede from the general Jewish community, in which Orthodox and Reform Jews jointly participated. Hirsch and his "secessionist" followers formed religious communities of their own with the declared objective of assuring their halakhic ordering.[50] Indeed, Hirsch's faction was willing to extend religious solidarity only to those Jewish organizations which recognized the ascendancy of *halakhah* in Jewish public life.

RELIGION DISTINGUISHED FROM IDEOLOGY

Hirsch focused upon the concept of progress to distinguish between religion and ideology, or, in his words, between "Torah" and "the spirit of the time." He recognized the present as an autonomous time-dimension in relation to the immediate past, and acclaimed its humanistic values. But he grounded the values of the present in symbols of the past that drew their basic sanction from Sinai. And inasmuch as the prevailing secular perception of these ideological values could easily blur their religious meaning, he emphasized the significance of the *mitzvot*. Because the *mitzvot* were rooted in the past, they stood for the ascendancy of religion over ideology in Torah-im-Derekh Eretz.

Hirsch identified ideology with progress and religion with the *mitzvot*, seizing upon the Reform movement's abrogation of the *mitzvot* in its avid pursuit of progress to drive this point home. "For them [the ideology of] progress is the absolute and religion is governed by it; to us religion is the absolute. For them religion is valid only to the extent that it does not interfere with progress; for us progress is valid only to the extent that it does not interfere with religion."[51]

A NEW RELIGIOUS SUBCENTER

It is beyond the scope of this work to evaluate German Orthodox Jewry's integration into general society.[52] But we note that, under the legitimation of Torah-im-Derekh Eretz, German Orthodox Jews internalized the general culture – including a strong awareness of science – and participated actively in the general economic and political institutions of society. Hirsch translated his religious perception of general life into practical terms in 1853, when he founded and directed an integrated school in his Frankfort am Main community, in which Jewish and secular subjects were taught in a unified religious framework. And, by admitting girls to his school, he championed "complete spiritual and intellectual equality" for women,[53] thereby preparing the ground for the entry of Orthodox Jewish women into the occupational sphere near the turn of the century, in the wake of German Gentile women.[54]

Traditional Orthodox German rabbis disapproved of Hirsch's innovative thrust,[55] but to no avail; even the very Orthodox center of

Torah authority in Eastern Europe eventually became reconciled to Torah-im-Derekh Eretz, even if it did not grant it explicit approval. Indeed, Hirsch's teachings led to the emergence of a new religious subcenter within Orthodox Jewry, composed of Orthodox rabbis who were positively oriented toward, and integrated within, Western culture and who at the same time acknowledged the halakhic authority of the East European rabbinic center. This new subcenter became institutionalized through the modern Orthodox rabbinical seminary that Rabbi Esriel Hildesheimer (1820–99) founded in Berlin in 1873.[56] Thus, in a space of less than forty years, Hirsch and the Torah-im-Derekh Eretz movement successfully effected the transition of the Orthodox Jew from a disjunctive, tradition-bound world to an integrated, modern, open one.

TOWARD THE RELIGIOUS PIONEERING MOVEMENT

In the 1930s German Orthodox youth constituted the dominant element of the religious kibbutz movement. Through this youth, Torah-im-Derekh Eretz made a far-reaching contribution to the modernizing thrust of the new movement. But it was the very familiarity of German Orthodox youth with the modern world, which they had gained through their secular education and participation in the institutions of the general society, that sharpened their sensitivity to the limitations of Torah-im-Derekh Eretz's attempt to integrate universal and particular cultures.

The structural dualism of Jewish-religious and general life was a subject of growing concern for Orthodox youth as early as the turn of the century.[57] The rewards of the objective observance of the *mitzvot* were overbalanced by the diminished awareness of the religious significance of the secular general life and, what is more, by the attenuation of the affective sources of religious life. Put differently, Derekh Eretz outweighed Torah, which was confined to a limited sphere of ritualistic, often formal, action. It was on the normative social level in particular that the Orthodox Jew could not integrate his two worlds. The problem centered around the fact that most of the institutions in which Orthodox Jews participated, especially in the economic and political spheres, were subject to, and molded by, non-Jewish authority and values. Thus, in the occupational sphere, Orthodox Jews were limited to positions where they did not have to work on the Sabbath or Jewish holidays. On the other hand, although they could exert control over the institutions of the more meaningful halakhically ordered community, these institutions affected only limited aspects of their lives.

In this context, it is significant that Hirsch did not attempt to rationalize traditional culture at the normative level; he refrained from cultivating an awareness of halakhic dynamics that might link religious law to the changing social institutions of the modern world. Instead, he clung to the notion that the universal polity operated in history to transform the world, and relegated the halakhically ordered community to an ahistorical role. Put differently, Hirsch enjoined Jewish action in the world within the universal perspective of the messianic vision, but he rejected such action within the particularistic perspective.[58] It follows that the Orthodox Jew could not fully integrate the universal and particular components of his identity. He could not live a "full and complete life" in a Gentile society, nor, for that matter, could he assume the responsibility for sustaining such a life; neither could he realize his Judaism fully in a non-halakhic social framework.

Indeed, it was this sharp division between civil life and particular religious life that spurred German Orthodox youth to seek a new form of polity, in which the two modes of life could be integrated in a modern, self-contained Jewish community. As stated in a 1932 bulletin of the Orthodox pioneering movement:

Judaism is becoming more and more a matter of cognition, observed artificially alongside of real life ... Orthodoxy ignores the fact that proclaiming "the dominion of the Torah" is condemned to remain merely a slogan if it is not accompanied by the obligation to struggle for a national, social, and cultural Gemeinschaft in a closed system. Only such a community can constitute a base for enabling Torah to constitute an all-embracing value influencing general culture and Jewish learning and a factor that molds the whole person.[59]

The Zionist movement, with its goal of creating a modern national Jewish society in which Jews could live full and complete lives, offered a potential framework for the Orthodox Jew to fulfill himself as a whole person, without having to compromise his observance of *halakhah*. Hence, it was toward this movement that German Orthodox youth began to turn.

CHAPTER 3

Religious Zionism

Religious Zionism constitutes a national response to the identity crisis which arose within Orthodox Jewry as a result of the confrontation between tradition and modernity. In contrast to the vigorous development of Torah-im-Derekh Eretz that was elaborated into an innovative cultural subcenter within Orthodox Judaism principally by one person, Religious Zionism was established by various figures and organizations over several generations. Crystallized for the most part in the pre-Emancipation setting of nineteenth-century Eastern Europe[1] – for it was not until the 1917 revolution that most East European Jews were awarded equal civil rights – Religious Zionism did not, generally speaking, develop an articulate and coherent modernizing ideology, as did Torah-im-Derekh Eretz in Germany. Thus, while it sought to overcome the dualism between the universal modern values fostered by East European Jewish Enlightenment, and particular Jewish values – a dichotomy epitomized by the slogan "Be a man in the street and a Jew at home"[2] – Religious Zionism never quite achieved a systematic integration of traditional religious and modern cultures.

This may have something to do with the fact that Religious Zionism matured under the shadow of traditionalistic rabbinical authority which looked askance at religious change. Notwithstanding the deterioration of the traditional Jewish order in Eastern Europe in the course of the nineteenth century, the religious leadership that constituted the supreme authority for most of the Jews in that region almost until the end of the century, refused to acknowledge modernity. Thus, while national religious thinkers – like S. R. Hirsch – expressed an awareness of the innovative potential of Torah in relation to modernity as early as the

1870s, it was only with the establishment of the Torah va-Avodah movement in Eretz Israel some fifty years later that this potential was realized. Unlike Hirsch, however, nineteenth-century national religious thinkers were sensitive to the need to rationalize traditional religious norms within the framework of a national polity, and they also favored religious solidarity with non-observant Jewish organizations. It therefore follows that, while Torah-im-Derekh Eretz nurtured a deeper identification with modernity than did Religious Zionism, the latter was to become more involved in the "nitty-gritty" of modern life.

In discussing Religious Zionism up to the formation of the Religious Kibbutz Federation in 1935, I shall draw upon (1) national religious thinkers of the nineteenth century; (2) ideologues of Mizrahi, the national religious party established within the framework of the Zionist movement in 1902; and (3) ideologues of ha-Po'el ha-Mizrahi, the religious workers organization affiliated with Mizrahi, which was created in 1922. Although these thinkers expressed differing responses to the challenge of modern life, they all played a role in attempting to meet that challenge. In delineating their attempts to chart – and build – a modern national religious culture, I shall address those values upon which the Religious Kibbutz Federation was to draw.

THE INTEGRATION OF RELIGION AND NATIONALISM

A new perception of the messianic process

At about the same time that Samson Raphael Hirsch was beginning to develop Torah-im-Derekh Eretz in Germany, a Jewish religious–national ideology emerged in Eastern Europe.[3] While the socio–cultural milieu of its fathers – Rabbis Tzvi Hirsch Kalischer (1795–1874) and Yehudah Hai Alkalai (1798–1878) – was the traditional Judaism of Eastern Europe, the nationalist message of these men stemmed from their fascination with the new reality created by West European Emancipation and with the contemporary national awakening in the Balkan countries.[4] Equal civil rights, and the belief that the persecution of Jews in Western Europe had ceased forever, induced them, as it had Hirsch, to regard Emancipation as a turning-point in the messianic process, and to call for rational human activity in advancing it. But in contrast to Hirsch, the fathers of Religious Zionism viewed this activity in terms of Jewish collective action in the world of modern nationalism.

As Kabbalists, Rabbis Kalischer and Alkalai gave a new interpretation to the Lurianic Kabbalistic interpretation of the *Zohar*'s notion that dependence of the "awakening from above" on "the awakening from below" was a call for human action in the inner, psychic, sphere that would hasten redemption (see pp. 15–6); under the influence of Emancipation, and within the perspective of European nationalism, the two rabbis shifted the focus of human action to the outer, empirical sphere. The messianic process was now conceived as consisting of a "natural," or rational, stage, which involved the return to, and settlement of, Eretz Israel, and the rebuilding of the Temple, as necessary preconditions for the "supernatural" stage that would consummate the process. It was this new interpretation of the messianic process that gave religious legitimation to the return of the Jewish people to history, in order to shape its own future.

The religious value of Jewish peoplehood

The national message emerging from the messianic theme was only rudimentarily charismatic, in that it constituted a response to the disarrayed Jewish worldview following Emancipation. This message, elaborated about the middle of the nineteenth century, coincided with the rise of East European Jewish Enlightenment. Exposing repressed Russian Jewry to modern values, Enlightenment legitimated abandonment of traditional religion and assimilation into Russian society. The ties which bound the Russian Jewish community began to unravel. The anxiety generated by the growing defection from Judaism was compounded toward the end of the century, by the pogroms of 1881–2 in south Russia and the intensification of the Russian government's repressive policy toward the Jewish minority. As a result, the charismatic message of Jewish nationalism became full-fledged.

Jewish survival was a secondary source of religious legitimation for modern nationalism. In 1872, the writer and public figure, Yeḥi'el Mikhal Pines (1843–1913), expressed the intrinsic religious value of the survival of the Jewish people as the carrier of Torah in the following words: "The Holy One, blessed be He, wants us to survive as a nation, having set His name in our midst ... through the Torah and the covenant that He made with us ...".[5] Three decades later, the Mizraḥi founder, Rabbi Yaakov Reines (1839–1915), employed more trenchant terms to express the message of religious succor contained in the national movement:

All the paths of life are progressively barred to us. Our Torah is being forgotten, the divine commandments ... are violated more and more ... Our entire Jewish being is becoming reduced to nil ... The younger generation strides with giant steps towards assimilation ... It is within the power of Zionism to bring about, with divine help, a radical transformation in our abnormal state, to provide us swiftly with material and spiritual healing.[6]

East European Jewish Enlightenment also constituted the seedbed of secular Jewish nationalism. For those adherents of Enlightenment who renounced traditional religion but felt committed to the future of the Jewish people, secular nationalism was perceived as an alternative framework for Jewish peoplehood. Notwithstanding the anti-religious stance of the secular nationalists, religious nationalists joined forces with them, first in the Ḥibbat Tzion ("Love of Zion") movement that originated in Russia in 1881, and later in the World Zionist Organization that was founded in 1897. They held that Jewish peoplehood constitutes a religious value in its own right, and that only through nationalism could religious and secular elements work together for Jewish survival.

The stress on Jewish peoplehood as a religious value in its own right constitutes the most distinctive feature of Religious Zionism within Orthodox Jewry. Whereas traditional Judaism regarded the people of Israel and the Torah as religiously interlinked, Religious Zionism, reacting to the emergence of secular national Jewry, distinguished between Torah and peoplehood, and transferred the primary source of Jewish solidarity from the former to the latter. Indeed, there were national religious thinkers who awarded a higher religious valence to Jewish unity than to the practice of the commandments. Such views led to a policy of tolerance toward the non-observant.[7]

The religious value of Jewish peoplehood was especially significant in the face of the anti-Zionist Orthodox condemnation of religious nationalist solidarity with secular Zionists. The traditional rabbinic leadership – headed by those rabbis who were considered "the sages of their generation" – was initially ambivalent toward the budding nationalist movement. Toward the end of the century, however, as it became clear that the secular nationalists were gaining the upper hand in the Zionist movement and championing a secular national Jewish identity, ambivalence turned to outright reprobation: Zionism was condemned as an heretical movement.[8] Religious nationalists were accused by the anti-Zionist Orthodox of being accessories to the secularization of Judaism. In rebuttal the religious nationalist leaders argued that all Jews are considered members of the Torah-bearing people and, as such, secularist abandonment of the *mitzvot* was to be regarded as no more than a passing phase.[9]

The innovative potential of Torah

Nineteenth- and early twentieth-century religious thinkers sought to delineate a national religious culture within the context of the return of the Jewish people to the world at large. The fathers of Religious Zionism broke with the insular view held by the traditional Jewish community, and viewed the national society as complementary to Enlightenment and Emancipation.[10] The cognitive and institutional boundaries of particular Jewish life would be extended in accordance with the newly acclaimed universal standards, thus making it "full and complete." And like their secular counterparts, the religious national thinkers regarded West European society as a model for the new national Jewish society. Indeed, since Western Europe's cultural and organizational patterns represented humanity in its most advanced stage, these patterns were considered worthy of being religiously legitimated.[11]

It was a maxim of Religious Zionist thought that a "full and complete life" within the national framework would be organized according to the injunctions of the Torah. Prior to the appearance of secular nationalism on the Jewish scene, the compatibility of Torah with national life was not questioned. However, once the adherents of secular nationalism began to disparage Jewish traditional culture as being anachronistic, religious national thinkers were spurred to defend the continuity of Torah as the national Jewish culture, by invoking its innovative potential.[12] Even after Jewish national settlement had begun in Eretz Israel in the 1880s, and it was evident that traditional religious culture could not fully support all aspects of the new national society,[13] Religious Zionists continued to nurture the belief that traditional culture could be transformed to the point where Torah would be able to sustain such a society.

The basic rationale for the transformation of traditional culture derived from Torah's inner relationship with Jewish peoplehood. While some Religious Zionist thinkers accorded the Jewish people an even higher religious value than Torah – thereby implying that Torah must be open to the needs of the people – Religious Zionism more characteristically regarded Torah and peoplehood as the "soul" and "body" of a unified religious system.[14] Rabbi Shmu'el Mohlewer (1824–98), the leading religious figure in the Hibbat Tzion movement, delineated this relationship when highlighting the non-institutionalized precept of *yishuv Eretz Israel* ("settlement of Eretz Israel").

> The settlement of the Land, that is, the purchase of land and building houses, planting orchards, and cultivating the soil, is one of the fundamental commandments of our Torah; some of our ancient sages even say that it is equivalent to the whole Torah, for it is the foundation for the existence of our people.[15]

Indeed, the concept of a unified religious system implied a dynamic relationship between the components of the system; in this light the transformation of traditional culture was viewed as the corollary of a self-regulating mechanism for maintaining the unity of the system. In other words, if a modern national society was necessary for strengthening the religious "body," Torah as the "soul" was obliged to prove its ability to sustain such a society. For otherwise, as Shlomo Zalman Shragai (1899–   ), a leader of ha-Po'el ha-Mizrahi, wrote in 1942, that would mean

> forfeiting complete life and leaving the building of the land to the secular Jews, confirming thereby the popular notion ... that there is a contradiction between Torah and life ... and that it is impossible to establish a Jewish state that will also be a Torah state.[16]

It was the partial release from the authority of the traditional past and the openness to the "spirit of the times"[17] that quickened the urge to revitalize religion, and encouraged Religious Zionist thinkers to believe that universal and modern national values could be adopted within the parameters of Torah. The perception of the present as "the beginning of divine redemption"[18] accorded it a higher religious valence than that of the immediate past. This perception was further warranted by events that acted to advance national goals. In 1891, for example, Rabbi Joseph Jaffee of Gordz, Lithuania (1845–98), evaluated the Russian government's authorization to raise money for the settlement of Eretz Israel:

> Those opposing the colonization of Eretz Israel argue: ... If colonization is good and desirable in God's eyes, why did our fathers never engage in it? ... [They claim:] "The new is forbidden by the Torah.".... We, in turn, reply: Our fathers did not do it because the time had not yet arrived; but now, when we have been privileged to obtain the permission of our mighty government ... to aid our brethren who have settled in the Holy Land, who can fail to concede that it is incumbent upon us to fulfill the will of God and to colonize the land of our fathers?[19]

The religious vitality that conferred the authority to create new values, drew upon symbols from the Second Temple period; Religious Zionist thinkers perceived Torah as inherently related to the full and complete life that had prevailed during this period. Through recourse to midrashic–Kabbalistic sources, they portrayed the return to Eretz Israel as a return to the "spiritual center of the Torah of Moses,"[20] a metaphysical–geographic center charged with creative religious power. In 1903, the historian and educator Ze'ev Yaavetz, elaborated upon the notion that the return to Eretz Israel would bring about the realization of "a complete Torah, of a complete life."[21] Noting that the pre-eminent mark of Torah is "the profusion of vitality that flows from it,"[22] Yaavetz stated:

> The sense of unity that dominates the spirit of our religion ... embraces life in its entirety ... Only in the land of our fathers can our Torah branch out in its own way, without hindrance. For there it will be mistress ... Only there will our Torah be able to live once again and restore its people to a real life, a life of complete unity.[23]

Modern national reality and halakhah

The major challenge to the projected renewed religious culture lay in *halakhah*. For nowhere in established religious law could sanction be found for a self-sufficient modern society, in which all roles are performed by Jews;[24] the needs of such a society were far more complicated than those of the pre-Emancipation local community. However, according to the postulates of religious national thought, if a modern national society is necessary for continued Jewish existence, and if *halakhah* is incapable of accommodating the roles and institutions necessary for its orderly functioning, the flaw does not lie in the structure of that society; the burden of proof rests with *halakhah*.

Religious Zionist ideologues held that the gap between halakhic and national norms was only temporary; it existed because the Rabbinate had not exercised the creative power latent in Oral Law to come up with solutions to problematic situations. Here, too, they could point to the example of the Second Temple period, claiming that the Sanhedrin[25] succeeded in maintaining the unity between *halakhah* and national life by recognizing the need for continuous halakhic adjudication in face of changing conditions of life.[26] Thus Ze'ev Yaavetz could state:

> You ask about the operation of the railroad, electricity, and the telephone on the Sabbath. I can give you an answer in general terms as I can for all matters on which the ability of the people to sustain itself on the land depends... just as [the Talmudic sage] Hillel answered the sons of Bateyra when confronted by a need for which he had not yet found a solution, advising them to rely on the ... wholesome intelligence of the people, who always found the proper way ... In the words of Hillel [Tractate *Pessaḥim* 66a]: "Let Israel be, if they are not prophets, they are the sons of prophets."[27]

In the meanwhile, if there were halakhic norms that hindered the independent functioning of the national society, the value of Jewish peoplehood made it possible for the Religious Zionist movement to endorse the full gamut of national roles – even if its members' commitment to *halakhah* prevented them from fulfilling some of these roles themselves – and to justify facts that were created in a secular framework.

To sum up: Religious Zionism held that the key to the transformation of traditional religious culture in a national context lay in the relationship intertwined between peoplehood and religion. National revival bore the seed of a dialectical thrust toward the rationalization of religious culture.

MIZRAHI

The Mizraḥi organization,[28] founded in Vilna in 1902, did little to advance the rationalizing thrust. Characteristically, it objected for many years to the inclusion of cultural activities in the program of World Zionism. Regarding itself as a political vehicle within the

Zionist organization to advance the national religious ideas that had been developing for decades in the Jewish world, Mizraḥi was a largely middle-class, Diaspora-based political party with chapters in many countries, founded and led primarily by rabbis.[29] It was as members of the institutionalized religious elite that these rabbis could build a new religious subcenter among traditional Jewry in the Diaspora; at the same time, however, they were too deeply involved in the disintegrating traditional order to be able to discredit it. Furthermore, Mizraḥi's dependence on the masses of Orthodox Jewry in the Diaspora for political support did not encourage openness to far-reaching change in religion. And, having been repudiated by most of the traditional rabbinic leaders for joining hands with secular Zionism, Mizraḥi assumed a defensive position within Orthodox Judaism that forced it to curb the impulse toward religious change.

After Mizraḥi became established in Eretz Israel – it founded a chapter there in 1918, and two years later moved its world headquarters to Jerusalem – it was also confronted by the traditionalistic religious leadership of the old Jewish community there. The "Old Community" (old *Yishuv*), centered in Jerusalem and focusing its life on Torah study, included most of the Orthodox population in the country. While modernization encroached upon this community, particularly as the new national society sprouted in the 1880s, and many of its members had cut loose from it to take part in the Jewish national life, its structure remained largely intact. When, in 1921, the new British mandatory administration initiated the creation of a Chief Rabbinate in order to rationalize rabbinic authority in the Jewish community, Mizraḥi supported this action, hoping, *inter alia*, that the Chief Rabbinate's authority would extend over the entire Jewish population. However, the "Old Community" seceded from the national society and did not accept the Mizraḥi-sponsored Chief Rabbinate. Furthermore, the traditionalistic authority of its rabbis was to cast a shadow over the national society; the latter's community rabbis who had been educated in local and East European *yeshivot* (Talmudic academies) – including those rabbis who were members of Mizraḥi – deferred to the traditionalistic authority in matters of *halakhah*. Indeed, even the first Ashkenazi Chief Rabbi, Abraham Isaac Kuk (1865–1935), in whose thinking a Jewish nationalism that integrated tradition and modernity was central, followed the traditionalistic line when halakhic issues arose.[30]

Thus, while Mizraḥi accepted modernity and was open to the stirrings of religious revival induced by national awakening,[31] it did little to translate them into social and cultural religious patterns that would accommodate modern life. As a result, there was only a nebulous integration of traditional religious values with modern national culture in the ideology of Mizraḥi. Its most significant contribution to modernization was the educational system that it initiated in Eretz Israel in 1909, which offered a curriculum combining sacred and secular subjects to girls as well as boys. But even here Mizraḥi did not integrate the subjects into a unified religious system. Mizraḥi also supported women's suffrage in the Jewish national society, in the face of opposition from the "Old Community's" rabbis and the disapproval of Chief Rabbi Kuk.

The fact that the buds of a religious–cultural revival that sprouted within Mizraḥi did not come to fruition is related to Religious Zionism's development. The kabbalah-nurtured progenitors were the ones who made the breakthrough to modern religious nationalism. The founders of Mizraḥi, on the other hand, were down-to-earth;[32] committed primarily to the practical needs of Zionism, they added little new impetus to the impulse of religious renewal inherent in the message of "national redemption."

HA-PO'EL HA-MIZRAḤI AND TORAH VA-AVODAH

This was not, however, true of the labor wing of Mizraḥi, ha-Po'el ha-Mizraḥi (the Mizraḥi worker), which was born in 1922 within the radical ambience of the national community in Eretz Israel. The founders and leaders of ha-Po'el ha-Mizraḥi did not belong to the rabbinical elite,[33] and, as we shall see, had already severed their attachment to the traditional order by joining the pioneering element in Eretz Israel. Their Hassidic background provided them with established mystical channels and symbols for fomenting the religious fervor needed to transcend the here-and-now and undermine institutionalized patterns. Their fervor was to crystallize in the symbol of "the holy rebellion."

The father of this symbol was Shmu'el Ḥa'im Landau (1892–1928). Reared in the Kotzk branch of Hassidism, and the leader of Tze'irei Mizraḥi (Mizraḥi Youth) in Poland before migrating to Eretz Israel in 1926, Landau was to emerge as the outstanding ideologue of ha-Po'el ha-Mizraḥi.

Significantly, the point of departure of Landau's thinking was Samson Raphael Hirsch's evaluation of Jewish peoplehood as secondary to Torah.[34] Landau argued that Hirsch's endeavor to justify Jewish collective existence in post-Emancipation European society emphasized the universal dimension of Torah at the expense of its national dimension. By divesting Jewish peoplehood of material trappings and predicating its existence upon the fulfillment of a universal mission, Hirsch eviscerated Jewish peoplehood. It was in this vein that Hirsch asserted that Israel was created for the sake of Torah.[35]

Landau rejected this view. On the contrary, he argued, "Torah was created for the sake of Israel."[36] The Jewish people must be grounded in material life and on its own soil in Eretz Israel; it is only in such circumstances that the Torah could be fully realized. By awarding Torah valence to manual labor in all facets of productive life within the context of national revival, Landau's thought constituted a foundation-stone of religious pioneering ideology.

The birth of the religious pioneering movement

Ha-Po'el ha-Mizraḥi represented an attempt to dissolve the tension between the disintegrating traditional social order of Eastern Europe and the national order that was materializing in Eretz Israel. Many of its founders had only recently been "pushed into the practical world" from their Hassidic *shṭibels* (places of worship, i.e. of prayer and study) by the accelerated breakdown of traditional society during World War I and by the centrifugal pull of the universalistic national states created in its wake. Torn between the values of traditional religion and those of the general society that Emancipation had suddenly opened to them, these young people were attracted to Zionism as a corrective. Thus they joined the postwar wave of pioneer immigration to Eretz Israel, kindled by the Balfour Declaration and the San Remo Conference,[37] to join the Jewish national community that had recently come under the jurisdiction of the British mandatory administration. National redemption with its messianic undertones generated new religious impulses and suggested new religious contours for reordering their lives.

While still in Europe, these immigrants were also affected by the social values of the Bolshevik revolution. The loosening of their moorings from the crumbling traditional order, together with the message of national redemption, made them particularly receptive to the revolutionary fervor in the air. Thus, upon joining the national society in Eretz Israel, they readily adopted such prevalent Socialist Zionist values as personal labor, equality, non-exploitation of others, and mutual aid.

The principal social–cultural absorption framework for the stream of post-World War I pioneer immigrants was the newly founded Histadrut (General Federation of Labor) that was sponsored by the dominant Socialist Zionist sector of the national society.[38] The Histadrut eased the absorption of the new immigrants into the life of the national society through employment bureaux, worker-kitchens, social services, and various co-operative and communal groups organized under its aegis. Most of the religious immigrants also gravitated to the Histadrut and were introduced to physical labor in its work-camps, building squads, and farm-worker groups. However, the completely secular atmosphere that prevailed in the Histadrut estranged many of the religious pioneers.

Mizrahi also established an absorption framework, but it was far more rudimentary than that of the Histadrut and proved to be inefficient. Mizrahi also looked askance at the radical orientation of the newcomers. Thus the religious immigrants lacked a social milieu that would support both their traditional and their ideological symbols, a milieu through which they could "foster and create a unified and coherent worldview."[39]

It was in the new rural and urban primary groups – groups characterized by face-to-face interpersonal relations – that came together to form ha-Po'el ha-Mizrahi that the inner sparks coalesced and the revitalizing experience heightened. A new religious message was born: Torah va-Avodah (Torah and labor).[40] The innovative subculture that was to crystallize around this message expressed the transmutation of the tension between exile and redemption into active sacredness through physical activity directed at nation building; it also spelled out the return of the Jewish people to history in active religious terms.

Vital layers in the past

Guided by the ideological symbols that structured their daily reality, the aroused religious consciousness of the Orthodox immigrants harked back to pristine sources for guidance in reordering their religious life. In the words of the founding proclamation of ha-Po'el ha-Mizraḥi:

> The religious worker ... arrived in Eretz Israel ... with a deep aspiration for the renewal of the life of the [Jewish] people, here in its homeland, after it had become frozen and ossified in the lands of the Diaspora ... We seek a Judaism of Torah and labor, through which Judaism can come in contact with nature, with life in its fullest sense, and with the nation, a Judaism that is more than tradition and the residue of a legacy, but also a live inner feeling stemming from the heart. We seek to return to the ancient Hebrew life, to original biblical Judaism, based on justice, righteousness, and morality.[41]

Ha-Po'el ha-Mizraḥi founders thus took the representations of the golden ages of the past as models for the realization of a true religious life that accorded with their labor-pioneering values. It was in this context that they turned to the biblical and talmudic periods as the "ancient social orders of the people of Israel, [who lived] a life based on physical labor and social justice, as described in the Torah and prophets."[42] Indeed, "the historical figures of our Sages of the Mishnah and the Gemarah, who combined Torah and labor,"[43] constituted a reference group for the religious pioneers, a model from which they derived their standards of conduct. The teachings of the prophets in particular certified the legitimacy of ha-Po'el ha-Mizraḥi and its pursuit of a "just" society. Hence the young labor organization could claim that its new values were originally religious values "that were blurred in the course of time." As stated in an early issue of *Ha-Po'el Ha-Mizraḥi*:

> We have not come to innovate ... If we have engraved on our banner "Religion and Labor," we have done so not because it is a new concept for us, but, on the contrary ... one of the very fundamentals of Judaism. "When you eat the labor of your hands, you shall be happy" [Psalms 128:2] ... "He who enjoys the fruit of his hands' labor is more worthy than the pious" [Tractate *Berakhot* 8a] ... We are enjoined to labor by the Torah ...[44]

When the historical layers were viewed through the prism of Kabbalah, they invoked metaphysical elements. Thus participation in the building of a national society represented the beginning of the return of the *Shekhinah* (Divine Presence) to its geographic source in Eretz Israel.[45] Similarly, the new socialistic reality invoked "original Hebrew socialism" as a reflection of the "source of supreme justice residing in the Divine."[46] From this perspective the biblical social precepts were construed as an indication of the social "intention of the Torah" – a diffuse norm that manifests social justice as the divine essence. For the Hassidic-bred ideologues of ha-Po'el ha-Mizrahi, a constantly renewing Creation – an order in which interpersonal relations are spontaneous and free of social barriers, and in which economic activity is conducted by personal labor – symbolized the ideal social order:

> The Jewish people never accepted the notion of ... a division according to classes. "Why was man created singly? So that one would not say my father is greater than yours." [Tractate *Sanhedrin* 38a; see also Rashi's comments there.] This exalted moral notion stems directly from faith in the innovation of the world and creation *ex nihilo* ... the two elements upon which the Hebrew moral world is generally based.[47]

> The Jewish ideal is "What is mine is thine, and what is thine is thine" [*Chapters of the Fathers* 5:13] which is a repudiation of the principle of property ... Man owns nothing and everything belongs to the Creator, while we are merely sojourners on earth ... The only possession that man has in the world is labor, and only that which he has acquired through labor belongs to him ... Even here, however, he should always keep in mind that it is God alone who has given him the strength to succeed. Hence, when he helps his fellow and gives him of his money, he should remember that he is not giving him of his own, "for thou and what is thine are His" [*Chapters of the Fathers* 3:8].[48]

And, when the symbols of historical and metaphysical layers joined together, they illuminated the "original ancient Hebrew simplicity ... pure Judaism, unsullied by *galut* dross."[49]

Thus ideological symbols, charged with vitality drawn from the religious symbols of the past, infused the members of the new labor organization with a sense of pristine religious power.

> "Torah and labor" is no more than a single life-pattern, as exemplified in the perfected society of the past ... We hold that the channel of religious inspiration continues to distill into our souls an ever-renewing fount of life ... And when we return to our country of *origin* ... we renew our days of old and build our *original* view ... Our mandate is: *not to stifle the divine voice that speaks from our throat*.[50]

The holy rebellion

What gave the Orthodox workers' feeling of religious power particular vigor was their sense of a direct affinity with God, through Torah as the primeval divine vitality expressing the "holy order." Thus perceived, Torah constituted the source of the "holy rebellion" of ha-Po'el ha-Mizraḥi.

> Judaism holds the holy rebellion as the end-goal of the world ... held captive by routine and in the confines of habit ... Wherever there is routine, habit ... there is no ferment to give meaning to life ... The opposite of all this is holiness, which freshens man's soul so he can feel the constant renewal of creation ... and of man as part of it ...
> What is the source from which we are to draw the will and power for the holy rebellion? It is the Torah ... of the continuous world revolution ... The people of Israel spurns routine ... This revolutionary people was vouchsafed ... the Torah of the holy revolution, of the holy order, the Torah that quickens all ... and never becomes reconciled to stagnation... This Torah ... calls on the people to be constantly at odds with what exists if it is evil ... This is the Torah which [according to *Breisheet Rabbah* 1] the Holy One, blessed be He, consulted [before He] created the world ...[51]

The ideologues of ha-Po'el ha-Mizraḥi directed their "holy rebellion" against the traditional religious order, and especially against its economic institutions and class-structure. They held that these established patterns, rather than being sanctioned by Torah, represented its perversion. In Landau's words, Torah could not be properly realized in the traditional order because of

> the negative outlook on life and the world ... and ... lack of productivity ... Necessity forced a life of idleness on us and that became a habit, and thus hallowed by the sacredness of tradition, to the extent that whoever revolted against it was regarded as one who denied the fundamentals of Torah.[52]

The pre-eminent expression of the holy rebellion against the traditional order was articulated in a statement directed at Mizraḥi by a leader of ha-Po'el ha-Mizraḥi's "left wing":[53]

> A revolution must take place in our life. The *galut* has moved us so far from the path of the Torah that today Torah ... is invoked [by Mizraḥi] to battle against those Jews who seek to follow its path in full ...
> Only because of the terrible economic pressures were the parasitic life, loans upon interest, usury, commissions, and trade permitted. It is those who invoke the Torah against us who placed the people that practiced these professions along the "east wall" [of the synagogue, where prominent personages are seated] and looked down upon the *ba'al melakhah* [mere artisan] ... the productive person who enjoyed the fruits of his own labor. And it is they who invoke the same religion to rebuke and censure those who struggle against ... exploitation and refuse to allow it in our rejuvenated land ...

> We will rebel against this with all our strength. We will ... invoke the reverence that we feel in our heart for our Torah legacy ... for all that is pure and sacred, for all that is true and just by the imprint of Torah. We will forcefully protest against those who dare to profane the splendor of its sacredness and darken the glow of its light ... We have proclaimed the great revolution in the life of Judaism ... We believe that with common forces ... we can remove all that is rotten in the life of the *galut*, all the fraud that was introduced into religious Jewry in opposition to its essential nature.[54]

But Torah in its pristine form is a constructive force as well. National revival creates the conditions for clarifying the religious consciousness and, in the words of Landau, for renewing Torah as "the spirit of the nation and the source of its culture, which appears in the very building process and revival of the people." In fact, the two prime movers of national revival, namely Torah renewal and personal labor, were conceived as interdependent. Torah as "the national spirit" constitutes the source of inspiration for personal labor, which connotes the creation of "a national life ... total creative independence ... activism ... and sovereignty." In this sense Torah inspires Jews to fulfill all the economic roles necessary to maintain a self-sufficient society. Labor, in turn, is conceived as capable of stimulating Torah to embrace "life in all its ramifications, from the most profane to the most sacred, from the most mundane to the most spiritual, all of which are illumined and hallowed by its light."[55] Indeed, in ha-Po'el ha-Mizrahi ideology, labor was perceived as a religious norm, a *mitzvah*, and as the very incarnation of divine vitality in the social roles and norms of national–pioneering.[56]

Thus it was Torah in the sense of religious charisma that imbued the religious workers with the authority to dissolve the established religious order and build a new order, comprised of religious institutions which they considered more valid and authentic than the ones abrogated.

In this context, ha-Po'el ha-Mizrahi established its own labor unions and encouraged its members to organize artisan, building, and especially settlement co-operatives that, in our terms, may be considered new religious institutions into which charisma had been cast. Here, it is of interest to note that, although a newly arrived woman pioneer was denied admission at the founding meeting of the first ha-Po'el ha-Mizrahi group in 1921 – "because it is forbidden that a woman be present among us"[57] – not very long afterwards, influenced by the dominant pioneering–socialist milieu, the gender barriers had diminished to the point where women were accepted as equal members.

Far removed from the surveillance of the traditionalistic rabbinic leaders of the Diaspora, and under the protective wing of the World Mizraḥi Organaization,[58] the religious labor movement developed and strengthened the religious cultural subcenter of Religious Zionism, thereby enabling Orthodox Zionist youth to integrate into the labor–pioneering fabric of the national society. A significant milestone in this integrative process was the Histadrut's recognition of the independent existence of ha-Po'el ha-Mizraḥi in 1927, a right hitherto denied them. Ha-Po'el ha-Mizraḥi also took part in the political process; in the 1927 elections to the Fifteenth Zionist Congress it polled more votes than Mizraḥi, and its electoral margin over Mizraḥi was to increase steadily.[59] In 1929 ha-Po'el ha-Mizraḥi created its own youth movement, Bnei Akivah (Sons of [Rabbi] Akivah). In short, in the course of the 1920s, the religious labor organization became the major Religious Zionist force in Jewish national society.

The nature of religious ideology

By investing the national and social norms of the Zionist secular labor movement with Torah valence, ha-Po'el ha-Mizraḥi drew upon the transcendent center of the present. But, by adhering to *halakhah* at the same time, it anchored the whole religious subculture in the transcendent center of the past, thereby affirming the supremacy of the past over the present in the ordering of national reality. It was in the halakhic context that S. Z. Shragai confirmed the religious grounding of the moral precept "Love your neighbor as yourself," which Socialist Zionism conceived as an ideological *mitzvah*: "It is only when one observes the [ritual] precepts that one can fulfill this precept as part of the Torah from Sinai."[60]

That ha-Po'el ha-Mizraḥi ideologues were well aware of the distinction between Torah as an innovative religious ideology expressing divine reality, and Torah as institutionalized religious culture embodied in *halakhah*, may be seen in both its national and social thinking. In the national context, this distinction was expounded by Shmu'el Ha'im Landau as follows:

This "Torah" . . . has two basic meanings: The first refers to the Torah as a code of law whose realization is incumbent upon the individual; the second connotes the Torah as a totality, as the people's spirit, the source of the people's culture and life ... In its individual aspect Torah ... implies no specific essential connection to the process of rebirth in Eretz Israel. In the second meaning, Torah completely permeates the process of national renaissance ... and it is therefore ... related to the essence of the renaissance. A national renaissance is inconceivable without the national spirit. In this sense – but only in this sense – the Torah is not only a *mitzvah* ... for the builders of the land; it is also the efficient cause ... of national revival.

... The path that leads the Jewish people to Eretz Israel passes ... through Mount Sinai. The Torah that was given at [Sinai indicates] a return to complete, original Hebrew life based on labor.[61]

In the national context, then, the *mitzvah* inherent in labor was recognized as a religious–ideological precept whose immediate religious valence derived from the present, in contrast with the institutionalized *mitzvot* of *halakhah*, whose immediate religious valence derived from the past. However, the ideological *mitzvah* of labor called for the sanction of Sinai for its legitimation.

When leaders of Mizrahi contested the view that personal labor is a *mitzvah*, Rabbi Yeshayahu Shapiro, a leading ha-Po'el ha-Mizrahi ideologue, presented the most exhaustive representation of ha-Po'el ha-Mizrahi thought on the religious nature of the ideological symbols, based on the two concepts of Torah. It was on this statement that the Religious Kibbutz Federation was to draw when it sought primary religious grounding for kibbutz life.

The demand that proof be cited from *halakhah* as to the value of work would be justified if we argued that personal labor is required by *halakhah*. But no one has said that. If there were an explicit statement in the *Shulhan Arukh* [the sixteenth-century code of Jewish law] to this effect the debate would never have arisen in the first place. What we argue is that toil and manual labor are inherent in Judaism's aspiration; that apart from the value of labor for the sound functioning of society Judaism sees in labor the only possibility of living a thoroughly just life. And this aspiration of Judaism is expressed not so much in the letter of the law as in the principle *lifnim meshurat ha-din*, to go beyond the letter of the law.

According to Nahmanides [in his commentary on Leviticus 19:2], the observance of the *mitzvot* of the Torah cannot ensure that the Jew will truly live in the spirit of the Torah, for a man can be "a scoundrel with the sanction of the Torah." He can be steeped in his passions for things that are legally permitted to him; he can be a glutton and drunkard with permitted food and drink, and he can find warrant for exploiting his fellow without transgressing any specific prohibition. This is the reason for the warning,

"Ye shall be holy"; not to act only according to the strict letter of the law, but as Naḥmanides put it "to pursue the intention of the Torah." Or in the words of the Sages [Tractate *Yevamot* 20a] "sanctify yourself in what is permitted to you."

To follow the Torah wholeheartedly we should not content ourselves with the formal observance of the letter of the *mitzvot*, but we should enquire into the purpose of the *mitzvot* and try to fulfill that purpose. We should consider what is "right and good in the sight of the Lord" [Deuteronomy 6:15].[62]

Rabbi Shapiro then proceeds to present the ideal religious reality in the light of primeval reality (see second citation on p. 59). Accordingly, the religious impulses aroused by ideological symbols induced knowledge of "the intention of the Torah" with regard to the ordering of social life, as illumined by primeval reality. Thus, in the final analysis, the authority of the new ideological norms was grounded in religious symbols embedded in the past.

Appearance of the German Orthodox pioneers

Notwithstanding the modernizing impulse of Torah va-Avodah, its thrust towards the rationalization of religion was severely limited in the 1920s by ha-Po'el ha-Mizraḥi's Hassidic value-orientations, which focused on the inner life of the individual as distinct from the community. Thus the leaders of the religious workers' organization preferred the moshav – or smallholder co-operative village – to the kibbutz, because they considered the former better suited for the "perfection of the individual." By the same token, ha-Po'el ha-Mizraḥi dissociated itself from collective-oriented socialism because of the latter's emphasis on the community as an intrinsic value.[63]

Consequently, during most of this decade, ha-Po'el ha-Mizraḥi ideologists barely addressed the gap between halakhic and national norms. In situations where members of the religious workers' organization could not fulfill their national roles because of halakhic restrictions – such as prohibitions against working on the Sabbath and Jewish holidays – the focus was on how that individual could evade the problem rather than on community needs.

It was only in the first half of the 1930s that a solitary voice came forth in ha-Po'el ha-Mizraḥi literature that expressed a dynamic perception of *halakhah*; it pointed up the significance of establishing national religious settlements as public "cells" for the "Torah state," once the Jewish state came into existence.⁶⁴ In the conceptual context of halakhic dynamics, Shragai in 1934, invoked the symbol of the Sanhedrin and, what is more, took to task the traditionalism of the Eretz Israel rabbis:

> It is imperative ... to establish a Sanhedrin as the superior national institution that will ... clarify all the [halakhic] problems that will confront the [future] Jewish state and not defer the answers to all the questions that come up, as is customary in our time ... If the time is not yet ripe for a Sanhedrin in its original historic form, then some other institution possessing the authority of Torah should be established.
> Should one say, but we have a Chief Rabbinate? Woe is us if we speak up, and woe is us if we remain silent. Indeed, the Chief Rabbinate possesses one great personality, our own Rabbi Kuk, and it also has several other exceptional individuals. However, the atmosphere and people surrounding the Rabbinate prevent these outstanding persons from rising [above the others] to truly minister to us ... They are as limited in their activities as most of the rabbis who continue the roles and confine their jurisdiction to those spheres that they were wont to in the Diaspora, and forget that one day they will have to be rabbis of the Jewish state ... We must entreat our rabbis: Instruct us! Then they will be obliged to remove Torah from the confines set for it in the study house, take it out to the city streets and village fields ... reach out ... and get to know life there.⁶⁵

Meanwhile, however, German Orthodox youth, representing a second wave of religious national revival in a pioneering framework, had begun immigrating to Eretz Israel. To these pioneers, with their explicit socialist awareness, the kibbutz life-pattern seemed to offer a dynamic rational instrument for reviving religious culture on a communal level. In choosing the kibbutz form of life, Orthodox pioneering youth from Germany were adding a national collective dimension to the rationalized Judaism of Torah-im-Derekh Eretz. And by so doing they created conditions for advancing the rationalization of traditional Judaism in a halakhically ordered community that would embrace all areas of life.

We have noted that, although Torah-im-Derekh Eretz called for Jewish activism in history, it did so on an individual basis within the context of the universal dimension of the messianic vision and the framework of the European state, and regarded the halakhically ordered community as existing outside history. Religious Zionism, on the other hand, rationalized Jewish activism within the context of particular dimensions of the messianic vision and in the framework of a Jewish polity within history. And even though religious Zionist ideology did not explicitly relate the Jewish polity acting in history to the halakhically ordered community, this relationship is implied in its basic religious and national premises.

The Religious Kibbutz Federation would transfer the universal messianic orientation of Torah-im-Derekh Eretz, with its concomitant value-orientations, to the socialist component of kibbutz life, and the particular messianic orientation of Religious Zionism to the national component, thereby complementing Torah-im-Derekh Eretz on yet another level. And together the two strands of thought produced a religious polity that would constitute a "lever" for universal action in history, in the spirit of the Sinaitic covenant.

PART THREE

The religious kibbutz movement

CHAPTER 4

The foundations of the religious kibbutz movement

In a summary of the settlement achievement of ha-Po'el ha-Mizraḥi groups published in 1931,[1] two communal groups of religious immigrants are mentioned, "Rodges" and "Shaḥal."[2] Each of these groups – the former from Germany and the latter from Eastern Europe[3] – chose the kibbutz life-style independently, and they symbolized the two major geographical–cultural streams that were to converge in the founding of the Religious Kibbutz Federation. (A third, subsequent, component of the RKF in the pioneering period was the Bnei Akivah movement in Eretz Israel, which was to build kibbutz life within the mold cast by the major streams.)

In declaring for a kibbutz pattern of life, the members of Rodges and Shaḥal could draw upon the twenty-year experience of the secular kibbutz movement, which by 1931 had consolidated in three ideological federations. Thirty kibbutzim had already settled on the land. Many of them had originated as pioneering "nuclei" in the Diaspora, usually consisting of graduates of Zionist youth movements who had prepared themselves on training-farms sponsored by he-Ḥalutz (the Pioneer) movement. Upon immigrating to Eretz Israel, the members of a pioneering nucleus would set up temporary quarters in a work-camp, in anticipation of settling on Jewish national land. Jewish-owned land was scarce until 1948, and a pioneering nucleus would usually have to wait from five to ten years for its turn to settle. In the meanwhile the group would endeavor to "flesh out" its kibbutz structure. A rudimentary farm would be set up, and members would be sent to veteran kibbutzim for vocational training. Communal institutions would be formed incorporating the principles of collective property and management, as well as equality in consumpton. To strengthen its settlement capacity, the group would absorb new members – both immigrant and local pioneering youth – as individuals, or as part of another nucleus. Rodges and

69

Shaḥal were two such pioneering nuclei that built kibbutz life in their respective work-camps, in anticipation of settlement.

Although the basic motivation of both German and East European pioneering youth for choosing the collective life pattern was to join national secular youth at the forefront of Zionist endeavor, a nebulous religious–ideological idea did underlie their choice of the kibbutz from the beginning. Sensitive to the inferior status of religious Jewry and of its traditional culture within the national community,[4] religious pioneering youth sought to prove their ability and the vitality of their religious culture at the highest stage of national fulfillment, by establishing their own kibbutzim.[5] At the same time, they sought to consummate the integration of the universal and particular components of their identity. The image of self-sufficient socialist–pioneering communities ordered by Torah suggested the ability to go beyond the bounds that Torah-im-Derekh Eretz and Torah va-Avodah had reached in rationalizing traditional culture.

As with ha-Po'el ha-Mizraḥi in the 1920s, the sources of the new religious values in the incipient religious kibbutz movement were tapped in new primary groups. These groups began to form in Germany in the mid-twenties, and in Eastern Europe at the beginning of the thirties. In both regions World War I and its aftermath threw the accepted life-patterns into disarray, leading wide sectors of Orthodox youth to seek new perspectives for existential reintegration. The radical social ferment among them, as well as the message of national revival, opened up such perspectives.

In Germany, where Orthodox Jewry was largely exposed to general life, the established worldview was jarred by the war itself, as well as by the ensuing social instability. The strong radical ferment of postwar society affected large segments of Orthodox youth, and the religious socialism of figures like Paul Tillich endowed this youth with the self-confidence to pursue its goal of originating a new religious order on a broad universal basis. Indeed, it was the clear-cut socialist orientation of the German Orthodox pioneering movement that impelled its members to declare themselves unequivocally for the kibbutz pattern.

In Eastern Europe, where the accepted religious worldview was jolted by the sharp postwar transition from a largely closed traditional framework to a universalistic national state, Orthodox Jewry had not yet become reconciled to the general culture and to

Emancipation. Hence the East European stream of Orthodox pioneers approached the creation of a new social order from a narrow cultural base, and had to grapple with the very legitimacy of the kibbutz form of life. Indeed, this stream anchored its kibbutz view in Torah va-Avodah ideology. At the same time, however, members of the East European stream were no less enthusiastic about the kibbutz as a unique social framework for the integration of combined Jewish religious and universal values,[6] than their German counterparts. If we discuss the latter at greater length, it is not only because they were to constitute the dominant sector in establishing the RKF, both in quantity[7] and in quality, but chiefly because the German Orthodox youth expressed these combined Jewish and universal elements in more clear-cut terms from the perspective of furthering the rationalization of traditional religion.

The new primary groups were generally formed in youth movements, along the cultural and social patterns of the German youth movement,[8] and crystallized in the communal ambience of training farms. Typically, cultivating a new group consciousness through close association with like-minded comrades, Orthodox youth would seek out their existential roots in an attempt to uncover fundamental values for the formation of an authentic life. National awakening and social renewal disclosed these roots at the particular and universal levels respectively, and these roots in turn were envisaged as anchored in religious well-springs.

For when the members of the youth movements opened up to one another in the spirit of "equal beliefs and opinions," they began to conceive a transcendent image of a communal pioneering order that became charged with divine vitality, charisma, when it was enlivened by collective religious experiences. And that vitality permeated one's personality, transformed one's identity, and urged one to find release in a pioneering life within the framework of "communal life with all the power hidden therein,"[9] as a way of fulfilling divine will. Projecting a "full and complete life," the transcendent order, furthermore, inspirited this youth with the ideal of realizing such a life in terms of Torah. As they put it: "We shall redeem our land from the desolation of generations, and we shall redeem the life of Torah, which did not have the opportunity to become manifest in the life of the Diaspora."[10] The validity of the new symbols and the "objective" reality that they created was strengthened through the intense interpersonal relations that the members developed while they supported one another in the new roles and norms, as partners in a collective consciousness and a new religious identity. This partnership they sought to continue in Eretz Israel, in the mutual realization of the transcendent order.

THE RELIGIOUS PIONEERING MOVEMENT IN GERMANY

"We are partners in the general culture; we view this partnership as an existing fact and we neither wish nor are able to throw it off."[11] This statement of Yeshayahu Leibowitz, a leader of German Mizraḥi Youth,[12] expressed the strong internalization of universal values among German Orthodox youth organized in their religious pioneering movement, Bachad (which is an acronym for Brit Chalutzim Datiim or Union of Religious Pioneers). Rational, scientifically oriented, possessing a strong predilection for organization and order, Orthodox youth could draw justification for the universal values of the youth movement and socialism from Torah-im-Derekh Eretz, the religious culture in which it had been bred. And, although the religious pioneering movement in Germany counted a wide circle of second-generation East European immigrants among its members, the more crystallized life-style of the established German members, as well as their higher social status, set them as a reference group for the others. Thus it was the latter's worldview that shaped the movement, and it was according to their value-orientations that the structural lines of an enduring kibbutz life were delineated.

The Gemeinschaft in Bachad

It was the general youth movement Gemeinschaft that constituted the emotive crucible of the religious pioneering primary groups in Germany. The same existential ferment that, at the turn of the century, led the German youth movement to upbraid the objectivization and superficiality of life, and called on its members to realize a new human identity, a "whole" person, through primary interpersonal relations in terms of a "return to the Gemeinschaft," permeated Orthodox youth as part of German Jewish youth in general. Indeed, the organizational framework through which this ferment was absorbed by the Orthodox youth was also formed along the model of the general youth movement; thus Jewish religious "Bunds" constituted a slender component of the "panorama of

Bunds"[13] of this period. Moreover, the methods of the Jewish groups for cultivating collective experiences and a feeling of a common psyche were borrowed from the general youth movement. In the words of one Orthodox youth movement leader:

> We, too, had to extract values from those of the youth movement and to adapt its goals to our own particular character... It was important for us to find a rapport between our being and our actions, so that the latter would not be merely mechanical, in which our being has no part... And in a completely consistent manner, the critical stance of the youth movement ensured that nothing was to be considered right merely because it had been considered right until then. But the subject of our critique was not the forms of our life, which were firmly established, but our very being, the only matter that was free to be molded by our will... on the path to Torah. Aspiring towards sincerity and consistency, people who were impelled to take moral stock by the change in the world order united, and this aspiration became the essence of our movement.[14]

The religious underpinning of the existential Gemeinschaft experience was provided by affective religious movements of Eastern Europe, especially Hassidism. Sons and daughters of German Orthodoxy came into contact with Hassidic groups – whose members had migrated from Eastern Europe after World War I – and their religious awareness deepened under the influence of Hassidic fervor. In the retrospective statement of one who had been bred in German Orthodox culture: "When the huge contrast between my rationalistic education and my religious longing reached a summit, I was able to overcome the former and experience closeness to God through the exaltation of my total feeling."[15] In other words, for German Orthodox youth, the innovative component of the religious consciousness pierced the crust of routinized religious culture[16] and led it to seek an unmediated relation to Torah in its pristine, creative manifestation, to replace the stereotyped observance of the *mitzvot* that characterized "frozen Orthodoxy."

Casting this religious ferment into Zionism and socialism, German Orthodox youth perceived Zionism as capable of "creating the conditions and clearing the path for the divine spirit"[17] in an autonomous Jewish social order, and socialism as the channel for "the religious revolutionary individual to answer *the* problem of our times, the social problem."[18]

Indeed, national, social, and religious values were inter-woven in all the German Jewish youth movements that provided the breeding-ground for the religious, as well as secular, pioneering movements. Thus Jewish youth movements whose members did not come from an Orthodox background looked upon their members' quest for religion as one for existential roots, and the two main Orthodox youth organizations shared in the national and social values of the secular groups.[19]

In Germany, then, the independent religious pioneering movement began to take shape outside the framework of organized Religious Zionism. The Orthodox youth who came to the first religious training-farm, Betzenrod, in 1924, were only seeking a religious setting for their pioneering training which they had not found in the secular Blau Weiss and he-Ḥalutz farms, where most of them had trained until then. However, "The shared labor, the Sabbath, the study together, the common age – all contributed to unite the members"[20] of Betzenrod into a cohesive group. The general religious tenor of the fellowship became apparent at the end of 1928 – by which time the group had expanded and moved to a larger training-farm, Rodges. It was this group that became the nucleus of Bachad, which defined itself as "the union of Torah loyal youth in Germany, irrespective of political affiliation."[21] The establishment of the junior Brit ha-No'ar ha-Dati, the religious pioneering youth movement of Mizraḥi Youth, at the same time, provided an organic understructure for Bachad.

It was also in the late twenties that German translations of Torah va-Avodah literature began to appear in Religious Zionist circles in Germany, and Orthodox pioneering youth began to cast its religious fervor into Torah va-Avodah's ideological symbols. Indeed, the religious effervescence among Bachad members, as expressed in such symbols, was to increase after their immigration to Eretz Israel, through personal and ideological interaction with the East European element of the RKF.

Bachad's religious ideology

We have thus far portrayed the Gemeinschaft as a social group whose members are bound together by the feeling of a collective psyche. However, influenced by German idealistic philosophy, general youth movement culture also perceived the Gemeinschaft as a closed social system that encompassed the total life of an individual in a unified framework of meaning. According to this perception, individuals can realize themselves as "whole people" only if they are "organically" integrated into a community whose members' shared value-system guides them in fulfilling all the social roles necessary for the independent existence of that community. The community is conceived as expressing the ideals of its members through the symbolic world and institutions that it forms and sustains.

Applying the concept of Gemeinschaft to contemporary Jewish Orthodox reality, Bachad members concluded that observant Jews who identified with modern life could not realize the unity between the universal and particular Jewish components of their identity, unless they participated in a society that was complete in the institutional sense and ordered by their religious values. And if Jewish religious culture proved incapable of sustaining the needs of a self-contained society, the closed system of a Jewish national Gemeinschaft would energize this culture, by contending with these needs. As stated by Leibowitz in terms of Torah:

The absence of a closed Jewish national and cultural Gemeinschaft prevents a Jewish perception of life based on the Torah ... We should not seek the blame for this situation in the Torah, but in our historical situation, which does not enable us to activate the tremendous forces hidden in the Torah. In this situation we must redeem the Torah by our own efforts.[22]

Hence the specific value of Zionism. As stated in 1934 by Ernst Simon, one of the spiritual mentors of Bachad: "The heart of Zionism is the restoration of the completeness of life to Judaism."[23]

In making a complete life a hallmark of the true religious life, Bachad members conceived of Torah as inherently related to such a life: "for without a complete life, there cannot be a complete realization of Torah."[24] Thus, in the words of Pinhas Rosenblueth, an Orthodox youth movement leader, "the aspiration for an authentic Judaism, enclosed within a self-contained system ... automatically leads to Eretz Israel, since only there can Torah encompass the entire present and, at the same time, constitute the base for our people's Gemeinschaft."[25]

In contrast to Torah-im-Derekh Eretz, Bachad highlighted Torah va-Avodah as a religious ideology, one that encouraged the creation of the primary economic roles necessary for sustaining an autonomous socio–institutional order:

Our slogan, "Torah va-Avodah," does not imply Torah plus a certain attitude towards labor and social problems. We perceive Torah as an [operative] method, a legal structure, and a form of life intended to encompass and define the occupational sphere, a life of labor as well as all the problems encountered in a social system.[26]

A corollary of this integral social–cultural outlook was the awareness that *halakhah* must not obstruct the functioning of the national Gemeinschaft. This goal in turn stimulated an awareness of the need for a "basic preoccupation with *halakhah* ... its formation, development, and the possibilities for its regeneration."[27]

The socialist values of religious pioneering youth were also perceived as Torah values realizable in social institutions. The educational program of Brit ha-No'ar ha-Dati gave clear expression to this in 1933:

> The awareness that the realization of Torah is a collective task should be included in an early stage of our educational work. This awareness should be deepened by the explanation that the Torah cannot be fully realized in every Jewish collective, but only in a Gemeinschaft of free workers, in which there is no exploitation. The universal goal of education for socialism complements the specific [national–religious] Jewish goal.[28]

The enthusiasm that the vision of building a better world aroused among Bachad members, along with their sensitivity to the political climate of the Weimar republic, led them to identify with the leftist parties in Germany, and to regard themselves as part of the "working class" that would fight capitalism in Eretz Israel, once they arrived there.

Kibbutz Rodges

The ideas discussed above were developed during Bachad's formative years in Germany. But they had not yet been worked out into a coherent system when the first training-farm graduates immigrated to Eretz Israel at the end of 1929 with the intention of establishing a kibbutz.[29] What the new immigrants did all have in common was a vague feeling that the socialist structure of the kibbutz would help them attain the life of religious unity that they sought. Put differently, if it was beyond their control to achieve this unity on a national scale, they could utilize the collective structure of the kibbutz to achieve that unity on a micro-national scale. Thus, immediately after the group's arrival in Eretz Israel, one member wrote in a letter the following:

Ever since we established Betzenrod and Rodges, we have been working for the creation of a communal group of Orthodox workers. We believe that this is the only way to live a productive and independent life according to the spirit of the Torah. Today, Orthodoxy is content if it can maintain its position against other streams; if it can save the ... Sabbath from the complexities of the economy. We cannot rest content with that. We aspire to a Jewish atmosphere that is central to our future – one that encompasses the whole person in his economic and cultural life. We believe that this constitutes the only direction that the Orthodox offensive must take.[30]

The Bachad work-camp established upon arrival in Eretz Israel was called Kibbutz Rodges, after the training-farm in Germany. Kibbutz Rodges was to become the epicenter of religious pioneering in Germany, as well as of the entire religious kibbutz movement. It was toward Rodges that the few religious collectives that formed in the early 1930s looked, until they combined into a united religious kibbutz movement in 1935. By this time, Rodges had joined ha-Po'el ha-Mizrahi, and the German component of the religious kibbutz movement had formally attached itself to the Torah va-Avodah movement.

THE RELIGIOUS PIONEERING MOVEMENT IN EASTERN EUROPE

The confusion within Orthodox youth, from which ha-Po'el ha-Mizrahi emerged in postwar eastern Europe at the beginning of the twenties, became more pointed in the thirties. For, even though the Orthodox youth of this decade had undergone secular education and had become increasingly involved in the general economy, their traditional religious outlook compelled them to remain on the sidelines of general life. Such states as Poland and Romania had formally awarded their Jewish minorities equal civil rights after the war; in practice, however, this policy was not carried out. Thus, while young Orthodox Jews suffered from the same wide gap as secular Jewish youth between civil equality in theory and social and economic discrimination in practice, unlike the latter, they were prevented by their traditional religion's passive orientation toward reality from joining the radical movements that were thriving on the Jewish scene. Added to this, their refusal to work on the Sabbath and Jewish holidays aggravated their unemployment. Hence the singular state of uprootedness of East European Orthodox youth in the 1930s, and their amenability to new social integration.[31]

And then suddenly we met together ... no one called us ... we the lonely, the ones devoured by a thirst for a new, different life ... Do you remember that first evening? Hearts were enlivened, arms were interlocked ... we burst into dance – the dance of the lonely, of those who had not known each other, and now are linked together by a chain of iron ... an unsnappable chain of common fate and organization.[32]

It was the charismatic message of Torah va-Avodah and the emerging religious reality being fashioned by ha-Po'el ha-Mizraḥi in Eretz Israel that created a new focus for this youth. For the symbols of Torah va-Avodah fostered a new religious worldview and ethos in the new groups being formed by this youth – in the training-farms of he-Ḥalutz ha-Mizraḥi (the Mizraḥi Pioneer),[33] and the ha-Shomer ha-Dati (the Religious Guard) and Bnei Akivah youth movements and training-farms.[34]

In the East European pioneering movement, the symbols of Torah va-Avodah fell on a cultivated religious seedbed. For most of this youth, like the founders of ha-Po'el ha-Mizraḥi, were bred in a Hassidic environment, and though they rejected their forebears' lifestyle, Hassidism supremely groomed them for cultivating religious–affective relationships and a transcendent world image. Thus they perceived Torah in the light of its pristine, regenerating essence. In this vein a ha-Shomer ha-Dati leader could state: "There is no notion more alien to the spirit of the Torah than that of conservatism and its trappings, for the very principle of Torah is a fierce desire and a mighty longing for advancement, for regeneration."[35] Indeed, it was such a perception of Torah that enabled East European pioneering youth to identify with the ideology of progress.[36]

The kibbutz was not a necessary corollary of this outlook. Indeed, there were those who doubted that the socialist life-pattern could be made to accord with that of Torah. It was only by resorting to primordial symbols that the communal way of life could be justified religiously, as a "social unit based upon the Torah of Israel ... that springs from the very roots of Israel's mission, from the very will of the Creator."[37] Translated into social terms, the kibbutz was seen as the basis for realizing an authentic Torah life, inasmuch as it is capable of fostering perfected interpersonal relations. As Shalom Treller (Karni'el), a ha-Shomer ha-Dati leader wrote:

It is possible to create an honest, harmonious society only by uprooting the evil of the extant social regime. The prevailing capitalist system constitutes evil ... "Turn away from evil and do good" [Psalms 34:15]. Only by removing the "evil" is it possible to attain the level of "good" – to create an improved society. This can be done only in the kibbutz. The kibbutz will deny one individual the opportunity to dominate another and exploit him, and will thus enable the creation of a just and honest life.[38]

Influenced by the example of Kibbutz Rodges, and grounding their kibbutz outlook upon a radical interpretation of Torah va-Avodah, the Eastern European pioneering movement envisaged the kibbutz as an "exemplary social cell" of an improved world, in which it would be possible "to give maximum expression to both the human and Jewish"[39] dimensions of individual being.

The first practical expression of these ideals by East European pioneering youth was the work-camp established by Kvutzat Shaḥal[40] in 1930.

BNEI AKIVAH IN ERETZ ISRAEL

While the religious pioneering movements of Germany and Eastern Europe repudiated their societies of origin, both Jewish and non-Jewish, the Orthodox members of Bnei Akivah in Eretz Israel identified with the pioneering cultural center of society at large. However, this positive response to the supreme values of the national community served to sharpen Bnei Akivah's sensitivity to the wide gap between it and secular national youth in the realization of national values. For its members, kibbutz "realization" not only expressed good citizenship in the national society of the thirties and forties, but also symbolized the solidarity with secular pioneering youth. Inasmuch as Bnei Akivah also grounded its kibbutz ideology in the radical interpretation of Torah va-Avodah, it adopted the collective pattern almost from the outset. But it was only in 1938 that the first viable Bnei Akivah communal group was formed.

CONSOLIDATION OF THE RELIGIOUS KIBBUTZ FEDERATION

The basic organizational move toward the consolidation of a religious kibbutz movement took place in 1935, when representatives of the dominant religious collective groups, Rodges and Shaḥal, got together, while still in their work camps, to form the federation that was to become known as ha-Kibbutz ha-Dati, the Religious Kibbutz Federation. The self-identity of the federation as a movement sharpened in 1937, after the members of Kvutzat Shaḥal joined up with a group from Rodges (and a third group, also from Germany) to settle on the land as Kibbutz Tirat Tzvi. In 1939, a second group, "Krutzat Aryei," composed of youth who had belonged to Brit ha-No'ar ha-Dati in Germany, moved from its work camp to settle on the land as Sdei Eliyahu. And, in 1941, the rest of the Rodges group moved to its permanent settlement as Kibbutz Yavne. This process continued, so that by the eve of the creation of the State of Israel in 1948, the RKF numbered ten settlements.

Until Israel's creation, most RKF settlements were established in relatively isolated areas, where there were few or no other Jewish settlements. While the basic reason for this was the RKF's desire to create blocs of kibbutzim that would enrich the economic, educational, and social framework of its individual settlements, the choice of these regions was also motivated by the desire of religious youth to prove its ability to undertake primary pioneering roles. Indeed, the founding of Jewish settlements under tenuous security conditions, in regions that were largely *terra incognita* to agriculture and, in some cases, in unusually severe climatic conditions, served to test not only the economic capabilities of the settling groups, but their religious culture as well. And the fact that some settlement sites were associated with religious–historical memories only enhanced their attraction.

In any event, by extending the pre-1948 borders of the national community, in the Beit She'an Valley and the Negev, as well as to the Hebron Hills, the religious kibbutzim deliberately placed themselves in the forefront of Zionist enterprise. The peripheral location of these settlements stood out in bold relief in the Israel War of Independence in 1948. Six of the ten existing settlements were destroyed; five of them were later rebuilt in other parts of the country.

Appendix A lists those kibbutzim of the RKF that left their historical imprint on the movement.

The religious kibbutzim followed the pioneering and socialist pattern of the secular kibbutz. Hence the normative course of the religious collective groups was already established when they set about realizing kibbutz life. However, in order to become firmly established, these groups had to legitimate the communal life-pattern in meaningful religious terms. The manner in which they did so will be the subject matter of our next chapter.

CHAPTER 5

Charisma and rationalization

In the last chapter I referred to the charismatic experiences that inspired members of the new religious primary groups to envisage a full and complete life within the religious communal framework. In this chapter I shall discuss the relationship between charisma as an ordering power and rationalization as an ordering process, as this relationship unfolded in the thrust of the Orthodox pioneers to build such a life. Insofar as it was rationalization that systematically ordered the social reality which was prompted by the charismatic vision, on both the ideational and behavioral levels, rationalization acted as an agent of charisma. The workings of primeval and institutionalized charisma, as well as the relationship between the two modes of charisma and rationalization,[1] can be seen in the efforts of the RKF leaders to define the specific religious kibbutz role on earth, within the perspective of a worldview shaped by ideological and traditional religious values.

The numinous power of the charismatic religious experiences has been described by Ḥanokh Aḥiman, a member of Kfar Etzion, as follows:

Primal influences exert a secret, almost mysterious power. Thought at certain moments of the primeval period of creation exerts influence for an extended period through an immense force of inspiration. The vast measure of awe before the manifestation of the creative and regenerative force greatly determines a person's attitude.[2]

It was highly charged religious illuminations of a transcendent order embracing national and social values "on special occasions" – to use Whitehead's phrase (see p. 1) – that integrated the worldview of the members of the new primary groups, led them to feel a renewed unity in their religious consciousness, and enjoined them to realize themselves religiously through building "a complete and unified life, whose character, giving it its unified coloring, is religious."³ A graduate of Brit ha-No'ar ha-Dati described the world-view that was projected from the charismatic religious experience and its imperatives in the following terms:

> We realized the demand to create a complete life ... not divided into separate spheres, a unified life ... since He who is Commander, commands us to be there, where we are needed, where a task awaits us ... The unity of God as a task, a demand! ... Life, in its entirety, with all its questions and demands, stands before us. You shall be holy unto me! ... The worship of God is a demand to live such a life ... a complete fully responsible life, towards something, towards the task, preparing for God.⁴

However, as enlightenment through momentary religious illumination allowed the beneficiaries of such religious experiences only a glimpse at how their diverse values could be ordered within the kibbutz framework, they found it difficult to articulate that ordering through ideational symbols. Thus, in the early years of the religious kibbutz movement, pioneering and communal values were entangled in traditional religious values on the intuitive level of cognition, to the point that they could not be co-ordinated to form a uniform system. As a leader of Kvutzat Shaḥal put it in 1935: "It is still not possible to speak of clear cognition: everything is still within the bounds of a feeling that ties the members together for shared realization."⁵ The nebulous content of the religious illumination, as well as its exciting and ordering moment, is well exemplified by the statement of a new member of Kibbutz Rodges. Referring to the slogan of "Torah va-Avodah" as a master-symbol embodying the charismatic message, he writes:

> As against sheer religion, whose world is somewhat confined, we strive towards a life of Torah and labor, a slogan that expands the outlook and includes solutions for heaven and earth, for man and society, for Israel and humankind ... Only ... the psychic dynamic forces beating in our hearts, towards a goal of which we are always aware, and which is imprinted and inscribed within us, can arouse a wave of enthusiasm in us, can elevate the dignity of our lives and *mend the tears in our psyches*.⁶

However, before clear cognition could be attained, the tangled strands of values had to be rationalized and articulated "for all occasions" – again in Whitehead's words – by separating and arranging them in accordance with an objective formulation of the glimpsed inner affinity between them, and establishing their relationship to kibbutz life. The symbol of Torah va-Avodah signified the point of departure for rationalization.

CHARISMA IN VITAL RELIGIOUS LAYERS

While it was the immediate relationship to God that created the charismatic religious experiences of the Orthodox pioneers, vital religious layers enlivened the transcendent reality projected by these experiences. These layers were embedded mainly in the primordial–mythical and historical golden ages of the past, but also in the messianic future, and they both legitimated the new religious kibbutz life and infused the Orthodox pioneers with their vitality. In what follows I shall specify the contents of these layers.

Although the primordial layers were enshrouded in metaphysical haziness, the fact that their power derived from a primal force associated with creation imbued the individuals with the feeling that they were reordering cosmic reality.[7] For the social order of "a world at 'Genesis' "[8] – a world without any division of class and property, and one marked by simplicity and primary interpersonal relations guided by the ethic of love – represented participation in primeval divine reality.[9] The shared life as well expressed primality, a new "family" whose sons were united by a common metaphysical root.[10] Manual labor, especially in the cultivation of the land, also symbolized participation in divine reality. For working the land not only allowed the individual to see himself "as a partner of God in Creation,"[11] but also aroused a religious feeling of "soul cleansing and body purification," and thereby moral rejuvenation of the individual personality. And cultivating the soil of Eretz Israel was of particular significance in creating the feeling of oneness with the religious ordering force. Thus the charismatic religious experience of the first plowing at Kibbutz Tirat Tzvi was described as follows: "With a quiver of holiness, the tractor opened the new land."[12] In short, by using the symbols embedded in the metaphysical past of Genesis, religious pioneers felt that they were participating in the perfection of the cosmic order.

Although the sacredness of such vital religious events as Creation, the Exodus from Egypt and the Giving of the Torah – also embedded in vital mythical layers – had crystallized in institutionalized patterns over the generations, the religious pioneers' heightened intentionality toward them tapped the sacred in its pristine manifestation. Hence the Sabbath was conceived as "the Sabbath of Genesis – the Sabbath of Creation, source of the regeneration of soul and spirit;"[13] the Passover Seder as a "bridge spanning the generations and the epochs to the source of regeneration";[14] and, in relation to the feast of the Pentecost, it was stated, "To us Sinaitic revelation is not only an event of the ancient and distant past, but a daily experience which casts content into our lives and shapes their features and image."[15]

As vital layers were embedded in the historical past as well, the pioneers could also find in them symbols laden with charisma and thereby with primal religious vitality. Thus parents were urged to give their newborn children "biblical names of earlier periods. For by doing so, we shall bring the spirit of those periods into our lives, act it out and activate it into a real force."[16] Similarly, referring to the security problems of his kibbutz when the group first settled on the land, a member of Kfar Etzion writes:"'We shall build and will not be a reproach' ... even if we must guard at night and labor in the day [cf. Nehemiah 2:17, 4:16]. How fortunate that we are worthy enough to resemble the generation of Ezra and Nehemiah."[17]

And, finally, the social and national reality that took shape in kibbutz life also marked a "breakthrough to the future," to the realization of elements of the messianic millennium. For the communal way of life was regarded as "the consummate stage of social life, the fulfillment of the vision of generations, a sort of reflection of the distant messianic period within present reality."[18] Indeed, one who participated in this life-order felt as if he were "actively participating in clearing the way for the King Messiah."[19] And the resettling of the land of Eretz Israel symbolized the normative realization of a religious reality embedded within the worldview of national redemption. In the words of one pioneer on the day his kibbutz settled on the land, "The vision reigns, and there is no trace of secular reality."[20]

One might therefore say that, for the religious kibbutz member, the mythical and historical past and the messianic future converged in the present.

In the scroll composed by Shalom Karni'el for the ceremony marking the planting of Kfar Etzion's first orchard, we find a strong echo of the present's role as meeting-ground for past and future.

We are setting out ... to plant fruit and woodland trees, to fulfill the Torah commandment, "When you shall come into the land, you shall plant it" [Leviticus 19:23]. "He did not create it a chaos; He formed it to be inhabited" [Isaiah 45:18] ... We have come here to build and to plant and to strike deep roots into the Judean Hills, for this planting constitutes a new opening for our redemption ... Thousands of years ago, the hills about us were resounding with the melodies of the woods and the joy of life. Now they stand bald in their desolation. Upon ascending Kfar Etzion, we took an oath: We shall not rest until we remove the disgrace of desolation from these mountains, and until we cover them with a blanket of fruit and woodland trees ... to fulfill the prophecy, "And you the mountains of Israel shall send forth your branches and give your fruit to the people of Israel – and you shall be tilled and sown and I shall multiply man, the entire House of Israel. And the cities shall be inhabited and the ruins shall be rebuilt" [Ezekiel 36:8–10].[21]

But the present was also infused with religious charisma of its own. For its direct linkage to the golden historic age of the past, as a discrete segment of historical time in the messianic time tract, established its status as an autonomous span of experience and legitimated its opening to the ideological transcendent center. It was in the light of this perception that Me'ir Or, a member of Tirat Tzvi, could write the following in relation to Passover:

Out of this feeling of "equal rights" with the ancients we re-enter the track of Jewish history. In no way do we feel inferior to early generations. We are molded from one clay and we share redemption with them. Our share implies what happens to us and what is our historical imperative. Through this comparison with the lives of our forefathers, we must achieve independence of thought and of creativity ... We, too, are interwined with and connected to the feats of redemption.[22]

Perhaps the pre-eminent example of the perception of the present as bearing religious autonomy – of being capable of inspiring legitimate religious creativity – is *Yom ha-Atzma'ut*, Israel's Independence Day. Created as an ideological holiday by the national community in response to the birth of the State of Israel, the religious kibbutzim perceive *Yom ha-Atzma'ut* as a religious festival by virtue of the direct affinity between the present and the sacred in its immediate transcendent center. Statements such as "We ourselves saw the miracle that was wrought. We shall be the first to hand it on to generations to come,"[23] and "We must adopt a pattern that appropriately expresses our appreciation of this day, and not impose the feeling on our members and our children that our prayer is capable of expressing only that which occurred thousands of years ago and not what occurs before our very eyes,"[24] expressed awareness of the independent religious standing of the present. (However, as indicated in Chapter 8, the normative patterns that the RKF members adopted for capturing and grounding this religious experience were derived mostly from the traditional past.) Basically, as we shall soon see, the present drew its principal religious significance from its position in the time order of the messianic process.[25] The creation of the Jewish state symbolized "political–material redemption" that creates the conditions for "spiritual redemption."[26]

THE CHARISMATIC POWER OF TORAH

From the foregoing we can see how the members of the religious pioneering movement turned the religious vitality that nourished their collective experiences into a new self-awareness, one that imbued them with the authority to create a new religious order by "transforming the values of the *galut*, including the religious ones, into values that are refreshed, rejuvenated, and creative."[27] The original power that enabled the communal groups to accomplish this transformation was conceived as Torah. It was Torah in the sense of divine vitality deriving basically from the center of the universe, a vitality that inspires and guides the regeneration of religious culture, that presses for realization in new social roles and norms, through which a reality that expresses God's will and essence can be molded. This was Torah as "the material from which we must extract the leading ideas around which to shape our lives."[28] The very ability to create a completely new social order gave the pioneers the feeling that in their meaningful reordering of reality they were activating the original force of Torah.

Indeed, such expressions as "according to the Torah," in the sense of Torah as a transcendent order, and "in the name of Torah," in the sense of Torah as an authoritative religious power, imply the source of the Orthodox pioneers' feeling that they had the authority to impugn the religious validity of the accepted socio-economic order, and to create a new, communal order. Thus, when a Mizrahi ideologist tried to disqualify religious kibbutz life on religious grounds by inveighing that

> there is no greater 'stubbornness of mouth' than the claim that the Torah strives for socialism, for the abolition and destruction of private

property ... since the Torah of Israel *sanctifies the institution of private property*[29]

the response was not slow in coming. Aharon Naḥlon, of Krutzat Aryei, phrased it in the following words:

Those who claim that the prevailing social situation and economic and political regime are in accordance with the Torah and are even *sanctified* by Torah ... must [also] claim that we have achieved the zenith ... of social development. But, for those who think otherwise, who think that there can be a better social situation and a more just political regime than the present one, it is their *holy* duty, according to Torah and in the name of Torah, to strive for that exalted state in the social sphere, as in the sphere of male–female relations, in the sphere of the Sabbath, and in all other spheres.[30]

In other words, in its pristine sense Torah expressed "the holy rebellion," the sense of authority to invalidate prevailing institutions and to build in their stead "purer" ones. And it was in this meaning of Torah that the religious pioneers sought legitimation for their new way of life.

For, although the RKF could justify many of its pioneering values and norms by basing itself on the ideology of Torah va-Avodah – which had already taken root in the national–religious community in the 1930s – the collective life itself was never given explicit sanction in this ideology. Since the religious pioneers were not able to justify communal living either on the basis of the norms and symbols of traditional culture at large or by any clear-cut historical precedent, they looked to the primeval charisma of Torah and the transcendent order projected by the primordial past for grounding. It was in this sense that they viewed the communal order as an expression of the "true spirit of the Torah," the "intention of the Torah," and "the will of God."[31]

To bolster this interpretation, the RKF drew upon a 1928 statement of a ha-Po'el ha-Mizraḥi ideologue, Rabbi Yeshayahu Shapiro (see pp. 63–4), even if it did not explicitly justify the communal order. Thus, in the words of Me'ir Or:

The general law is inadequate for ordering the life of the community and the state. For the law does not prevent the doing of evil *within permissive limits*, and it is possible for one to act in accordance with the explicit laws of Torah and still be a scoundrel. It emerges [then] that one must penetrate into the spirit of the law ... This assumption ... serves as the foundation for the very existence of a religious kibbutz. For, although it is evident that we cannot claim the Torah explicitly enjoins the communal way of life, we do claim that the general commandment, "And you shall do what is right and good" [Deuteronomy 6:18], leads us to the kibbutz, since absolute virtue and honesty cannot exist in a world based upon conflicting interests and competition.[32]

Within the affectively charged interpersonal field that expressed divine reality, the individual could feel that he was achieving salvation.

THE TRANSITION FROM THE BUND TO THE COMMUNE STAGE[33]

The sources of primeval charisma opened up to the innovative component of the Orthodox pioneers' religious consciousness in loosely structured modes of their life, notably in the incipient stage of the kibbutz, which the sociologists of the kibbutz call the Bund stage.[34] This was the period in kibbutz evolution that included the youth movement and especially the training-farm, and even part of the work-camp experience in Eretz Israel that preceded settlement on the land. In this stage, to which I referred when describing the coalescence of the communal group in Chapter 4, the group usually comprised at the most several dozen single men and women. Guided by the maxim "From each according to his ability and to each according to his needs," the group realized the socialist values of equality and shared living, through familiarity that bonded the individuals into a collective psychic entity. The precept of "Love thy neighbor" constituted the general guideline for interpersonal relations. Members circulated from task to task, the roles for which were undeveloped; indeed, differentiation between members was discouraged. All decisions affecting daily life were arrived at by consensus, usually – in the training-farms and work-camps – around the communal dining-tables, after the evening meal.

The significant mode of time in the Bund stage was inner time; and value-charged activities, characterized by their spontaneity, were aimed at promoting personal regeneration through the realization of expressive goals. While the individual member sought to improve himself through the purification of his soul, his religious consciousness was directed toward restoring its unity by drawing charisma from primal sources. Indeed, the dense symbolic field charged with charisma rendered transcendent reality the significant reality in the Bund stage. In addition to communal life and physical labor, even work tools, simplicity of dress and manner, and revived Hebrew speech were viewed as expressing the "intention of the Torah."

In the Bund stage, the collective consciousness was cultivated by the group at the expense of individual consciousness and it was meant to effect

> the complete identification of individuals with public affairs, mobilizing all of the individuals' strength, their talents and creative impulses ... for the realization of the common goals through the constant integration of the members' thoughts and actions with the common general goal ... .[35]

Thus the members of the Bund felt that they belonged to a charismatic community which acted as a single personality reinterpreting the values of Torah in order to restructure reality according to God's will; "to transform life in its various shades into a single mass of Torah."[36] It was its highly charged charismatic mood that rendered the Bund stage a social–cognitive springboard for the rationalization of traditional religion.[37]

For national pioneering goals would not allow the RKF to rest content with having cultivated a lofty religious reality. The kibbutz grew in size, and families were established. The increase in population, coupled with the need to grapple with outer reality in terms of economics and of security, brought the group's consciousness down to earth. Thus, at the more advanced stage of kibbutz evolution which generally began in the work-camp and was consummated after settling on the land, the accent of reality shifted from the inner to the outer life. This phase – which sociologists of the kibbutz term "the Commune stage" – marked the transformation of the kibbutz life-structure. Rational life-patterns began to emerge and to "flesh out" the socialist structure; social roles became more specific and impersonal, and daily life was routinized; "real" time became the principal mode of meaningful time. In short, the social reality began increasingly to diversify.

Differentiation in the group's political system constituted a significant feature of kibbutz transition from the Bund to the Commune stage. Ultimate authority continued to rest in the collective, but formal institutions began to mediate its relations with the individual. A weekly general assembly replaced the informal daily gathering, and day-by-day administration was delegated to an elected secretariat. Committees were formed to deal with all aspects of kibbutz life, ranging from work assignments and economic management to cultural activities and vacations. Rules and regulations were drawn up to define the obligations and rights of the individual member.

The transition was also marked by the differentiation of the kibbutz economic system from the social group and its rapid expansion. Communal "service" branches developed to meet consumer needs, such as the kitchen and dining-hall, the laundry and clothes store. The farm economy, encompassing the "productive" branches, became the central component of kibbutz life. It was launched with the support of the Zionist financial organs and aimed at economic viability to further the goal of Jewish national autonomy, in addition to providing for the members' consumption needs. The farm economy slowly developed into a multi-branched system, geared to large-scale productivity through a sharp division of labor and modern technology. The work ethic intensified, and physical labor, no longer perceived as an intrinsic value, became the overriding feature of daily life. Economic roles continued to be assigned on a daily basis – now by a work co-ordinator – and although they were increasingly specialized, the individual member could still be transferred from one branch to another, often against his will, in order to meet current work needs. Similarly, he could be assigned to security duty. For that matter, the entire community organization could be restructured to meet security needs, as they arose.

Compared to the Bund stage, equality and shared living became increasingly formalized and rationalized at the consumption level. As one member put it retrospectively:

The individual gives according to his ability, but ability is now determined by a machinery of rule-making committees; the individual receives according to his needs, [but] needs are now determined by committees and often by established norms.[38]

Thus food and clothing, housing and furniture, vacation allowance and financial "aid to [outside] relatives," were largely apportioned according to standard patterns determined by impersonal rules.

A further feature of the socialist structure of kibbutz life that materialized only in the Commune stage, was child care and education. From birth onwards, kibbutz children lived in separate houses, according to the various stages in their growth, under the care of especially assigned members; they would be with their parents only after work, several hours a day, and on the Sabbath and holidays.

Thus, in the Commune stage, the focus of kibbutz life shifted from individual regeneration to the building of the pioneering–socialist settlement and its farm economy. Transcendent reality continued to illuminate these objective, ideological goals, but its glow dimmed. While the individual was called upon to strengthen his self-awareness, and to rationalize his behavior and direct it toward objective goals, the integrative mechanism of kibbutz life shifted from diffuse values to specific norms of behavior. In brief, as daily life became increasingly rationalized and routinized, charisma became institutionalized.

THE PROBLEM OF COMMUNE STAGE LEGITIMATION

Among the statements in religious kibbutz literature that reflect the importance of this structural transformation for social stability, and that fit our conceptual framework regarding the transformation of primeval charisma into its institutionalized form, was the following one made by Moshe Unna, the RKF's prominent ideological leader, in 1946:

> The essential basis of the group is the free will of its members and the ardor created by the meeting between will and idea. This ardor must renew itself every day ... Human society, however, cannot remain in the sphere of enthusiasm and desire. The group's second step, of necessity, must lead to the sphere of form and measure. [For] the group will remain faithful to the ideal only if it knows how to transform the lava into building-blocks and capture and harness the will that presumptuously seeks to ascend to heaven and conquer it.[39]

Notwithstanding the awareness that this transition was crucial to the continued growth of the RKF as an agent of national redemption, the transition did not proceed smoothly. During most of the 1930s the Orthodox pioneers had to grapple with the problem of self-definition in view of the tenuous religious grounding for Commune life. For these pioneers, whose ulterior value-system was anchored in traditional religion, even the goal of national revival did not justify the extensive rationalization of daily life – as in the secular kibbutz. Neither the perception of social roles as "sacred pioneering roles," nor the definition of pioneering norms as "*mitzvot*"[40] – or even imbuing the national and social collective components of the kibbutz with religious value in their own right – was enough to integrate them meaningfully into traditional Judaism. And if these roles and norms – and ideological collective components – could not be so integrated, the Commune structure could not be adequately legitimated. Put differently, when ideational rationalization was unable to develop alongside practical rationalization, the meaning of kibbutz life became attenuated. A new path to salvation had to be devised that would fit the transformed rational life-pattern.

The inadequate ideological grounding for the growing rationalization was expressed by Avraham Herz, a leading member of Kibbutz Rodges, in 1934:

> In the course of realizing our ideal ... we arrive at a point where we must say that it is not enough to create the structures of a developed economy, or something similar. We cannot realize the life towards which we aspire if we remain content with the structures themselves.[41]

About a year and a half later, when the RKF had formed and four groups were already living in work-camps, Moshe Unna described the movement's ideological inadequacy in more comprehensive terms:

> Our irreligious environment and our small membership in the general kibbutz movement threaten our existence ... On the other hand, there are certain differences of opinion between us and the overwhelming majority of religious Jewry – from which we emerged and to which we are tied by many bonds. To be caught between the two camps, with each of which we not only share many ideas and matters but also differ in many spheres, makes it difficult for us to follow an original path. And, though we have made some progress in clarifying what this path will be, it will take a long time until we are able to reveal the natural link between the real and the ideal, until we find the blessed integration between the religious spiritual moment and the collective–realistic aspect.[42]

And at the end of 1937, when Kibbutz Tirat Tzvi had recently settled on the land and representatives of the groups that comprised the RKF convened to discuss strengthening their ideological grounding, their disquiet was expressed more forcefully:

> We still lack an intelligible path of our own. It is therefore not clear if we are experiencing "realization" and what we are realizing. Community, the conquest of labor, and of the land, agriculture, etc. – in all of these we have benefited from what others initiated ... We tend to let action precede

thought. Were we to remain content with defining a "religious kibbutz" as a kibbutz that is also religious ... one which from time to time must come up with answers to technological and economic problems for practices that the Torah prohibits ... we could speedily conclude the proposed ideological clarification. However, if we define the kibbutz as both a means and a primary condition for fulfilling the laws of the Torah, we have a wide latitude for thought and clarification.[43]

The ideological flabbiness and its ensuing snags were expressed in more trenchant terms by a member of Tirat Tzvi in 1939:

Not knowing what we want to create on the spiritual scene ... undermines the foundation of our endeavor. Kibbutz life, socialism, national roles, religion, Torah, prophetic mission, faith, etc., all of these concepts have not yet been properly defined for us. How are we to realize them and in what form? Are we to continue as usual or to rebel against the conventional and search for something new? Unlike the [secular] kibbutzim, we cannot divest ourselves of these concepts, since the psyche aspires to something exalted that will provide a mooring for the human soul.[44]

Since practice preceded a coherent religious ideology, the young movement was unable to crystallize its identity within the context of Commune reality, and the lack of such an ideology threatened to impair its vitality. As stated in 1938, at a meeting of an RKF committee that was formed for ideological clarification:

The RKF cannot constitute a significant and guiding factor for the public at large so long as its members are not clearly aware of the role they must realize in their life, so long as their form of life is adventitious, and is not grounded in a worldview.[45]

THE IDEATIONAL FRAMEWORK OF RATIONALIZATION

Before discussing how the RKF made a determinative breakthrough towards ideational rationalization, let us unfold the broad worldview that the Orthodox pioneers were to draw upon in systematizing their religious ideology. The central thread of this worldview was the mutual relationship between the Torah and the present, within the messianic perspective.

If the religious pioneers perceived the present as charged with its own religious charisma stemming from the ideological transcendent center, before the charisma could take hold in new religious–cultural patterns, it would have to revert back, in the stream of their religious consciousness, to the well-head of divine reality at Sinai, where a "Torah of life" was given. In the words of Shalom Karni'el of Kfar Etzion:

> Since our Torah is a Torah of life, it is possible to find innovations in it in every generation... In every generation... a person of Israel should feel as though he himself were standing at Mount Sinai and receiving the Torah.[46]

In the words of another formulation, which cites part of a passage from *Midrash Rabbah* (Leviticus 22:1): "We believe that whatever a veteran scholar is destined to innovate was revealed to Moses at Sinai, that the whole formative course of the Torah of Israel ... was indicated at its very outset."[47] In other words, by imbuing the present with religious status, the Orthodox pioneers were also, of necessity, implying recognition of historical change by virtue of Sinaitic revelation.

This conception of the charismatic power of Torah implies a premise that there is a pre-ordained harmony between Torah and the "full and complete life" of every generation. From this it follows: (1) there is a reciprocal relationship between Torah as an ideal reality and historical reality as it develops; (2) the contents of the Torah are, accordingly, subject to change; and (3) all the changing contents of the Torah were invested in it at Sinai. And, since the premise also implies that every historical period has a role to play in the messianic process, the Torah legitimates those changes in the reality of every period which "improve and elevate the complete life of the individual and community, and which subject ... them to the ideal of human perfection."[48] From the last, it follows that the cultural and social institutions of every period may constitute the ways in which Torah orders the life of each age according to its internal meaning.

It was in this context that the religious pioneers came to focus on the relationship between *halakhah* and history. According to this reasoning, if social institutions are transformed in the course of historical development, the judicial formulations of *halakhah* should also be modified to allow it to apply its stamp of sacredness to these institutions. In 1938, Pinhas Rosenblueth expressed this view as follows:

> In our view, the Torah does not contain laws and ordinances for one generation alone, but is an absolute imperative for the entire Jewish people

wherever they are in every generation ... We do not regard the Torah as a summary of a certain period in the development of mankind or even in the development of the Jewish people ... Although it was certainly the intent of Torah to order and perfect the life of our people in the period in which it was given, we find in it not only detailed laws and ordinances, but also general guidelines for generations to come. This is the basis of Oral Law. Every generation finds its own rationale in the Torah, reflecting its responsibilities and special needs. Furthermore, every generation finds in Torah possibilities of application that were not, and could not have been, apparent in former generations, although the potential for those possibilities was contained therein.[49]

And in a sharper formulation by Moshe Unna: "We want to renew the eternal possessions that are inherent in the past and the *present* of religious life ... As we understand it, religion is called upon to answer the problems of the time."[50]

It was from this worldview that the parameters for rationalizing religious kibbutz values emerged in the Commune stage. The key to the rationalizing process was national revival. For not only did national revival arouse a creative religious power that drew upon the historical past, but, nurtured by the ideological transcendent center, it was also perceived as capable of liberating the Jewish people from subjugation to the nations of the world. Thus an independent national life would nullify the conditions that had created the "contradictions between Torah and life," which had, in turn, led to distorted interpretations of the intention of Torah. Thus, in the words of Yosef Lutvak, of Tirat Tzvi:

If, indeed, at certain times *takkanot* [regulations] and legal fictions appear, which, in fact, abrogate certain *mitzvot*, it is an indication that the people of Israel are not leading an independent life, but are subject to an alien life-order. Inasmuch as the people ceases to create its own life ... an antagonism is created between Torah and life.[51]

Accordingly, the national movement itself was viewed as capable of activating the charisma of the Torah to the point where it would sustain the unity between Torah and life in the present. Because Torah had encompassed a "full and complete life" in the golden age of the historic past and is to do so in the present, the present can be linked to the golden age in a unified stream of consciousness that bypasses the *galut* period. "Therefore, the concept of national revival [encourages us] to strive to understand the Torah anew, to revive and restore it to the role it played before the Jewish people went into exile."[52] And therefore, RKF ideologues argued, the establishment of an independent Jewish life implied creation of the conditions in which Torah could express itself according to its true essence, by addressing the reality of the present directly and sustaining it in practice.

The dynamic perception of *halakhah* also colored the socialist worldview of the Orthodox pioneers. Regarding the dominant social structure of the contemporary world as immoral on account of capitalist exploitation, they perceived socialism as a religious antidote. To be sure, the Torah does not indicate explicit "methods for organizing society, [but] it highlights concepts and precepts [such as the sabbatical and jubilee years]. Each generation has to consider them and find the organizational way to realize them in life."[53] Socialism was perceived, then, as the pre-eminent contemporary social expression of the teachings of the Torah.

SYMBOLIC IDEATIONAL RATIONALIZATION

Within the framework of this worldview, it was settlement on the land that gave the decisive impetus to ideational rationalization. For it was when the religious consciousness of the Orthodox pioneers opened up to a differentiated social and natural reality, and addressed the building of religious pioneering communities, that the RKF was able to elucidate the logical relationship between the national and socialist components and the halakhic component of religious kibbutz life in abstract, objective terms of Torah. Through this rationalized perception the RKF could strengthen the concreteness of its worldview, clarify its definition of reality and, above all, stimulate its members to act on this reality systematically, through awareness of its specific role in the world.[54]

Moshe Unna wrote in 1939: "As a result of the meeting of the ideal with the real stemming from a desire for realization, it became possible to arrive at a lucid formulation of the idea and the role."[55] The "idea" and the "role" were the modern halakhically ordered community and its development. The scope of such a community was contrasted to that of the post-Emancipation, truncated, ritualistic community.

In his comprehensive description of the stages involved in the rationalization of religious kibbutz values, Unna begins with the religious experiences of the members within the framework of the new primary groups in the Diaspora and takes us, step by step, to settlement on the land.

> Our movement is not based on an ideal that was clear and evident from the start. We got to know ourselves through our development ... The first element of our religiosity was a private religious experience rather than theoretical understanding ... Then, we had only a desire for self-definition and for creating something of our own. We could not yet articulate all our thoughts and intentions. The second stage was the decision to adopt the kibbutz pattern ... We felt a need to prove outwardly and even to ourselves that it was possible to be a religious Jew even within a kibbutz framework. We sought to find the structure that would fit [both] our socialist convictions and our religious attitude. However ... there was still no ... content to guide us toward the future. We had not yet found the factor that would show us the way as a community and as a movement.
>
> The change occurred with settlement on the land. We demanded an unconquered area for our settlements, where we would be able to form an agricultural base and a bloc. [Although] community awareness heightened around the questions of settlement, we were not aware of the roles that we had taken upon ourselves until we were engaged in settlement of our own. As we made headway, a new world unfolded before us. We became acquainted with all the roles that a self-sustaining community must encompass: ties with the civil administration and Jewish national institutions, relations with our neighbors, security matters ... all became part of our sphere of activities ...
>
> We must see the kibbutz as a community in the making.[56]

Thus it was not until the late 1930s that the RKF began to carve out its unique field of action, within which it could define its identity.

Ideational rationalization involved differentiation between the traditional religious and ideological community-related values, and their arrangement into a coherent pattern. Organized into a hierarchy of means and ends, the pattern indicated gradations in the sacredness of those values. *Halakhah*, standing at the apex of the hierarchy, was subserved by national values. Thus, while the pioneering collective component of kibbutz life was conceived as of religious value inasmuch as it promotes the existence of the Jewish people, and as conferring its religious valence to all economic and security-related activities necessary for its functioning, its basic religious grounding derived from its role as social carrier, as provider of the substance of daily life for the halakhic order. The latter, on the other hand, impressed on the pioneering collective, awarded it its basic legitimacy, and consummated the religious community. This perception of the hierarchical and interactive relationship between the halakhic order and the pioneering collective is implied in the leading article of a 1939 Kibbutz Rodges bulletin:

In a war of survival, the major task of building a home for a persecuted and ravaged people begins with matter ... which is neither secondary nor incidental, as it was to our fathers in the Diaspora. It is for this reason that matter plays such a significant role in our lives. But we must remind ourselves again and again ... that in the final analysis, our mission ... is spiritual ... religious. Only the foundation appears secular. The upper layer will sanctify and elevate it. At first, one builds with the secular and only after that does one sanctify it.[57]

But the pioneering collective was also regarded as an agent for the restoration of the domain of *halakhah* to a full-fledged community in modern terms. For, by extending the basis of community life beyond the confines of the traditional religious community, the pioneering collective created the conditions for reviving halakhic dynamics. As stated by a member of Sdei Eliyahu in 1942:

We were aware that our religious position could only be set right if religion assumed real control over our entire life, and was expressed in every aspect of our day-to-day life. In order to enable such a development, we have set up micro-communities that take part in all spheres of life ... By assuming the roles imposed on every pioneering community by the reality of farm economy and general settlement, we confront *halakhah* with all the problems deriving from that reality and thereby create the first condition for the domination of the Torah over life.[58]

In other words, the RKF saw the pioneering collective as capable of creating a closed system for the direct confrontation between crystallized *halakhah* and modern social institutions, and the consciously created "clash" between them as forcing solutions to the problems that would arise. "Our creation as a community makes this clash possible. We live the gap between *halakhah* and life, and express this gap in our public life."[59]

What was the role of the socialist collective component of the kibbutz in this hierarchical scheme? At one level, the socialist component fashioned the national collective in an ethical pattern, thereby consummating the substantial purpose of the halakhically ordered community. (We shall elaborate on this in the next chapter.) However, the Orthodox pioneers also drew upon the kibbutz's socialist structure for reviving halakhic dynamics. For through its centralized authority and rational organization of social roles, the socialist collective rendered the national collective a controlled and "directed" community with which to confront crystallized *halakhah*. In the words of Eliezer Goldman, of Solei Eliyahu:

> We of the RKF have taken it upon ourselves to create a consolidated community that will conduct a directed experiment or a series of directed experiments so as to realize a Torah society under conditions of the present. We have embraced the kibbutz pattern for two reasons: (1) to mold the correct [religious] structure of society ... (2) because a directed social experiment is possible only in a directed society ... Our goal is to create a halakhic society in the actual conditions of our times. Our method is to create special conditions – kibbutz conditions – which will make this directed experiment possible.[60]

Within the controlled life framework of the national community embracing a "complete life," it was possible to examine different solutions to problems arising from the clash between halakhic and national norms. For, if "for the creation of a society subject to the absolute sovereignty of the Torah and its full control over all areas of life, it is necessary to become acquainted with all the facts operating within a society and adjust them to Torah governance,"[61] the national community organized in a rational socialistic structure was perceived as pre-eminently amenable to such adjustment.

The kibbutz structure served religious revival at the community level in the non-halakhic context as well. Composed of individuals seeking new expressive patterns for their religious experiences, the kibbutz constituted the central authority for controlling members' roles and time. Thus the kibbutz could encourage and direct the creation of new religious patterns. The ceremonies adopted by the religious kibbutzim to commemorate agricultural celebrations in Temple days – such as the first reaping of the grain harvest on Passover, and the bringing of the first fruits around Pentecost – or the prayer patterns for the Independence Day celebration, illustrate this communal ability.

To sum up: through the concept of the modern halakhically ordered community, the Orthodox pioneers were able to integrate their national, social, and traditional values and fix upon a methodically ethical way of life, in service of an ultimate goal prescribed by traditional religion.

INSTITUTIONALIZED CHARISMA AND RATIONALIZATION

Although the RKF was able to institutionalize the primeval charisma of Torah by infusing it into pioneering roles and norms, this transformed mode of charisma could find its full expression only through the rational co-ordination of those roles and norms in the concerted building of religious community life. Put differently, it was only through his participation in building this community's institutions that the Orthodox pioneer could feel that he was achieving salvation – living "a life of Torah" – in terms of Commune reality. Indeed, more than any other factor, the building of the religious kibbutz community determined the feeling of interpsychic partnership in the Commune stage. And the community, envisaged as embodying independent religious values, was perceived by its member–builders as investing them with its own religious power.

> In the kibbutz ... every small matter attains prominence ... when it is attended to by a like-minded community. Perhaps that is one of the sources of satisfaction in kibbutz life ... The social ability to elevate life to a shared height is the direct consequence of the efforts invested in daily living ... The premise of the religious kibbutz is that religion is capable of ordering all practical and spiritual matters in life. Whoever merges with this aspiration within the group famework, feels himself expressed by the shared life created with his help.[62]

Thus primeval religious charisma did not disappear from interpersonal life in the rationalization of the Commune stage. It continued to flow in the routinized patterns of activity as well as in interstitial areas not captured in a rational pattern. However, the intensity of this charisma abated. Indeed, the statement, "There is no romance in kibbutz life, but a lot of drabness and difficulty, and only occasionally can one draw a full measure of contentment," is an accurate description of Commune reality.[63]

In this chapter we have seen that halakhic Judaism is capable of meaningfully sustaining a highly rational social organization geared to modern ideological goals. In the next chapter we shall examine the ability of Judaism to sustain this type of organization at the structural and motivational levels.

CHAPTER 6

The halakhic–socialist collective

In this chapter I shall consider the rationalization of Judaism in the Religious Kibbutz Federation in terms of the value-orientations embedded within its world-transformative ethos. The religious kibbutz community saw itself as a social instrument acting in history, not only on the national level but also as a halakhic–socialist community designed to take part in perfecting the world.

The fact that many members of the Religious Kibbutz Federation were raised on Torah-im-Derekh Eretz as the religious culture of German Orthodox Jewry indicates the possibility of an immediate influence exerted by this culture on the RKF's religious worldview and the character structure of its members. Indeed, the religious value-orientations that co-ordinate with those of modernization – orientations that received unequivocal expression in Torah-im-Derekh Eretz – were similarly manifest in the religious kibbutz. The religious ethos of world transformation that was cultivated by Torah-im-Derekh Eretz, expressed in the urge to improve creation through scientific, and specifically halakhic, law, comes clearly through in the following description of the worldview of Gedaliah Unna, one of the early spiritual leaders of the RKF:

Torah treats the world's soul, while science treats the world's body. Both spheres are important for the problems confronting us in our difficult path through life . . . Through the study of Torah and observance of the *mitzvot* man frees himself from bondage to the physical world, learns to control it and render it sacred, as a means of divine worship . . . to perfect the world and its fullness in the Kingdom of God.[1]

But, while the religious transformative ethos of Torah-im-Derekh Eretz was embodied in the aspiration to perfect the world under the guidance of scientific and halakhic law, the ethos developed by the religious kibbutz was more varied. It integrated the scientific ethos, primarily within a socialist context, and the halakhic ethos with the pioneering ethos. Further, the fact that the RKF was a forceful socialist–nationalist movement, advocating Jewish action on the world within the framework of the Jewish religious community, marked a definite, qualitative change *vis-à-vis* Torah-im-Derekh Eretz as a religious–political system.

THE SCIENTIFIC–HALAKHIC ETHOS

The value-orientations bound up with the ethos of transforming reality are rooted in two intellectual traditions: rabbinic Judaism and scientific rationalism.

To analyze the value-orientations of rabbinic Judaism as a whole is beyond the scope of this discussion. However, since the RKF members quoted herein refer to the teachings of Maimonides, it is worth noting that many of the motifs that they expound are to be found in the writings of Maimonides, in systematic and elaborate form. These include: self-rationalization for worshipping God; the conception of the *mitzvot* as an instrument for self-rationalization; reason as the link between man and God; and a religious–political ethic based on self-rationalization and aimed at creating a perfected community through which individuals can realize their own improvement.[2] Indeed, many features of the RKF's religious ideology bear the imprint of Maimonides' teachings.

As stated above, the scientific ethos, as it relates to the halakhic ethos of the religious kibbutz, appears to reflect the Torah-im-Derekh Eretz ideology as internalized by the German-bred pioneers. Existence is perceived as having a rational structure, according to an order of law that issues from God, which can be subdivided into halakhic law and religious–scientific law, and the Jew is enjoined to know God by studying His order of law in the structure of existence. The purpose of scientific inquiry is to expose the laws of the universe, as set down in Creation, and the purpose of halakhic inquiry is to expose the laws of the Torah, as revealed at Sinai. Both types of inquiry proceed by reason, which is a divine quality given to man. Discursive reasoning, employed by men of science to reveal its laws, is also used in Torah inquiry, to reveal the laws of *halakhah*. In Torah inquiry, the researcher acts according to logical principles of hermeneutics, on which halakhic commentary rests: these are "the principles for expounding the Torah." Both the hermeneutical principles and the authority to use them autonomously derive from God. As stated by Eliezer Shimshon Rosenthal, of Kibbutz Rodges:

> Exegesis is subject to rules ... We have been given an investigative key that alone may be used for interpreting the divine word: the thirteen rules for expounding the Law ... In the same revelation of Torah He has given us its laws and the method to interpret them as explicit law. For whatever human perusal may discover through the faithful use of this investigative key is in itself absolute Torah.[3]

Moreover, just as scientific inquiry is not simply an end in itself but – in the worldview of the religious pioneers – also has technological application, so halakhic inquiry is not undertaken merely "for its own sake," but has practical application as well. In effect, this uniform religious–legal prism, through which the religious pioneers perceived the structure of existence, is what enabled the religious pioneers to integrate scientific cognition into their halakhic–religious worldview, within the context of the religious–socialist collective.

Furthermore, the concept of an essential link between *halakhah* and science, particularly science within the framework of socialism, paved the way for the religious kibbutz members to turn to "scientific education" in order to anchor the religious kibbutz movement, from the ethical–religious standpoint, in the solid ground of empirical reality. RKF thinkers attached particular importance to practical action for striking roots in this reality, as well as to meeting the challenge of the religious problems it posed. For it was conscious, practical action, which necessitated an immediate relationship with empirical reality, that enabled a clear-cut distinction to be made between the religious pioneers' vision and concrete social facts, and the adaptation of the vision to realistic possibilities. In the previous chapter we saw that, in Commune reality, the deed preceded the idea, and that it was on the strength of the deed that the RKF succeeded in developing a religious ideology suited to empirical reality. It may now be added that it was the halakhic perception of empirical reality as the essential domain of religion that grounded RKF members in a realistic religious footing.

The following passage underscores the consciously empirical nature of the religious pioneers' halakhic perception; it also sheds light on the religious–political ethic related to the halakhic perception:

> ...Jewish law is revealed to us ... as a law given to us by a supreme Lawgiver to rule the community and to mold the life of the individual

therein. It neither cancels out reality nor belittles its importance. Its purpose is to order reality and to found the Jewish people on permanent elements... The idea is completely embodied in the precepts of the Torah, which are aimed at establishing a social and political regime based on Torah. These laws therefore reveal the general guidelines for establishing an ideal society. Man, following the rule of law in nature, is enjoined to institute moral law in the social and individual spheres... According to Judaism, only by creating a certain type of person, living and educated within the framework of such a society, can man approach God.[4]

THE "IDEAL TYPE" OF RELIGIOUS PIONEER

What was the nature of this "certain type of person"? What were the qualities of his religious temper that corresponded to those of the successful socialist–pioneer type in Commune reality? These were a strong personal awareness, a highly developed abstract cognition, self-restraint, an impulse for action, and a collective orientation. These qualities made it possible to integrate the religious pioneering personality within the socialistic structure of the kibbutz community. And these qualities made up the "ideal type"[5] of religious pioneer, whose character is molded by *halakhah*.

First, the religious pioneer confronts the world and God through his unique consciousness. "His conceptual base is grounded principally in reason,"[6] and he perceives himself and his actions objectively. Then, on the social level, he inter-links with his comrades to realize religious collective aims. This activity is performed out of a conscious division of labor, with every individual preserving his own sense of self.

Such self-awareness, deriving from rational cognition, depends upon neutralization of feeling. The religious kibbutz member hones his emotional neutrality by self-restraint – by suppressing his emotional inclinations through constant self-discipline and obedience to guiding principles. The resultant self-rationalization constitutes the psychological foundation for active religious–pioneering asceticism. And that this self-imposed austerity became a vital principle in the religious kibbutz, can be seen in the following words of Eliezer Goldman:

"Asceticism" ... denote[s] the view that moral life, as well as religious life ... demands that man live in constant effort and tension in a struggle with his own nature and structure of habit. The desire for comfort and material satisfaction is likely to attenuate one's power to strive towards one's highest ends, and must often be suppressed. This view insists jealously on defining the boundary between that which is an end in itself and that which serves us as an intermediate end, as a means to still another end, and considers it vital to combat any attempt to attribute the character of ends to means.[7]

Or, as Aharon Naḥlon put it:

[In] a religious way of life ... life is ordered by a supreme precept, rather than by the individual's free and changing will ... Reason, rather than natural emotion, is the governing factor.[8]

Self-rationalization, then, equips the individual to rationalize his life toward the supreme mission: the worship of God.

Self-rationalization achieves its most distinctive expression in adherence to halakhic law. The halakhic system sets down permanent and interrelated modes of religious conduct, and the individual who accepts halakhic discipline subjugates his desires and emotions, and channels them toward objective paths of worshipping God. Thus it is not one's subjective, emotional tendency that determines religious activity according to *halakhah*, but one's conscious self-subordination to the system of heteronomous religious norms. Furthermore, *halakhah* demands psychological alertness; there is a constant tension between everyday situations and their definition in terms of the religious precepts that apply to them. And, although the observance of each precept tends to dissolve this tension, the tension recurs in permanent cycles as these situations repeat themselves. It therefore follows that the "practical *mitzvot* oblige man to direct life on the basis of a [conscious] idea, rather than to allow its development according to 'natural' laws."[9]

The result is that the halakhic–pioneering life serves as the focus for the encounter and integration of two self-rationalizing systems: the kibbutz system and the halakhic system. The first system is religious–ideological; the second, purely religious. Both systems are built on an effort to sustain a purposeful life by cultivating a methodical control of action by thought, an effort necessitating perpetual tension between natural impulses and one's unnatural transcendent sense of purpose. "The entire kibbutz endeavor is unnatural, and the moment that it becomes natural it will lose its pioneering quality. What especially characterizes it is that here we are contesting nature, contesting our inclinations."[10] Similarly,

"... who knows more than we that a meaningful life cannot be normal. [For,] is the observance of the *mitzvot* something normal?"[11] Nonetheless, each system may be regarded as a yoke willingly assumed by its bearers. For "the reward for the observance of a precept is the deed itself" [*Chapters of the Fathers* 4:2], and religious kibbutz life continuously demands that its members perform their religious duties as they do their economic and social duties. The individual assumes the yoke of the precepts not out of blind submission but out of conscious recognition that, in the words of the Talmud, "He who is commanded and observes a precept stands higher than he who observes and is not commanded" [Tractate *Kiddushin* 31a].[12] Through self-awareness, he attains an inner freedom, supreme independence.

While this psychological neutrality may seem passionless, such neutrality is not totally devoid of emotion. For obedience to God opens a route to know Him, and knowledge of God inspires a sense of religious exaltation.

Furthermore, the self-aware and self-rationalizing religious personality is motivated by an impulse to act on reality under the guidance of the law.

> We who seek to realize the Torah and its precepts in the life of the individual and the community ... demand [that] the act of the individual and of the community be performed in everyday life, in the drabness of the quotidian ... If to this one can add a deep feeling and an exalted intention, so much the better; but we will not forgo the act, even if it is not always accompanied by exalted thought.[13]

The impulse toward action is associated with the ethos of renewal and creation. The term *ḥidushei Torah* (new interpretations of Torah), which traditional culture attributes chiefly to the theoretical level,[14] is conceived by the RKF on the empirical level by virtue of the intrinsic and inescapable ties between reality and religious law. Just as the scientist questions nature in order to reveal its laws, so is the religious pioneer meant to question the Torah, when faced with the data of the new reality, in order to reveal laws hidden in the Oral Law and to determine the behavioral norms for implementing halakhic law.

> Study lacks influence and an abiding validity if one does not participate in creating social life in its entirety ... Study lacks purpose if it does not lead to action. According to our outlook, study exists for its practical application to

all aspects of practical life... The only form of Torah study "for its own sake" [Tractate *Taanit* 7a] that we acknowledge is that of the working man.[15]

THE TRANSFORMATIVE ETHOS OF THE HALAKHIC–SOCIALIST COLLECTIVE

The foregoing brings us to the technological consciousness of the religious pioneer, through which he remolds reality in a new form. It is in this remolding that the ethos of rational conquest achieves its pre-eminent expression. According to the worldview of the religious kibbutz members, knowledge of reality is not an end in itself; it is incumbent upon the religious pioneer to know reality in order to act on it and to perfect it in the religious sense. To put it differently, just as it is possible to control reality by applying the law of science, reality can be controlled through the theoretical law of *halakhah* and its practical applications. In the words of Gedaliah Unna:

Just as the natural sciences are not of theoretical concern to the farmer, but are practical studies closely related to the reality of the community that earns its livelihood from the plant world, so knowledge of the religious laws and understanding of Jewish ethics embrace ... the first principles for establishing a religious society.[16]

The theme of applying the law to reality, then, embraces not only the technological–scientific ethos of both pioneering and of socialism, but the halakhic ethos as well. In this vein, the Orthodox pioneer set technological–scientific conquest in the context of "prevailing over nature's inflictions and subduing them for the sake of the public weal. 'He did not create it a chaos; He formed it to be inhabited.'"[17] By the same token, the "colonizing instinct," which "none of us can or, indeed, wish to shed," is directed "to the arch-precept of Zionism ... building up the land ... working the soil and redeeming it from its wilderness."[18]

It was in the socialist context, however, that the ethos of scientific conquest came to the fore in the ideological literature of the RKF. The ethos of scientific conquest was stated in these general terms: "Within its religious conceptual framework, the RKF requires that all the means placed at man's disposal by modern science be used to uplift and improve the life of the community and the individual."[19]

The specific manifestation of the ethos, however, was in the realm of social reality. Whereas a purely "scientific law" of social reality states that economic relations among people are the chief factors in shaping their moral interaction,[20] the religious–socialist collective is perceived as the "technological" vehicle for the application of this law. It therefore represents "the implementation of scientific advancements in the war waged by mankind for a just order" through the establishment of rational social institutions aimed at guiding ethical behavior and personal correction.

Indeed, in the religious kibbutz, the concept of the actual religious–socialist collective integrates with that of the potential halakhic–socialist collective. As such, the RKF pioneers apprehended the occurrence of these concepts both in substantive terms, insofar as they were perceived to share an ethical–social trend, as well as in terms of common value-orientations. The substantive sense derived from the divine social law common to both, which was to "order and perfect [man] and the world." In this sense, not only socialist–scientific law, but halakhic law as well, was conceived to be ethical–social. *Halakhah* embodied "the reality-perfecting and social aspiration of the Jewish religion [which] was most pronouncedly expressed in the words of the prophets [and which] *halakhah* in its entirety aims to validate and actualize in daily life."[21] But, because the Torah could not receive its true and essential expression in the Jewish life of the Diaspora, "the framework of *halakhah* ... today ... has lost much of the [social] realistic significance it once had."[22]

This brings us to the unique social role of the religious kibbutz: since the "precepts of the Written and Oral Torah are meant to establish a perfected social order," kibbutz life must "reveal and develop the profound, social, reality-grounded message embodied in the Torah for our own time and for all time."[23]

What is more, the religious kibbutz community is seen as the social instrument best suited to realizing the ethos of perfecting the world, by applying halakhic law, in its socialist garb, to the social reality. In the words of Eliezer S. Rosenthal:

It is evident that we have ... effected a change ... in the interpretation of the religious value of the *mitzvot* ... Traditional religion regarded them as a *means* to a final end, to refine man ... *This approach was oriented to the individual and not to the world.* And, while "most of the precepts" concern man's relation to the world, they come not to serve the world, but to serve man, so that he will conquer his instincts ... rise and prepare [himself] for the worship of [God] ... For man is "me," and the world is all that is external to me, the other person, the community ...

But we cannot accept this view ... We aim not at man alone, but at the world ... "Fill the earth and subdue it" [Genesis 1:28] is the mission of man who instates his King's reign over the world ... "To perfect the world in the Kingdom of God" [the daily *Aleinu* prayer] is the sincere wish of our religious outlook. The world, the real world. To perfect it, for there is no perfection in the heavens above for creating the new heavens and earth until *we* perfect and renew below. This theocratic view expresses nomocracy ... for this King ... rules only by His Torah ... as was made clear at revelation: "You shall be unto Me a kingdom of priests and a holy people" [Exodus 19:6].[24]

If, then, as Max Weber saw it, the worldview of traditional Judaism deflected the aim of the observance of halakhic precepts from the biblical mandate of transforming the world to the very observance itself, the religious kibbutz explicitly reinstated the original trend. For the religious pioneer was enjoined to co-operate with God in perfecting the world: (1) on the social level – by applying "scientific" ethical laws to social reality; and (2) on the halakhic level – by "extending the framework of *halakhah* over the whole of our lives, and invoking its authority when adopting a stand and handing down a judgment on any social issue."[25] In so doing, the religious pioneer serves not only autonomous human objectives but also religious objectives. He obeys God to enhance His glory in the world. Thus these two tendencies – the autonomous–human and the heteronomous–religious – which are ostensibly mutually exclusive, converge on the level of reason, both theoretical and practical, in the idea of a partnership between man and God to perfect the world.

THE RELIGIOUS–POLITICAL ETHIC OF THE RKF

We shall consider the religious–political ethic of the RKF from the point of view of the halakhic–socialist collective residing in the religious kibbutz community. This ethic is focused on the community, inasmuch as it is manifested in the halakhic law that applies to the community and imparts sanctity to it. Just as God instituted order in the universe by means of law, so the community is to institute order in social reality by means of the religious law that expresses divine justice. The individual's role is to cultivate the social institutions determined by the law.

What, then, is the nature of the relationship between the individual and the community in the religious kibbutz? First of all, the individual is viewed according to his objective quality, particularly his objective activity "in the community, for the community, and together with the community."[26] Only through his participation in the life of the community can the individual attain complete religious fulfillment; on the other hand, the collective imparts its sanctity to the individual.

The community assumes independent religious responsibility both in its relations with the world beyond its boundaries, including God, and in the relations among its members, within its boundaries. Religious responsibility connotes the mutual religious responsibility of the members for one another, and this principle conforms with that of mutual responsibility in kibbutz life as a whole. By virtue of his religious conduct, the individual thus assumes responsibility not only for himself but for his community as well. Thus, since the RKF kibbutz community constitutes the point of reference for most of the kibbutz member's actions, the individual is, indeed, conceived as a *shli'aḥ tzibbur* (community emissary) in the literal sense.[27]

And within the religious community, personal precepts such as donning phylacteries or lighting Sabbath candles, have a collective aspect as well, since the individual abides by the precepts also as a member of the community:

... the distinction between the religious life of the individual and of the community is perforce narrow in the religious kibbutz; religious life cannot be the personal domain of the individual. In this respect, too, there must be mutual responsibility and equality of duties.[28]

The fact that the collective controls the individual's economic resources, including the time that is necessary for observing these personal precepts, underscores the fine interweaving of the personal and the collective dimensions in the actual performance of the precepts.

It follows that the personal ethic sustaining the religious–political ethic of the halakhic–socialist collective is the ethic of duty. This ethic demands an assumption of roles and responsibility based on the self-rationalization of the personality; at the same time, it receives its specific expression in the conduct of the individual according to collective norms of the kibbutz framework. In his conduct, the individual preserves his personal awareness, and relinquishes his individual desires and inclinations out of a conscious yearning to conform his personality to his roles in the community. It is halakhic discipline that prepares the individual temper to obey the collective will. Indeed, the RKF's adoption of the term *middat ha-din* (the quality of justice) to denote the impersonal nature of the regulations of the kibbutz, rather than *middat ha-raḥamim* (the quality of leniency in judgment), clearly illustrates the close kinship between the halakhic patterns of consciousness and the "objective" normative patterns of consciousness of the religious kibbutz community in its halakhic–socialist character.

In this respect, perfecting the individual did not stop at the Bund stage in the religious kibbutz, but continued to serve as a goal of kibbutz life in the Commune stage as well. However, the religious– moral perfecting of the individual and the religious–moral perfecting of the community were conceived to be closely interwoven. As opposed to the subjective individual of the Bund stage, whose improvement derived from the purification of the soul (see p. 88), the improvement of the more rational individual of the Commune stage depended on the realization of the kibbutz's objective social goals. The community's institutions, upheld by the behavior of the members, were thus conceived as dialectically influencing the individuals in the moral sense. Indeed, the Torah was perceived as charging the collective to create conditions to ensure the perfecting of the individual: "It is not enough to set down the . . . rules of Torah and demand that the individual abide by them. It is necessary to create certain specific conditions that alone will allow the individual to progress on the right path."[29]

In the final analysis, "perfecting society is not an end in itself but a means to realize the purpose of mankind, which is, to comprehend God. We see kibbutz life as a means to realize this religious purpose."[30] Appropriate economic conditions, as determined by religious–socialist law, are a necessary condition for achieving the improvement of the individual seeking a closeness with God.[31] We thereby return to the confluence of *halakhah* and socialism: rational socialist–moral law is anchored in halakhic–moral law.[32]

The RKF ideology delineated a methodical pattern for rationalizing life towards the goal of divine worship. Through the rational political ethic, the individual religious kibbutz member is called upon to serve God by cultivating the ethical social institutions of his society. But, as we have indicated, through the rationalization of the personality and of the collective, at a second level, the individual is also called upon to serve God by realizing the modern religious community. Thus action becomes ethically unified when it is directed toward the final goal. The religious kibbutz acts "toward the fulfillment of [its] roles on earth,"[33] within the context of world improvement.

TORAH SCHOLAR AND PIONEER

What is the nature of cultural activity in the context of the pioneering–halakhic ethos? Although scientific studies are prominent in the RKF's cultural program, pride of place is given to Torah study, particularly to the study of Oral Law.

The affinity between the halakhic and the pioneering personalities was expressed in the incipient period of the RKF in a phrase coined by Ernst Simon: "Torah scholar and pioneer."[34] According to Simon, each component of this image lives in tension between his real life and the ideal reality that he seeks to realize. For the scholar, the ideal reality is the Torah reality expressed in the symbols of his study; for the pioneer, ideal reality is that of a rejuvenated Jewish and human society, in the building of which he participates. Simon indicates, furthermore, that the two types are perceived as sharing a similar temperament:

> It is not sufficient to regard the Torah scholar as one who knows how to study a lot. He is the Jew for whom the study of Torah is the supreme form of divine worship. That is to say, his intellectual preoccupation calls for a trained mind, and only for one who is capable of practicing this preoccupation at a refined level does it become identical with the most profound feeling of religious life... He studies prosaic, everyday matters. He does not possess pathos, but is often serious, refined and restrained. All matters of feeling in the Talmud are neglected by this type. The down-to-earth rational aspect is in fact the spiritual food of the Torah scholar. But behind his down-to-earth approach lies great pathos... The pioneer is the person who performs his multi-faceted everyday activities supposedly without pathos, but behind his down-to-earth approach rests a calm pathos. From the formal standpoint, then, he is very close to the Torah scholar. [For] both engage in self-realization through the variegated roles of everyday life.[35]

The ideal image of the Orthodox pioneer is depicted then, as a farmer who possesses the psychological traits of the intellectual elite of Jewish traditional society, as well as strong national and social awareness. This Torah scholar, however, "realizes the Torah and the precepts in the productive life of rural expanses."[36] By integrating the Torah scholar with the pioneer one could identify with past ideal figures: "an individual rooted in Torah, in community behavior patterns and in human life – an ideal fusion that existed in the past, in the days of the [Mishnaic] Tanna'im."[37]

Recognizing the high spiritual–psychological value of Torah study for the tone of the religious community, the RKF has always demanded "Torah training" of its members as part of their training for kibbutz life. Thus religious youth movements encouraged their members to attend *yeshivot*, and Torah study constituted a major item of the RKF agenda after the formation of the kibbutz groups. Although the RKF has not produced many members who correspond to the ideal type of Torah scholar and pioneer,[38] it has never stopped educating its children in accordance with this role-model. The resolutions adopted at the Tenth RKF Council on Education (1958), which stated that the religious kibbutz member "should be knowledgeable in Oral Law and comprehend halakhic proceedings," as well as capable of "understanding the fundamental principles of agriculture, from the scientific–technological, economic and social–organizational standpoints, and of agricultural innovations...,"[39] reflect the perceived affinity between the Torah scholar and the pioneer. But in effect, all the intellectual and practical activities championed in the RKF are those which "lead man to know his Creator and the world in which we live ... sacred and secular subjects, sport and art, they all contribute to activating man, to improving society,"[40] – so long as such activities do not conflict with *halakhah*.

How are these principles translated into practice? In the RKF school curriculum Jewish studies have set the base upon which humanistic and natural science subjects are grounded. At the secondary level, these three groups of subjects are taught in a forty- to fifty-hour school week. Many graduates of the RKF school system proceed, after their military service, to Israel's universities and technological institutions.

On the adult plane, a cultural program composed of religious and general studies is part of the weekly schedule, with sessions taking place in the evenings and in the case of religious studies, on the

Sabbath as well. Talmud study, at different levels, constitutes the core of the religious studies program, and is supplemented by classes in Bible and Jewish thought. General studies may range from literature and music to astronomy and photography. Since the 1960s, some kibbutz members also attend classes after work in universities and colleges close to their settlements. Members are also able to attend concerts and dramatic productions outside the kibbutz.

The compatibility between the halakhic ethos and the scientific ethos, by virtue of their common value-orientations, has been a primary focus of this chapter. However, the correspondence between *halakhah* and science in the practical scientific sphere as technology, and in the practical halakhic sphere as legal precepts, still remains to be seen.

For on the practical level there are sharp differences between the two due to their different frames of reference. The central sphere of reference of science and technology is empirical reality; that of *halakhah* is transcendent reality. Moreover, the significant norms in technology are practical–rational, while halakhic norms express intrinsic values. The operative system of technology is directed at achieving objective goals; the operative system of practical *halakhah* at achieving transcendent goals. The operative systems of both technology and *halakhah* have their own relation to empirical time;[41] they may also lack functional coherence. For all these reasons there is potential tension between *halakhah* and technology in their confluence in a single operative system.

The religious kibbutz sought to create a community both imprinted with *halakhah* and, as we have seen, characterized by a modern farm economy – a community that makes use of progressive technology to realize the values of the economic ethos of the national pioneering culture. In the following chapter, we shall see to what extent the RKF communities succeeded in rationalizing *halakhah* on the normative level.

CHAPTER 7

The confrontation between halakhah and external reality

In 1990 the typical "veteran" religious kibbutz – established before 1950 – had a population of about seven hundred. Its diversified farm economy included hundreds of milk cows and tens of thousands of chickens. It grew field and industrial crops, as well as fruit and vegetables, on about 2000 acres of land, most of which were irrigated. It also had a manufacturing plant. This socio-economic complex developed within a double value-frame: of national–pioneering and of *halakhah*. The Religious Kibbutz Federation is unique in that it set out deliberately to rationalize halakhic and national–pioneering norms by bringing about a confrontation between them.

When the Orthodox pioneers of the 1930s and 1940s undertook to mold a new social reality subject to the authority of *halakhah*, they were aware that problematic situations would arise that would thwart the attainment of their goal. But they were also aware that it was only through the process of building pioneering social institutions that the RKF could stage the confrontation between these institutions and *halakhah* that would force their mutual accommodation.

This chapter, then, is concerned with the meeting between new religious–ideological norms representing the needs of the present, and halakhic norms representing religious continuity, as well as with the influence of the former on the perception of the latter. This may be viewed as an encounter between two channels of religious charisma. One, deriving from the transcendent center of the present, carried a stream of spontaneous charisma that illuminated the ideological norms in a new religious light. The other, emanating from Sinai, carried charisma institutionalized in the patterns of *halakhah*.

We have noted that the Orthodox pioneers felt imbued with the authority to invest the national and socialist norms of the secular kibbutz movement with religious valence and to regard them as *mitzvot*. However, not all of these new *mitzvot* could be readily absorbed within the religious kibbutz cultural system. While the socialist, and most of the national, norms did not generally contradict those of adjudicated *halakhah*,[1] there were some national norms, in critical economic and security spheres of pioneering life, that clashed head-on with established precepts. But both types of norms had a claim on these spheres. The national–pioneering norms first shaped the secular reality, economically and in terms of security, under the guidance of science and technology. Thus, when *halakhah* was called upon to define this reality, it was not "raw." However, since halakhic norms were considered to be on a higher religious level than the pioneering norms, they were to provide pioneering reality with its full religious legitimation.

Identification with two sets of norms that were mutually exclusive in critical spheres of kibbutz reality subjected the Orthodox pioneers to an acute tension that had to be dissolved, or at least blunted, if they were to crystallize their religious–pioneering identity. If *halakhah* represented a horizontal co-ordinate for defining the identity, ideological–religious norms represented a vertical co-ordinate for this definition. The thrust to accommodate both the vertical and the horizontal co-ordinates within the framework of the religious kibbutz expressed the pioneers' determination to align the values of the present with the continuity of the past. Indeed, *halakhah* became the heart of the tension between traditional religion and innovative religious ideology.

In essence, the tension was between autonomous charismatic and heteronomous institutionalized religious authority. The first inspired the pioneers with the feeling that it was they who represented Sinaitic revelation; the pioneers consciously recognized the second as deriving institutionally from Sinai and vested in the Rabbinate.

THE DYNAMIC CONCEPTION OF *HALAKHAH*

The very staging of a confrontation between halakhic and national–pioneering norms within the bounds of a closed community attests to the Orthodox settlers' faith that the tension between the two types of norms could be resolved. We noted in Chapter 5 that the RKF's dynamic conception of Torah, focusing on *halakhah*, was perceived as capable of sustaining the historical changes in social life. Let us review this conception through the words of Moshe Unna:

Jewish religion ... aspires to contain within its framework every new reality that establishes itself in the world. It does not negate the new because it is new. The desire and attempt to flee from a new reality and its problems – as epitomized in the classical phrases, "The new is forbidden by the Torah," and "Sit and do nothing is preferable" – oppose the essence and character of this religion ... Oral Law within the system of Torah implies providing an answer for the new.[2]

Since Oral Law merely expresses explicitly that which was revealed *in nuce* at Sinai, new social institutions lead not to the creation of new rulings, but rather to the unfolding of new formulations potentially contained in the sources. Guided by rational investigation in accordance with the logical rules of hermeneutics, new halakhic formulations materialize to accommodate changing historical reality.

It follows that if *halakhah* imposed upon the individual and the community is heteronomous, halakhic formulations are subject to change by virtue of an internal ethos of renewal that finds expression in two types of autonomous activity: the creation of new facts in empirical reality, and interpretation of *halakhah* under the guidance of the rational human mind.[3] And, if new formulations are not revealed when new social institutions arise, this is because the relevant elements of established *halakhah* have not yet been correlated and applied to the new empirical facts.

This perception of the relationship between Torah and changing historical reality inspired the Orthodox pioneers to feel that they played a charismatic role: to participate actively in stimulating the inner dynamics of *halakhah* so as to co-ordinate religious law with the social reality of the present. Thus the pioneer's role was to fructify "not only the wasteland, but the laws of *halakhah* as well."[4]

Inasmuch as the pioneering institutional system was perceived as expressing God's will because it served the religious goals of sustaining the Jewish people and Torah, it stood to reason that *halakhah* could and indeed must be compatible with this structure. For "It is evident that *halakhah* is capable of coming up with the right answer to the exigency of the existence of the Jewish people, as God's people."[5] It was faith in the charismatic nature of Torah – "trust in the cogency of the Torah and its omnipotence" – that inspired the Orthodox pioneers to regard themselves as trail-blazers for *halakhah* within pioneering reality. And, inasmuch as the young religious kibbutz movement included members who were well-versed in *halakhah*, and even members who had been ordained as rabbis, its leaders regarded their movement as qualified to participate in halakhic investigation.

The roles that the first Central Religious Committee of the RKF designated for itself in 1938 reflect this state of mind:
(1) to point up problems as they arise; (2) to investigate them in a halakhic context, in terms of their factual reality as well as of applicable judicial rulings; (3) to bring about practical and uniform solutions to all these problems within the framework of the religious kibbutz.[6]

The RKF then took the innovative ethic inherent in theoretical *halakhah*, expressed in the concept of *ḥidushei Torah*, and extended it beyond the confines of the study-house. The religious feeling that inspired the Orthodox pioneers to grapple with "problematic situations" resulting from the incompatibility of halakhic and pioneering norms is exemplified in the discussion that preceded the establishment of the RKF's first mountain kibbutz, Kfar Etzion, in the early 1940s. According to the agricultural acumen of the period, the economic viability of mountain settlements depended on the cultivation of orchards. However, only hybrid fruit trees could grow in the mountain soil, and hybrids are forbidden by the Torah.

> The question of hybrids faces us in all severity. Again, we have to ask ourselves: will we be able to rise to the task? Isn't it more realistic to postpone the plan for a mountain settlement? However, this is not the course for a religious pioneering movement... Questions of that sort will not be solved ... as long as they are not put to practical test. We are the religious group ... upon whom their solution depends.[7]

Another statement in this context attests to the members' depth of belief in the charisma inherent in the Torah and their sensitivity to its dialectic implications: "Here one must not say that 'sit and do not act' is to be preferred, for 'sit and do not act' in this case implies 'arise and uproot.' "[8]

The charismatic self-confidence of the Orthodox pioneers notwithstanding, the Rabbinate was the decisive factor in creating new halakhic formulations. While exegesis of *halakhah* by a Torah scholar is conducted according to logical, objective rules, the application of the law is the province of the Rabbinate, which has sole authority to rescind established halakhic formulations and legitimize new ones. Therefore, RKF members could supply the Rabbinate with data pertaining to problematic situations and suggest new solutions, but the Rabbinate was not obliged to accept them.

And, as we shall see, the Rabbinate did not share the RKF's religious–ideological vision. Indeed, the disparate perceptions of national and religious reality of the RKF and the Rabbinate were an ongoing source of frustration to the former.

BETWEEN HALAKHIC AND RATIONAL–TECHNOLOGICAL NORMS

The concrete problems that confronted the RKF on the normative level were created by the clash between two sets of halakhic and three sets of rational–technological norms. The halakhic norms related to the observance of the Sabbath and holidays and to the farm economy. The national norms involved farming and defense as well as the provision of "municipal" services, such as water and electricity on the Sabbath and holidays. The following were the major "problematic situations" caused by clashes between the two sets of norms.

Problematic situations related to the Sabbath and holidays:
Milking cows; collecting eggs; carrying arms; mounting patrols on horseback and motor vehicles; activating a spotlight; extinguishing a fire; repairing power failures, including those affecting incubators and brooders; irrigation; summoning a veterinarian.

Problematic situations related to agriculture:
The sabbatical year; "mixed seeds" and hybrids in the fields, groves; "uncircumcised fruit," i.e. the prohibition against using the fruit of a tree or vine during the first three years after planting; first-born cattle.

Two of the situations related to Sabbath and holiday observance – milking and defense – will serve as examples of the nature of the difficulties confronting the Orthodox pioneers.

When dairy farming was introduced into the Jewish agricultural sector of Eretz Israel in the 1920s, cows were milked by hand.

However, established *halakhah* forbade Jews from milking on the Sabbath and from using any of the milk produced by Jews. Before the establishment of the religious kibbutzim, Orthodox farmers who kept dairy herds solved the problem by employing Arab laborers to milk their cows on the Sabbath. But such a solution not only created security problems for the farmers, but also rendered their herds susceptible to diseases prevalent among Arab cattle. The rabbis to whom this problem was first addressed proposed that the Jewish farmers milk onto the ground to prevent both suffering by the animals and the use of the milk. However, wasting one-seventh of the milk produced threatened the economic viability of the Orthodox farmer; and, indeed, there were Orthodox farmers who abandoned dairy farming because of this problem. But the young religious kibbutz members felt that a "full and complete" Jewish life that realized the intent of the Torah should be able to find justification for milking on the Sabbath within *halakhah*.

The second example concerns defense on the Sabbath. When Kibbutz Tirat Tzvi settled on the land in 1937, *halakhah* prohibited the carrying of arms, the activating of electric appliances, riding a horse, or driving a vehicle on the Sabbath for security purposes. Observant Jews would turn to the Rabbinate with this problem, but to no avail. But once settlement began, the problem demanded a solution.

The problem that confronted the RKF was, then, how to modify halakhic norms in the face of the exigencies of national pioneering norms, without gainsaying traditional religious authority.

MEANS AND ENDS IN THE RATIONALIZATION OF *HALAKHAH*

The problem of the clash between charismatic and institutionalized religious authority involves the social structure of Orthodox Jewry, which we shall address in Chapter 8. Here, however, we shall deal with the question of how pioneering rational–technological and ritualistic actions – what Pareto terms "logical" and "non-logical" action – can be accommodated meaningfully and functionally in a unified system.[9]

Both types of action address empirical and transcendent reality. However, whereas the rational–technical pioneering norms primarily address empirical reality, the ritualistic halakhic norms primarily address transcendent reality. In order to attack the problem, then, we must break it down by distinguishing between the ends of these two systems and the means for their realization.

The realization of the defined ends of pioneering – high and efficient economic production and full security of life and property – can be objectively ascertained. For it is possible to determine the most efficient means toward these ends in accordance with practical–rational criteria of technology. On the other hand, one cannot ascertain objectively when the end of halakhic action is realized; i.e. whether God's will is fulfilled in transcendent reality. The only cognitive measure for ascertaining such realization is the symbolic ritualistic action itself. It therefore follows that halakhic norms cannot be rationalized in problematic situations unless the empirical ideological and transcendent halakhic ends are mutually accommodative, as should be the rational–technological and religious–ritual means.

It should now be apparent that the core of the problem in rationalization of *halakhah* did not lie in the ends of the halakhic and technological actions. For, since the RKF views the national collective, as embodied in the kibbutz, as both a means for the preservation of the Jewish people and an undercarriage for a halakhic community encompassing a "full and complete" life, the national collective is charged with religious valence. Therefore, *halakhah*, as an expression of God's will, should support the modern technological activity upon which the building and orderly functioning of a national community is contingent. Even if the normative national and halakhic systems that render certain situations "problematic" primarily address different planes of reality, the respective empirical and transcendent ends of the two systems should be capable of integration in the realization of God's will. This means that, if the RKF disputed the Rabbinate's perception of its problematic situations on the level of ends, its disagreement stemmed from its differing perception of the meaning of the actions that led to these ends. But, since there is no prescribed rationale for the ends of halakhic action, RKF members felt free from the religious standpoint, to interpret such ends from their ideological perspective.

And, in fact, the problem deriving from the clash between the two sets of norms focused on the means – on the ability of technology and *halakhah* to integrate in the same action, or systems of action, on the functional level. For if, as noted above, the end constitutes the touchstone for the correctness of the means of the technological act, the reverse holds for the halakhic act; only the correct ritual execution of a halakhic act can constitute a cognitive touchstone for evaluating the realization of the goal of that act. And as noted, such a touchstone is defined by specific religious laws. On this level, there is no difference between precepts carried out in a purely ritual context – such as the correct use of the citron and the palm branch on the Feast of Tabernacles – and those precepts that mix with technological acts – such as milking on the Sabbath. In terms of the rationalization of *halakhah*, however, we are concerned here with precepts of the second type, upon which the orderly functioning of technological norms was contingent.

THE DIMENSIONS OF CORRECT SOLUTIONS

In the attempts to attain "correct" solutions for problematic situations, the source of the RKF's difficulties with the Rabbinate was related, then, not to the need to find a rational solution, but to the difference in both parties' interpretations of "correct" solutions according to Torah – at the level of means. From the religious–ideological standpoint of the RKF, any correct solution would have two principal dimensions: (1) it could be universally applied in every Jewish autonomous community, whether religious or not, and (2) it would accord with the relationship between the given law and the real situation in which the problem arose, from the cognitive–meaningful stand-point.

The first dimension springs from the view that *halakhah* is carried by the entire Jewish people, specifically by every Jewish community. And if the community is not organized according to Jewish law, *halakhah* does not recognize such a reality. However, inasmuch as *halakhah* regards the community as an entity in its own right, and since from the national–religious perspective the Jewish community should be self-sufficient with respect to its public needs, *halakhah* is bound to enable the functioning of such a community through Jewish role-occupants, whether or not they are observant. In the words of Tzuriel Admanit:

A [Jewish] religious community views itself as an organic whole and not simply as an aggregate which may characterize any association of religious people in town or village. It does not shirk from making decisions on matters of religion in which one individual or more may be involved in any activity which elsewhere would appear to be a religious transgression... It must provide for the orderly functioning of all its services: sanitation ... security, communications, water, electricity, and so forth. It cannot leave part of these functions to non-religious people ... for the entire Jewish people bears responsibility for their acts.[10]

The second dimension of a correct solution was aimed at avoiding ethical–existential "duplicity" between *halakhah* and empirical reality as perceived through the national–symbolic prism. This dimension was directed particularly against the tradition of "legal fictions": the *ad hoc* creation of artificial empirical situations in order to circumvent real problematic ones, for example, the pretense of "selling" a field to a Gentile to circumvent halakhically prohibited planting or harvesting. "At the beginning of our departure from the Land, we started the practice of legal fictions; at the beginnings of our return to the Land, we must start to undo this system," said an RKF member in 1937.[11] The duplicitous solutions were based on a rigidly formal perception of *halakhah*. But in the view of the RKF, the temporary suspension of a *mitzvah* by means of such a solution contradicts the intent of the Torah:

The overwhelming majority of the public, both religious and non-religious, view such dispensations as pious frauds. Such dispensations, therefore, may debase the dignity of the Torah to the public at large ... It is evident that just as we are enjoined to observe each and every *mitzvah* we are enjoined to observe the Torah's honor.[12]

Both these dimensions particularly bar the use of Gentiles – "a signal *galut* arrangement" that had become institutionalized in traditional culture – in order to solve problematic situations. For the halakhic system is borne by the Jewish people alone; "It is inconceivable that the Torah was given to Israel from the outset to be observed only with the help of others who are not required to observe it."[13] Thus, from the RKF's stand-point, the use of a Gentile disrupted the existential unity that its members sought to realize in their lives, and curbed the charismatic–creative thrust meant to actualize this unity. In the words of a member of Massu'ot Yitzḥak in 1946:

The kibbutz framework ... means joy of creation, ideals ... Symbols play an important role in our lives. Those related to building the land and tilling the soil are particularly important. We settle and conquer the wasteland. The fictitious sale of the land to an Arab, even if no more than symbolic, leads to derogation of values and to self-scorn. The rule for joy of creation is: let your actions match your heart.[14]

The Rabbinate's failure to provide solutions for a considerable number of the problematic situations brought to it over the years meant that halakhic norms severely blunted, or even prevented, the functioning of technological norms.

In order to circumvent these impasses, the RKF began to look to an alternative approach: if problematic situations could not be resolved from the point of departure of the *halakhah*, perhaps they could be resolved from that of empirical reality. To put it differently, the burden of change was transferred from *halakhah* to empirical reality, and new technological means were sought for realizing the defined economic or defense goal without violating established *halakhah*.

All those who talk of the need to adapt to the demands of general life ... forget one thing: it is man who shapes his own life ... Our direction should be one of harnessing the scientific and technological achievements of our time for the great role of blazing a path for the rule of Torah in human life. We should not run to the rabbis ... but to the technicians and scientists.[15]

As to the variable factor, technology would serve religion; given its methods and tools it could advance the actualization of the desired ideological goal without touching the given halakhic norm.

SOLUTIONS IN PRACTICE

Generally it took years before a rational–technological norm became established in a problematic situation, and even then the solution did not always accord with both of the desired dimensions. For our purposes, it will suffice to present the lines along which solutions were usually worked out, and to present in detail the solution to one central problem – milking on the Sabbath.

Solutions relating to the Sabbath
The key to the solution of defense problems on the Sabbath was rooted in the general halakhic precepts of "saving an endangered life" and of "a suspicion of saving an endangered life."[16] As these norms were regarded as being on a higher religious level than accepted halakhic norms, they suspended the latter in situations where human lives were endangered on the Sabbath, thereby

enabling the rational–technological norm to take over. This same formulation – which was compatible with the RKF's two ideological dimensions – would also suspend accepted halakhic norms when the electricity or water supply was disrupted on the Sabbath.

Problems that concerned the functioning of the farm economy on the Sabbath – for example, collecting of eggs in the henhouses, technological malfunctioning of the hatcheries and brooders, and treatment of sick animals – could not be solved in as clear-cut a fashion as the defense issue. However, over the years, solutions that satisfied the two dimensions were found for almost all these problems.

Egg collection on the Sabbath and on holidays is an example of a problem whose solution was long in the making. Chickens lay their eggs in special boxes, and in the course of a day fowl movement tends to break eggs accumulated in a box, thus necessitating their frequent removal. However, *halakhah* forbids a Jew to handle an egg that was laid on the Sabbath (or a holiday); by Saturday night, when eggs can be removed, many may be damaged. And if a holiday falls immediately before or after the Sabbath, the damage multiplies. The problem was particularly acute in Kibbutz Yavne, whose chick breeding industry became the major component of its farm economy.[17] As long as the number of layers was small, the kibbutz reconciled itself to the Sabbath egg breakage. But when thousands and even tens of thousands of eggs were broken on the Sabbath, the kibbutz, in the late 1960s, resorted to a rabbinic dispensation to employ Gentile labor for egg collection on this day. The introduction of automatic egg collection in the chicken houses in the 1970s obviated this expedient and finally led to a satisfactory solution.[18]

Electric automation has enabled the mechanical performance of most farm activities forbidden on the Sabbath and holidays. And although an automated system may malfunction, this innovation has acted by and large to neutralize the clash between halakhic and technological norms. On the other hand, in regard to problems that are not amenable to solution through automation, such as the prohibition against using a telephone to call a veterinarian and ask him to come on Sabbath, considerable economic losses are still being incurred.[19]

The maxim *yishuv Eretz Israel* (settlement of the Land of Israel) was an ancillary consideration in solving many problematic situations. In some instances this formula constituted the sole basis for a rabbinic dispensation to suspend an institutionalized *mitzvah*. Thus, in the Mandatory period, when Arab neighbors in the Beit She'an Valley would divert channeled irrigation water from lands of the religious kibbutzim on the Sabbath, the kibbutzim received a dispensation to perform all labor necessary to protect their water rights.[20] Similarly, Kibbutz Yavne received a dispensation to activate a generator in case of an electricity stoppage in the hatcheries on the Sabbath – a frequent occurrence in the 1940s and 1950s. In both cases, the reasoning of the rabbis who gave the dispensations was that the disrupted farm activity would jeopardize the physical existence of the kibbutz which, in turn, would impair the settlement of Eretz Israel.

Halakhah forbids the extinction of fires on the Sabbath. In the religious kibbutzim this prohibition is modified by the *yishuv Eretz Israel* maxim. In case of field fires on the Sabbath, the dispensation to extinguish them is grounded on the Talmudic injunction (Tractate *Eruvin* 45a) that Jewish frontier villages bordering hostile neighbors should take all necessary measures on the Sabbath to protect their fields; almost all religious kibbutzim are frontier settlements. This injunction also legitimates mounted armed patrols on the Sabbath – at first on horses and later in jeeps – to protect kibbutz fields.[21]

The operational guide-lines for fires that break out in the residential or workshop areas of the kibbutz on the Sabbath are less clear-cut. The consideration of whether or not the fire endangers the viability of the settlement provides a rule of thumb for how to proceed. One legitimate line of conduct would be to hasten and consult a halakhic authority in the kibbutz; another, no less legitimate line of action, would be to extinguish the fire at once, before it spreads. The immediate decision is left to the individual (or individuals) on the spot.

In view of the short rainy season in Eretz Israel, irrigation is a central component of kibbutz farms. In those regions where the average annual rainfall is substantially low – such as the Beit She'an Valley and the Negev, where RKF kibbutzim are located – crops may have to be irrigated all year round. But *halakhah* allows irrigation on the Sabbath only when the operation begins before the Sabbath. Thus, if a mishap in the system on the Sabbath necessitates the temporary closure of the water flow, it is forbidden to reopen the system, and in particularly hot weather crops may wither. This problem has largely been solved by automatic regulation of the water flow. Some religious kibbutzim have even computerized their irrigation systems.

Solutions relating to the agricultural mitzvot
The most recalcitrant problematic situations of the RKF settlements stemming from the clash between halakhic and pioneering norms have been those related to agriculture, specifically *mitzvot ha-tluyot ba-Aretz* (agricultural precepts that are observed only in Eretz Israel).[22] Inasmuch as these precepts had lain dormant for hundreds of years and were revived only with the beginning of Jewish national settlement, the RKF lacked a grounded tradition for developing patterns of their observance.

"Gifts for the poor" ("gleanings," "forgotten sheaves," and "corners" of the field – see Leviticus 19:9–10) are a case in point. The abrupt transition from a Talmudic to a modern socio–demographic setting and technology makes the literal observance of these precepts difficult. The religious kibbutzim have therefore availed themselves of the halakhic ruling that if the "poor" tend to mar the donor's property when gathering their "gifts," the gifts may be converted to cash by the donor. In this vein, the kibbutzim donate each year to charity, as a minimum, the equivalent of "one part in sixty" of their fruit, vegetable, and grain produce.

The problems of the other agricultural precepts have proven to be more complicated, and the solutions proposed for resolving them have not been able to accommodate the two ideological dimensions, thereby creating a dilemma: whether to vitiate the universalistic dimension of the solution by weakening the validity of the national norms, or to vitiate the symbolic dimension by duplicity, usually through the use of a Gentile. In situations such as these, decisions have never been consistent; they have been, and still are, based upon the specific precept involved and the significance of its suspension.

For example, the laws of "uncircumcised fruit" (Leviticus 19:23–24) have always been observed literally. And although the Rabbinate has allowed the sale of such fruit to Gentiles, accepted policy is to destroy it, to ensure that the fruit will not eventually be eaten by Jews. On the other hand, first-born animals – which according to *halakhah* are to be sacrificed in the Temple (Leviticus 27:25) – are sold fictitiously to Gentiles in advance, inasmuch as the objective condition for observing this precept – i.e., the existence of the Temple – is lacking.

The precept concerning the sabbatical year (Exodus 23:11; Leviticus 25:4-7) poses a particularly acute dilemma for religious kibbutzim. Based on the Torah's rationale for this precept (Leviticus 25:23), that man holds his land merely as a trust from God, plowing, sowing, and normal reaping of crops is forbidden every seventh year, while the crops growing in the field are to be treated as ownerless, and at the disposal of the needy. Thus, while the sabbatical year precept has a wide social significance, the suspension of farming every seven years could severely impair the farm economy. RKF settlements are wont to join the national arrangement, based on the rabbinical dispensation given in 1889, and fictitiously sell the land to a Gentile.[23] The original dispensation obligated the plowing and sowing in the sabbatical year to be performed by Gentiles. However, in advance of the sabbatical year of 5705 (1944-5), the Chief Rabbinate acceded to the entreaties of the RKF (and of the smallholder co-operative settlements of ha-Po'el ha-Mizraḥi), and ruled that the settlers may work the land themselves in the sabbatical year, "in cases where there is no possibility of Gentile labor being employed." As awareness of the sabbatical laws has heightened over the years, there is a growing tendency in RKF kibbutzim to observe some of the precepts related to it, for example, by abstaining from new plantings and by circumventing the letter of the law through introducing automated sowing machinery. Every kibbutz also symbolically excludes one tract of land from the formal sabbatical sale of its land, and leaves it fallow.[24]

The solution to the problem of "mixed seeds" in the field crops (Leviticus 19:9) exemplifies the effective use of new technological means to circumvent a problematic situation from the standpoint of empirical reality. When the first religious kibbutzim developed their farms, vetch was the prevalent fodder. But, as it was difficult to reap the vetch alone since it grows close to the ground, the accepted procedure among Jewish farmers was to sow barley or oats together with the vetch, to provide support for the latter. However, vetch is a legume, while barley and oats are cereals, and such sowing is considered "mixed seeds," which is forbidden by the Torah. Orthodox farmers, therefore, often circumvented the letter of this prohibition by having two different people, one to sow each seed, supposedly without each other's knowledge. In this case, the reaping difficulties notwithstanding, RKF settlers chose to sow vetch alone, while they experimented with other types of legumes in an attempt to find a satisfactory fodder that could be reaped together with vetch. And, indeed, certain varieties of clover and peas did prove to meet these requirements. On the other hand, settlers in the Hebron Hills in the 1940s, unable to find a satisfactory alternative to the accepted practice of grafting fruit trees of diverse species, were compelled to sell some of their lands fictitiously to Gentiles.

Sabbath milking.
The problem of Sabbath milking provides the most comprehensive example of a drawn-out process involved in finding a solution that accommodated the two ideological dimensions. The solution involved three stages, each of which was considered technologically and halakhically superior to its predecessor.

The dairy farm is one of the key branches of the mixed farm economy in the Jewish national community, and when the first Orthodox kibbutzim set out to build their farms, they were loath to forgo it. However, the pioneering norm called for an optimum milk output, and the Holstein milch cattle had to be milked several times a day. We have noted that *halakhah* forbade normal milking on the Sabbath by a Jew, and that the Orthodox pioneers were reluctant to accept the Rabbinate's solutions to the problem. Thus, when the first dairy barn was established at Kibbutz Rodges in 1933, its members were faced with the need to find a way to milk on the Sabbath without violating *halakhah*.

The first stage of the solution (1934–42) – milking into a vessel containing a cereal – was based on a dispensation that a member of a Frankfort rabbinical court, Rabbi M. Kirschbaum, had given the kibbutz, conditional upon its endorsement by a local rabbi. And, since the Ashkenazi Chief Rabbi of Tel Aviv, Rabbi Shlomo Aronson, gave his verbal approval to that dispensation, the dairymen in Kibbutz Rodges would milk the kibbutz's small herd into pails containing oats, rice, or some other cereal on the Sabbath. This solution was not considered duplicitous, inasmuch as the mixture of milk and cereal created porridge, which was consumed by the members of the kibbutz.

However, when word of this dispensation spread in 1934, it was impugned by Rabbi Avraham Y. Kuk, the Ashkenazi Chief Rabbi of Eretz Israel, as well as by other leading figures in the rabbinical world.[25] As a result, the Tel Aviv Chief Rabbi withdrew his endorsement, and no other local rabbi was willing to support this solution. Nonetheless, the Rodges dairymen continued to milk in this way on the Sabbath, and other religious kibbutzim that were establishing dairy herds followed the same pattern during this period.

Although this Sabbath milking practice was approved in 1937 by Rabbi Eliezer Shimshon Rosenthal, whom Rodges then appointed to serve as its religious leader, the general rabbinical consensus continued to oppose it. However, the RKF members were aware that such a solution was only temporary, from both the halakhic and economic standpoints; not only did the rabbinical consensus reject it, but it would not be practical once the dairy industry expanded.

The growth of the dairy herds in the religious kibbutzim led to a second stage in the search for a solution (1942–50). Basing his decision on halakhic research conducted by Torah scholars within the RKF, the Chief Rabbi of Jerusalem, Rabbi Tzvi Pessaḥ Frank, gave a dispensation in 1942 to milk on the Sabbath into a pail containing chlorophyll, a material that prevented its consumption as milk, but not its use in the manufacture of other dairy products. Indeed, Tnuvah, the national marketing agency of the co-operative settlements, purchased this milk for this purpose. However, although this dispensation was issued by a highly esteemed rabbinical figure, other important rabbis opposed it.

The introduction of automatic milking-machines into the dairy barns of the religious kibbutzim around 1950 constituted the third and final stage. The machine was introduced because economically it was more rational; however, it was also endorsed by the general rabbinical consensus. The introduction of the milking machine was the culmination of a sixteen-year search for a solution to the problem of Sabbath milking that would be both economically sound and legitimated by the entire Rabbinate; it enabled the complete integration of halakhic and rational–technological norms.

AVENUES FOR RATIONALIZATION OF *HALAKHAH*

The above examples of how the RKF arrived at solutions to problematic situations that involved modifying accepted halakhic norms equip us to respond to the two questions posed by this chapter: (1) how the RKF was able to resolve the tension between the autonomous charismatic and the heteronomous institutionalized religious authorities to which it felt bound; and (2) how it was possible to undo problematic situations by integrating the halakhic and the rational–technological norms, without impairing the functioning of the latter. (We shall not discuss solutions arrived at through altering empirical reality.) In effect, these two questions are intertwined, and can be jointly formulated: how could the RKF maintain orderly technological activity within the framework of the desired ideological–religious dimensions, and at the same time maintain halakhic discipline?

The solutions arrived at can be divided into three types: (1) those that complied with both of the RKF's ideological–religious dimensions; (2) those that did not comply; and (3) those that complied and found some rabbinical support but were not accepted by rabbinical consensus.

Carrying out defense or municipal service-related activities on the Sabbath, on the basis that it "saves an endangered life," complies with both dimensions because it implies the displacement of an accepted halakhic norm in favor of a superordinate halakhic norm that suspends the ritualistic dimension of the former. And although the Rabbinate has generally regarded the principle of "saving an endangered life" as pertaining to an individual or a number of individuals, whereas the RKF interpreted this principle as pertaining to the existence of a Jewish national community – or of the Jewish people through this community[26] – the rational action involved is the same in both instances. In other words, the RKF could grasp the rope at both ends: it could act rationally according to its religious interpretation of reality and still remain within the bounds of established halakhic authority.

Furthermore, a cognate principle was applied to many other problematic situations in connection with the Sabbath in which the activation of a rational–technological norm is justified by virtue of "a suspicion of saving an endangered life." In cases such as these, however, the rational–technological norm was generally compounded by a non-institutionalized halakhic norm of *shinuy* (modification). For example, in 1942 the Tirat Tzvi bulletin reported that the Rabbinate had authorized operation of the wireless station on the Sabbath – "if possible with a modification" – if its use was essential for the defense of the settlement.[27] In this case the modification – a slight change in performance – lent the rational action a ritual increment to ensure awareness of the transcendent end towards which the action was directed. Another example of *shinuy* is actualization of the technological norm by two people instead of the normal one in problematic situations connected with the Sabbath, as in the reactivation of a generator that had ceased working. In situations involving defense and orderly functioning of municipal services, the ritual increment did not impair the rational action. The addition of food or chlorophyll to the Sabbath milking-pail was regarded in this light.

Thus, through solutions of the first type, the RKF advanced the rationalization of *halakhah* without having to wrestle with the problem of conflicting authority.

The legal fiction – generally entailing the use of Gentiles in problematic situations involving the sabbatical year and first-born animals – constitutes an example of the second type of solution. While this type of solution enables orderly, rational action, the benefit gained by such action is offset by neutralization of the relevant precept. For, unlike the dispensation based on "saving an endangered life," which is inherent in *halakhah* and where one precept is displaced by another, the utilization of Gentiles introduces a foreign element – a sort of *deus ex machina* – to solve a problem that cannot be solved by the known givens. While the RKF accepted the solution of the Rabbinate in such cases because its members identified with the ends of the rational action made possible by the dispensation, they disapproved of the means. Thus here, rationalization of *halakhah* is deficient.

Solutions of the third type, those formally based upon a "solitary opinion" of a recognized rabbi or upon the opinions of several rabbis, but which are not approved by the rabbinical consensus, are perhaps the most interesting from the sociological viewpoint; they generally constitute stopgaps, in anticipation of solutions that will eventually be approved by the rabbinical consensus.

The first dispensation for Sabbath milking, onto food, is the preeminent example of this type of solution. Indeed, this solution was not illegitimate, even though it did not have the approval of the rabbinical consensus, because halakhic dynamics are not rigorous and one-directional; more than one halakhic solution may be proposed for a problematic situation when, in the words of the Talmud, "both these and these are the living words of God." Thus, although there may be differences of opinion as to which is the "superior" means for achieving the goal of the halakhic precept, in terms of interpreting the intention of the Torah, the halakhic means that is functionally most compatible with the technological means of an economic or defense-oriented action may be adopted, even if it is a "minimum" norm that is determined by a "lenient" rabbi. "Just as we cannot solve all of the social and political problems immediately upon coming to Eretz Israel, so it is natural that the religious problems will be solved only gradually,"[28] said a leading member of the RKF in the 1930s. In the meantime, until a complete solution can be reached, one that will be agreeable to the Rabbinate as well as to the RKF, it is permissible to employ a "minimum" halakhic norm that can integrate functionally with a rational–technological one. In this respect, solutions of the third type also advance rationalization of *halakhah*.

And, indeed, in a situation where it is impossible to reconcile the ritual halakhic with the rational–technological norm, one might invoke Kingsley Davis' insight, that a person acting irrationally may be under the illusion that he is acting rationally, since his attention is given to the means at his disposal, and not to all of the means available.[29] Awareness of the halakhically approved means suppressed awareness of autonomous rational means in RKF consciousness. The fact that many Orthodox kibbutzim have demonstrated a high level of economic performance from the beginning, and, what is more, that this performance continues to be outstanding, encouraged and continues to encourage RKF members in their belief that they are not handicapped economically because they choose to live in accordance with halakhic precepts.

A further point concerning the openness of *halakhah* to change within the context of modernization is related to the existence of "metahalakhic" principles, namely basic principles that guide the interpretation of *halakhah* according to the intent of Torah and thereby influence adjudication. If, in the course of building and sustaining its pioneering settlements, the RKF was able to institutionalize rational–technological and halakhic norms without one type of norm invalidating the other, this was often possible because the physical existence of a Jewish community, especially one that takes part in settling Eretz Israel, is a metahalakhic principle.

If a certain response to the pressure of exigencies is of necessity legitimate, this is so because of metahalakhic norms that postulate the halakhic system as a framework for the normal existence of a Jewish community. This norm pertains to the special affinity between the Torah and the community meant to observe it, for without the existence of such a community, Torah cannot exist. It behoves us, therefore, to activate halakhic technique in such a manner that will ensure the basic existential needs of the Jewish people.[30]

The data in hand are too scanty for drawing general conclusions as to the significance of metahalakhic principles in deciding the adjudications of the rabbis to whom the Orthodox kibbutzim turned for the solution of problematic situations. However, within the context of the transformative capacities of traditional Jewish religious culture with respect to modernization, the existence of such diffuse principles should not go unmentioned.

TIME-LAG BETWEEN NEW INSTITUTIONS AND NEW HALAKHIC RULINGS

Problematic situations in the initial period of settlement could have thwarted the RKF's enterprise, had not adequate solutions been found for most of them. The Orthodox settlers were able to draw upon the experience of the secular kibbutz movement and to receive, ready-formed, many of the technological norms developed by that movement. Indeed, the experience of the secular movement made the RKF aware of many of the difficulties involved in reconciling rational–technological and halakhic norms. Even so, there was a distinct time-lag between the RKF's new social institutions and new halakhic formulations that legitimated their functioning. The new social institutions, then, preceded the new formulations of *halakhah*; the latter rounded them off, religiously speaking. It was religious daring grounded on charismatic authority that inspired the RKF to plunge into the halakhically disarrayed reality, out of faith that *halakhah*, as interpreted by institutionalized authority, would accommodate the rational–technological norm *ex post facto* in problematic situations.

Regarding the time-lag, one might argue that the relationship between *halakhah* and empirical reality could be compared to that between mathematics and physics.[31] Just as mathematics employs deductive rules in order to determine the formula for an empirical phenomenon, so *halakhah*, operating in accordance with such rules and its own given laws, may determine the religious formula for a new empirical phenomenon *a priori*. In practice, however, it seems that the probability of preparing halakhic formulations in advance for new empirical situations is very small. For changes in empirical reality, whether intentional or haphazard, are far more varied and frequent than the new halakhic formulations made by a small group of scholars bound by well-defined laws and rules. The possibilities for creating new empirical situations are therefore infinitely greater than those for determining in advance new halakhic rulings that will fit such situations.

Despite its innovative ethos on the theoretical level, then, *halakhah* as a normative system tends to restrain the innovative thrust on the practical level. The precepts of the Torah are regarded by the observant as absolutely binding, and they enjoin great caution in defining new empirical situations that may clash with them. One could even argue that the halakhic norm discourages the creation of new situations that might involve its transgression. The new situations are generally created by the unobservant, and it is only when the observant get to know them at first hand, generally after the situations have become institutionalized, that halakhic definitions may be called for after the fact.

And since changes in formulated *halakhah* are made only after a specific question is brought before a halakhic authority, without the latter having anticipated the question so as to study the problem in advance, the time-lapse between the genesis of a new situation and its halakhic treatment tends to widen. In short, the *halakhah*-observant do not tend to initiate the creation of new social situations.

It was the RKF's principle of forcing *halakhah* to confront new empirical situations directly that marked its unique path among modern Orthodox movements for religious renewal. The RKF's perception of pioneering reality as an expression of the "intent of the Torah" legitimated the building of these pioneering institutions and nurtured the belief that *halakhah* was bound to sustain this reality. This pragmatic approach to reality was expressed by Avraham Herz in 1934:

> It is not ideologies or theories, schools of thought or lectures, that are decisive in creating the national–religious reality in Eretz Israel. It is the life that one lives that calls for a practical solution to all its problems and activities – only such a life can determine the form of the synthesis between Torah and labor.[32]

And in 1939, two years after RKF settlement had begun, it was possible to state:

Our group enterprise would not have come into being had we not acted upon our will to create by boldly taking matters into our own hands, and had we waited for a formal solution ... When we first began our enterprise, we were taken to task, regarded as transgressors in the accepted traditional sphere. Then traditional Jewry became reconciled to us, and finally, today, many religious circles look upon us as the creators of a new religious reality.[33]

Perhaps the outstanding example of this daring approach involved the problems of defense on the Sabbath. We have noted that, when Tirat Tzvi settled on the land in 1937, *halakhah* did not permit the carrying out on the Sabbath of the very activities needed to ensure the security of the autonomous Jewish settlement.[34] However, when *ex post facto* security problems arose that jeopardized its very existence, the settlement managed, over time, to obtain the Rabbinate's dispensations for defense activities on the Sabbath. As stated retrospectively by Me'ir Or:

Just as a rabbi to whom we referred the question of milking on the Sabbath answered: "Do you really have to maintain a dairy barn? Why don't you occupy yourselves with other matters, without becoming involved in matters of *halakhah*?" ... we probably would have received an answer in the same vein had we asked rabbis whether we were permitted to settle in the Beit She'an Valley and thereby place ourselves in situations which would compel us to violate the Sabbath for reasons of security. But we did not ask the Rabbinate whether we were permitted to settle there. And, when we created facts, the Rabbinate proceeded to confirm them, permitting the violation of the Sabbath for security reasons by the rationale of saving an endangered life. Many other problems of this sort were not solved *a priori*, but only after we created facts.[35]

By plunging into the halakhically disarrayed reality, the RKF served as an intermediary group between pioneering and halakhic institutions, and could integrate the two in a unified social system.

ECONOMIC ACHIEVEMENT OF THE RKF

We return to the question of the relation between Jewish religion and modernization in terms of economic activity. We have noted Sombart's view that Judaism encourages economic achievement. We have also seen that the ethos of world transformation, which according to Weber was latent in pre-Emancipation rabbinical Jewry, is clearly expressed in the Orthodox kibbutzim. It therefore seems reasonable to expect that this ethos can influence economic performance positively. But we have also seen that halakhic restrictions can impair economic activity. One may ask, therefore: what is the net influence of Judaism on the RKF's economic performance?

To answer this question properly, it would be necessary to compare the economic performance of the Orthodox kibbutzim with that of the secular kibbutzim in the period under study. The 1930s and 1940s were a period of settlement and economic entrenchment in the life of the RKF, as well as one of halakhic groping, and pioneering norms had not yet been institutionalized in many of the problematic situations. And, inasmuch as the years before the establishment of the State of Israel also constituted the pre-eminent ideological period in the life of the secular kibbutzim, it stands to reason that the influence of national collective goals on the economic ethos in these kibbutzim was particularly strong then. We do not have reliable economic data for comparing the religious and secular kibbutzim in this period, but we can assume that the economic performance of the RKF settlements was no better than, and perhaps even fell below, that of the secular kibbutzim.

On the other hand, a study covering the 1958–82 period seems to provide an answer to the question of the influence of religion on the RKF's economic performance in its second twenty-five years. This study indicates that the economic achievements of the RKF group of settlements in this period have increasingly surpassed those of each of the secular kibbutz federations.[36] The gap between the economic performance of the RKF and that of the secular federations has become particularly evident since 1983. For, while the two major secular kibbutz federations have sunk into financial difficulties due to heavy borrowing and ill-judged financial investments, the RKF, having practiced a tight investment policy and adopted a lower standard of living than the secular kibbutzim all along, has remained economically sound.

To compare the RKF economic performance with that of the secular kibbutz federations, let us address a typical year within the above time-span – 1972.[37] A comparison made for this year between the economic performance of the then existing thirteen RKF kibbutzim and the eighty-three kibbutzim of Ihud ha-Kevutzot veha-Kibbutzim Federation indicates that, for the same level of productivity per member, the religious kibbutzim rated higher than the secular in net income (1.3 times more per member), savings (3.2

times more per member), and net worth (2.6 more per member). These results were achieved despite the Orthodox kibbutzim's higher birth rate (1.3 more children per couple) and lesser dependence on industry, as well as the halakhic restraints under which they operated. Since the economic standard of the Ihud farms in that period was characteristic of that of the other secular kibbutz federations – ha-Kibbutz ha-Me'uḥad and ha-Kibbutz ha-Artzi[38] – and since the standard of productivity of all the kibbutzim excelled by international standards, the economic success of the RKF seems to have been outstanding.

Yaakov Goldschmidt's detailed analysis of the RKF's economic performance within the kibbutz movement attributes its success to extra-economic factors.[39] After pointing to the economic handicaps of the RKF – among which he includes the less favorable geographic conditions of the RKF settlements and their younger age – he proceeds to single out three interrelated factors that appear to account for the RKF's success: (1) its relatively smaller size among the kibbutz federations; (2) the German cultural background of most members of the RKF's veteran kibbutzim; (3) its religious value-system. While the smaller size enables a closer supervision of the economic behavior of the individual kibbutzim and tends to enhance solidarity and mutual aid among them, and the German background is conducive to an orderly regimen, in the final analysis it is the value-system that nurtures the RKF's economic success.[40] In other words, the RKF's economic success seems to be rooted in religious factors.

In the past three chapters, a basic theme recurs: in the life of the RKF, ideology serves religion, which is embodied in *halakhah*. Both the socialist–religious and the national–pioneering communities encompassed within the structure of the religious kibbutz were perceived by the Orthodox pioneers as intermediate, rather than final, goals, serving the transcendent goal of worshipping God according to established patterns of traditional culture. If, for the secular kibbutz movement, national revival and independence constituted the ultimate goal of kibbutz life, this goal was largely realized with the creation of the State of Israel in 1948. In the RKF, on the other hand, modern nationhood was conceived as a means for religious worship, both before and after the creation of the state. As Eliezer Shimshon Rosenthal stated in 1942:

Our Zionism does not view the free development of the national treasures ... [as] an essential matter of independent value. It wishes to view all of them established towards religious worship, to constitute a vehicle for the Divine Presence. In this sense ... it is incumbent [on us] to lay the economic–sociological and political foundations, whose corollary can only be the observance of the *mitzvot*.[41]

And, although the life-style of the Orthodox kibbutzim has undergone changes since the establishment of the state, as it has in the secular kibbutzim – changes expressed, among other things, in a considerably higher standard of living – it seems that the halakhic framework of religious kibbutz life constitutes a powerful, meaningful structure for rational organization of everyday activity toward the ultimate transcendent goal, thereby informing the ideological norms with its authority. Our analysis suggests that the economic success of the RKF may best be explained by its religious–political ethic grounded upon religious self-rationalization. Indeed, the maintenance expenditures per person (adults and children) of the RKF in 1976 – indicating a higher measure of self-restraint – were 80 percent of those of the Ihud.[42]

Again we turn to RKF literature to show that the relatively ascetic personal norms in effect in the RKF are grounded in its religious ethic, and to examine the possible effect of this ascetic orientation on the political ethic and its economic results. The passages below are quoted from the published proceedings of three RKF seminars held between 1961 and 1970, which were devoted to the broad relationship between the individual member, the farm economy, the polity, and the general value-system of the RKF.

The seminar proceedings reveal that in the 1960s, just as twenty or thirty years earlier, the kibbutz member was directed to practice restraint so as to regulate his life and behavior methodically in order to realize his ultimate values. Thus the seminar on self-imposed austerity urged self-awareness in consumption as a means for self-rationalization in the service of an ultimate religious value. As stated by Dov Rappel:

We may apply to the question of the consumption standard that which Maimonides stated in a comprehensive and well thought out form many generations ago. Man builds his life according to his task in life... The general rule determines the secondary rules, and these determine the details, down to the very last one. It is not the quantity of consumption that is important, but its designation within the context of man's role in general.[43]

In the framework of religious kibbutz life, "man's role in general" is conceived as divine worship within the context of the community. In the words of Efrayim Ya'ir:

> We all agree that asceticism is not an intrinsic value of the kibbutz movement. However, we hold for restraint, self-control, moderation, and modesty in demands, not because we cannot consume ... nor because we do not have something to consume, but because the satisfaction of needs is only a means for the realization of what is essential. What are our essential goals? As religious Jews, we emphasize the religious principle of "cultivation of society as against cultivation of the individual." We must add immediately that this stands in opposition to an orientation towards consumption. The moment that one establishes society as a preferred value, the individual must forgo his private demands.[44]

In the same vein, the economic norms of the kibbutz are specifically related to religion. "In our viewpoint, religion is a broad concept, covering precepts between man and his fellow man, between man and God, and devotion to the farm economy."[45] This idea is expressed even more specifically in the communal context: "With us, everything is religion. Life and religion cannot be separated. Work and farm economy and society – they are all part of the community."[46] Again and again, the proceedings stress the normative mutual responsibility of the members to the community as an ontological religious entity.

If we look for the specific element in the religious–political ethic of the RKF that influences its economic performance, it appears that the basic halakhic structure of kibbutz life reinforces commitment to the norms that regulate the relationship between the community and its individual members, and infuses them with religious cogency. Indeed, kibbutz norms are focused on, as well as derived from, a religious polity whose dynamics are nourished by the biblical charge of reshaping the world. And, since all the economic norms in the kibbutz are community-oriented, they are harnessed to the political ethic and focus on religious–political goals.

In sum, religion appears to stimulate and tighten the functioning of the socialist organization of the RKF kibbutzim. In these rationally organized communities, religion enhances self-discipline, strengthens the collective aspect of daily life, augments the shared responsibility toward a transcendent Being, and reinforces the kibbutz norms – including those involved in production and consumption – with the cogency of halakhic norms.

CHAPTER 8

Between heteronomous and autonomous authority

In the course of building its institutional order, the Religious Kibbutz Federation established a social base – a "plausibility structure" – for its specific symbolic world, a world that integrated traditional–religious and innovative–ideological cultures. In this chapter we shall discuss both these cultures as embodied in the RKF's two basic reference groups: Orthodox Jewry and secular–national Jewry.

Had the RKF confined itself to its social boundaries and nurtured its symbolic reality within them, in all likelihood its seclusion would have advanced the crystallization of this reality. However, since the RKF regarded itself as a pioneering movement that aspired "to be among the molders of the Jewish people as a whole, and not to confine itself to elite sects,"[1] its involvement in general society tended to stretch its cultural fabric in opposing directions. This is because both of the RKF's reference groups recognized a different transcendent center as the source of authority for its cultural system and identity. Moreover, these groups had mutually exclusive cultural centers. For Orthodox Jewry, the transcendent center of the past was focused on *halakhah* and mediated through the Rabbinate. For secular Zionism, the transcendent center of the present was mediated through radical national ideologues and quintessentially expressed in the secular kibbutz movement. And, although Mizraḥi, and especially Ha-Po'el Ha-Mizraḥi, were largely able to blunt the antipathy between these cultures and their elite carriers, the very fact that the RKF constituted part of the "realizing" pioneering camp, and directly experienced the cogency of the transcendent ideological center, sensitized its awareness to the gulf between them.

INTEGRATIVE GOALS OF THE RKF

In the previous chapter we focused on the RKF's normative system as the meeting-ground of the horizontal religious co-ordinate of RKF identity, which extends from the past, and the vertical ideological–religious co-ordinate, which stems from the present. In this chapter we shall concentrate on the social system of the RKF as the meeting-ground for these two co-ordinates, as embodied in its two reference groups.

Just as the RKF sought to align the halakhic and ideological co-ordinates by resolving the discord between their normative systems, it also sought to align them by unifying its two conflicting reference-groups – Orthodox Jewry and secular Zionism. These two groups were not closed to one another. They met in the ideological and political arenas and wrestled over molding the image of the national Jewish community, both in the pre-state period, when Orthodox Jewry was represented by the Religious Zionist parties, and after statehood, when Orthodox Jewry was also represented by non-Zionist religious parties. Inasmuch as the RKF adopted the view that "the merit of the kibbutz lies in its sense of responsibility towards society at large,"[2] it did not shrink from taking sides over the points of contention.[3] Indeed, as the religious kibbutz members strove to crystallize their specific cultural system and identity, the RKF's sense of responsibility to both reference groups became a source of structural tension which compelled it to switch sides from time to time on public issues.[4] But, since the weight of the RKF within the national community was always minuscule compared to that of both its reference-groups, it never had the resources to develop the broad base necessary to support a policy that would be independent of both groups. The upshot was that RKF solidarity with these two groups tended to weaken the integration between the two cultural components of its identity.

But the coin of contrasting reference-groups had a second side. For, by virtue of belonging to both groups, the RKF felt an integrative social mission. Thus it sought to draw the two groups together through the integration of Torah and peoplehood, conceived in modern national terms – Orthodoxy was to incorporate the national culture *in toto*, while secular Zionism was to adopt religious culture – so that they would eventually coalesce. As stated in a RKF seminar "Bringing hearts closer to the Torah and *mitzvot*," conducted in 1967:

Bringing the secular and religious closer together expresses the desire to draw closer to one another as brethren in one people, as partners in a common destiny... Bringing them [the secular Zionists] closer to the Torah and the *mitzvot* is based upon the religious belief that we must bring all our brothers of Israel closer to the Torah and *mitzvot*... These two concepts do not contradict each other; they both draw upon a love of Israel and of the Torah of Israel...[5]

The RKF aimed to realize this social–integrative goal in two ways: first, through the model of a religious pioneering community which would deepen the involvement of Orthodox Jewry in the institutional structure of the national community and, at the same time, prove to secular Jewry that it is possible to sustain a modern community in a religious framework; second, through active participation in the respective cultural centers of the two groups: membership in the kibbutz center of national society and co-operation with the Rabbinate in renewing the unity of Jewish religious community life in a modern framework.

THE RKF AND SECULAR ZIONISM

As the cutting edge of Religious Zionism, the RKF constituted its point-group in reaching out to secular Zionism to cultivate religious solidarity with it. Indeed, the RKF went far beyond the Religious Zionist parties, Mizraḥi and ha-Po'el ha-Mizraḥi, in recognizing the legitimacy of the secular Zionist camp which constituted a majority of the national public. Acknowledging that the existing *halakhah* was incapable of meeting all the functional needs of national society, the RKF rejected the slogan of "Torah rule" that the religious parties were wont to flaunt, especially after the founding of the Jewish state. As Moshe Unna stated in 1952:

The [religious] political endeavor should be directed not toward the establishment of "Torah rule," but toward enhancing respect for the Torah and avoiding an inner conflict between tradition and state... A complete imposition of Torah laws as they are today is unrealistic and even quixotic... One should therefore take pains to instil within the secular public an understanding for the religious public's views and position and not rest content with indicating the halakhic ruling and rabbinic authority... "Even the transgressors in Israel are as full of *mitzvot* as a pomegranate,"[6] notwithstanding their anti-religious trends.[7]

It was with socialist Zionism that the RKF particularly identified. From its very inception, the RKF emphasized its socialist identity, which found expression, *inter alia*, in the celebration of May Day in most religious kibbutzim, until the outbreak of World War II. And, although the RKF affiliated itself to ha-Po'el ha-Mizrahi instead of to the Histadrut – the overall organizational embodiment of socialist–Zionist values – it strove for ha-Po'el ha-Mizrahi's joining the Histadrut. From its inception the RKF constituted the hard core of successive factions within ha-Po'el ha-Mizrahi that worked towards this goal. However, the political weight and influence of these factions – the longest-lived was "la-Mifne" ("Towards a Turning Point"), formed in 1946[8] – was never sufficient to lead ha-Po'el ha-Mizrahi into the General Federation of Labor. Consequently, there was very little real interaction between the RKF and the general socialist–Zionist movement.

The RKF, however, was able to develop direct ties with the secular kibbutz movement, the heart of socialist–Zionism – at first at the economic level, through common economic enterprises. Already in the early 1940s, a joint kibbutz co-operative was formed in the Beit She'an Valley, which in time was to encompass transportation, purchasing, marketing, and processing of agricultural products for all the kibbutzim in the area – both religious and secular. Similar ventures were established in other parts of the country. Then, in 1964 the secular kibbutz federations took the decisive step of inviting the RKF to join the newly formed Kibbutz Movement Alliance, which was to concern itself with comprehensive kibbutz policy. In short, the RKF gained entrance into the epicenter of national society through its communal–pioneering venture.

In the perception of RKF members, partnership with the secular kibbutz movement opened a window for the penetration of religious influence into the secular movement. The RKF sought to advance this influence, first because it was in keeping with the RKF's social–integrative role; influence within the elite of secular society would radiate to society at large.[9] A second reason concerned the legitimation of the RKF in national society. For since, as we shall see, the RKF never enjoyed the position of an elite within traditional Jewry, nor even within Religious Zionism, as did the secular kibbutz movement within the secular Zionist movement, RKF leaders' fear of becoming a "sect," recurrently expressed in religious kibbutz literature, could only be allayed by membership in the general kibbutz movement. Hence the desire to identify completely with that movement.

However, in the first two decades of RKF life, the secular kibbutzim influenced the values of the RKF more than the other way around. The RKF adopted not only social institutions that originated in the secular movement, but also ideological expressive patterns, such as those for celebrating the agricultural aspects of traditional holidays (see page 99). Insofar as the RKF did radiate religious influence onto the secular movement, it was diffuse and dispersed. The fact that the RKF never constituted more than five to six percent of the total number of kibbutzim, and what is more, that the secular kibbutz movement constituted the hard core of secular national consciousness, was not conducive to intense religious influence. If the secular kibbutzim, upon sharing economic enterprises with the religious kibbutzim, deferred to the latter's demand that no activities conducted within the framework of these enterprises would transgress *halakhah*, this applied only to limited external aspects of secular kibbutz life.

In effect, then, the close solidarity with the secular movement acted to attenuate the religious valence of the ideological values in RKF culture, and thereby to impede this culture's crystallization. As stated by Me'ir Shilo'aḥ in 1957:

As opposed to the generations preceding us, we have broadened the framework of religion to include the various national and social values, such as labor, building the country, language, social equality, non-exploitation, and so forth – matters that, in our opinion, are elements of the Torah's outlook as a Torah of life. However, since these values do not possess a clear-cut external religious stamp, and are shared with the secular–kibbutz sector of the population, our member, in the course of his multi-faceted realization, does not feel the sway of religion in the national and social reality of our life. There is no doubt ... that ties with the other kibbutz movements – and it cannot be otherwise – contribute to the weakening of religious tension. ... And our closeness to them somewhat clouds the sphere of religion that is unique to us.[10]

It follows that the identification of the RKF with the secular kibbutz movement had a two-edged implication with regard to its self-identity.

THE RKF AND ORTHODOX JEWRY

While the body of the RKF leaned towards secular national Jewry, its roots were planted within Orthodox Jewry. And, in the final analysis, its identification with the ultimate values of traditional culture, and its commitment to the continuity of historical identity according to these values, determined that its ties with Orthodox Jewry would be deeper and more essential than those with secular–national Jewry. Moreover, the RKF's ingrained attachment to Orthodox Jewry defined its specific pioneering social role: to constitute a vanguard for this Jewry in bridging the gap between secular–national and traditional–religious cultures.

Given this definition of its role, the RKF as a charismatic religious movement saw itself as a new subcenter within Orthodox Jewry. By way of background, let us review the central features of the self-identity of Orthodox Jewry as a group within contemporary Jewish society. The point of departure is Sinaitic revelation. Three internal religious elements extending from Sinai coalesce in Orthodox Jewry's self-identification: (1) a pure cultural element – *halakhah*, the contents of which were revealed at Sinai as the Written and Oral laws; (2) a broad social element – Orthodox Jewry itself, a social group that regards itself as a link in the chain of generations extending from Sinai and sustaining the religious mission of the people, namely, observation of the Torah crystallized around *halakhah*; (3) a limited social element – the Rabbinate, the cultural center of Orthodox Jewry, which possesses institutionalized authority deriving explicitly from Sinai to interpret the Torah as focused on *halakhah*.

We have noted that the Rabbinate's authority derives first and foremost from the charisma institutionalized in the social roles of its members. However, this authority has a secondary dimension, which is spontaneously charismatic because it derives from the personal individual qualities of individual rabbis. It is especially those rabbis considered to be "the greatest in their generation" in knowledge of Torah who are deemed capable of apprehending divine will and interpreting it as *daat Torah* (the opinion of [the bearers of] the Torah). It is they who determine the general rabbinical consensus in matters of *halakhah*.[11] Inasmuch as the Rabbinate as a consensual body draws its authority primarily from the continuous past, it is lodged, of necessity, in tradition.

Orthodox Jewry, then, grounded in halakhic continuity and tradition-bound rabbinic authority bears, as a matter of course, a strong conservative orientation.

The RKF saw its duty as tempering the conservative orientation of Orthodox Jewry in the period of national revival. At the cultural level, this entailed revamping the symbolic and normative systems, so that they could accord with modern national reality. It was in this spirit that the RKF subjected the *Shulḥan Arukh* itself, the authoritative compendium for religious behavior, to critical evaluation. As Moshe Unna wrote in 1947:

> If we wish to free ourselves from *galut* reality, it is inconceivable that a certain estrangement will not take form between us and the formulations of the *Shulḥan Arukh*. In order for a natural tie to form between *halakhah* and our reality, it is necessary that the halakhic formulation fit our lives and take into consideration the new reality of Eretz Israel.[12]

At the social level, allaying Orthodoxy's conservative orientation entailed getting Orthodox Jews to identify with modern institutions. However, as we have noted in the first chapter, only a small percentage of the Orthodox Jews in Eretz Israel in the 1930s and 1940s had been brought up in post-Emancipation Jewish communities and integrated into modern life; the great majority were of Eastern European origin. And it was chiefly in national society that the latter became conversant with modern institutions.[13] But since this was a gradual process, in the thirties and forties Orthodox Jewry generally continued to perceive religious life within the perspective of traditional society, and thereby remained largely oblivious to the implications of national revival for reconstructing this life. It was wary of any religious change that was not sanctioned by the Rabbinate.[14] In the words of Eliezer Goldman in 1943:

> The departure from the ghetto has not broadened our horizons as observant Jews. We still lack the approach to broad cultural problems... "Practical" problems of religion are still, for most of the Orthodox public, questions of arranging the ritual bath, [kosher] slaughtering, and teaching Torah, rather than how to arrange the entire technical, economic, organizational, and theoretical complex of our society according to Torah.[15]

Mizraḥi, and particularly ha-Po'el ha-Mizraḥi, did seek to broaden the religious horizon of Orthodox Jewry and involve it more deeply in national community life. However, according to the RKF conception, "Those parties . . . which assumed the mission of realizing a life of Torah under conditions totally different from those of their forebears, demonstrated a great lack of confidence in the rightness of their public course."[16] By the 1930s, the RKF claimed, ha-Po'el ha-Mizraḥi's regenerative ethos had spent itself, and the radical religious line dividing the workers' organization from Mizraḥi had blurred. Through the factions that it championed within ha-Po'el ha-Mizraḥi, the RKF, accordingly, sought to renew the parent organization's innovative religious thrust. However, these factions' minority position precluded extensive RKF influence on Orthodox Jewry. As a result of the inability of the Religious Zionist parties to transform Orthodox Jewry, the latter remained incapable of sustaining a national community life by its own power. As Moshe Unna put it in 1939:

The sterility of the enterprise . . . is the salient characteristic of Jewish Orthodoxy in our times. Its origin is Orthodoxy's unwillingness to assume responsibility for deciding on every basic religious problem; its outcome is the absence of an independent religious community that can live its own life without being dependent on others . . .[17]

In its perceived capacity as an integral component of the Orthodox cultural center, the RKF did not intend to impugn the dominance of the Rabbinate, but to complement it. Representing the quintessence of the new national reality by virtue of its pioneering community, the RKF would co-operate with the Rabbinate in co-ordinating *halakhah* with national life through a division of labor.

There are two foci: the great in Torah and the organized community. These two elements acting in tandem can create a reality of community that lives according to the ideals of the Torah.[18]

In this respect, the RKF envisioned the kibbutz community as a laboratory at the disposal of the Rabbinate. The ability of the kibbutz to manipulate social roles and economic resources so as to create a controlled meeting-ground for empirical reality and *halakhah* would render it a pre-eminent social instrument for harmonizing religion and modern life at a communal level.

THE CHARISMATIC–RELIGIOUS COMMUNITY VERSUS THE RABBINATE

The fallacy in the RKF's reasoning lay in the fact that since the Rabbinate did not recognize the religious significance of national revival, it was oblivious to the religious significance of a pioneering community. "Some of the problems they do not understand to this day, and they regard others in a completely different light than we do,"[19] said one RKF ideologue. And in the words of Simḥa Friedman, a member of the second Central Religious Committee, in 1946:

> Our rabbis have not been touched by any revolution; they are unfamiliar with national life, and lack a perspective of statehood. They do not know that, in effect, they are fulfilling [today] the role of the Sanhedrin.[20]

By shirking responsibility for the needs of the national community, the Rabbinate, from the RKF's perspective, was derelict in its role of religious leadership. "Those possessing [religious] authority are not entitled to exert their prerogative if they are not responsible for the consequences of their adjudication," as Tzuriel Admanit put it.[21]

This led to instances where the RKF would defy rabbinical authority. Hence, when the RKF pitted its autonomous charismatic authority, deriving from the transcendent center of the present, against the heteronomous authority deriving institutionally from Sinai, it felt that it was expressing the "true Torah" according to Sinaitic revelation. This feeling, stemming from "a religious responsibility towards the reality around us ... in the spirit of the Torah as we understand it ... according to the needs of the Jewish people,"[22] infused the RKF with the authority to act, in the spirit of "the holy rebellion ... against accepted religious perceptions" according to "the great rule, 'It is time to act for the Lord, for they have violated your Torah.' 'There are times that the suppression of Torah is its very foundation.' 'And you shall live by them.' "[23]

In Chapter 7 we showed how, during the pioneering period, the RKF acted independently of the Rabbinate in accommodating halakhic precepts to milking and security activities on the Sabbath. The period of statehood witnessed several other instances where the RKF took stands on religious issues that contravened those of the Rabbinate.

One such instance, involving the integration of Orthodox Jewry into the national community, concerns military service of girls and of *yeshiva* students. In the early 1950s, when the Knesset was about to pass a law prescribing military service for all women, the Chief Rabbinical Council proclaimed its opposition to the service of religious girls as *daat Torah*. The RKF, however, taking public issue with this position, announced that it "enjoins ... recruitment of women to the aid of the Jewish people in all ways that ensure their concentration in separate religious units."[24] As stated by Simḥa Friedman:

Despite the strong criticism directed against us, we firmly stood our ground ... When we were asked how we, as a religious group, could act in such a manner, our reply was that as long as the Chief Rabbi did not state that the prohibition was based upon *halakhah*, we could not regard his decision as being more than an expression of a certain point of view on a matter of public interest; and on matters of public interest, we had just as much right to voice opinions as he.[25]

And until this day, the RKF, contrary to the stand of the Rabbinate and the religious parties, continues to denounce the practice, in effect since the early years of statehood, of exempting *yeshiva* students from military service.

A second example, indicative of the RKF's solidarity with secular–national Jewry as against the Rabbinate, concerns partnership with secular kibbutzim and moshavim in the Marbek meat company, which was founded in 1964 as a large-scale enterprise for slaughtering meat produced in the southern district of Israel and marketing it throughout the country. Inasmuch as nation-wide distribution would violate the traditional rule that meat marketed in a certain community has to be slaughtered under the supervision of local religious authorities,[26] the Chief Rabbinical Council refused to issue a country-wide *hekhsher* (certificate of purity) for Marbek's meat. However, the RKF, whose kibbutzim in the southern district are partners in this enterprise, rejected the Rabbinate's position, claiming that such a parochial approach is typical of *galut* life and inconsistent with the universalistic reality of a Jewish state. The Rabbinate eventually retracted.

A third example involves the adoption of prayer patterns institutionalized by *halakhah* for expressing the religious experience of *Yom ha-Atzma'ut*. In Chapter 5 we presented the basic ideological nature of this holiday of Israel's independence. The RKF, seeking to capture the religious feeling invoked by the newly restored Jewish sovereignty, sought to express this feeling through institutionalized religious patterns, the adoption of which would require the sanction of the Rabbinate. And, although the Chief Rabbinical Council did confirm the religious nature of the holiday in 1949 and established a special prayer service for it, the RKF rejected the Rabbinate's service on the grounds that it was of a "hybrid" nature, lacking those benedictions and practices that characterize Jewish religious holidays. Hence the RKF composed its own prayer service in 1950, publishing it as a special Independence Day Prayer Book in 1968.

While the RKF has blurred the line of defined allegiance to rabbinical authority through these and other actions, it has never overstepped the boundaries of *halakhah*. Instead, it has resorted to three legitimate avenues for adopting positions that contravened those of the Rabbinate.

The first such avenue consists of restricting rabbinical authority to matters of *halakhah*. That is to say, while the RKF accepts the institutionalized charismatic dimension of the Rabbinate as binding, it does not accept the secondary, personal charismatic dimension, as expressed in *daat Torah*, when it is not grounded in *halakhah*.

If by *daat Torah* is meant that when a Torah scholar expresses an opinion on non-halakhic matters, his opinion should be viewed as a conclusion influenced by his wisdom, which is the wisdom of Torah – this perception is completely justified. But, if one claims that such an opinion has halakhic validity, as though it were a ruling – it must be stated very clearly that this claim has no basis whatsoever.[27]

In non-halakhic spheres, therefore, the RKF views its ideological–religious norms as possibly expressing the intent of the Torah more fully than those declared by the Rabbinate.

Daat yaḥid (the opinion of a single rabbi), which we encountered in the last chapter, constituted the RKF's second avenue for advancing independent religious positions. Inasmuch as every rabbi is formally authorized to interpret *halakhah* according to his own understanding, the opinion of a single rabbi who overpasses the halakhic consensus is not considered illegitimate.

No less interesting from the sociological viewpoint is the third avenue: the autonomous religious authority of a Jewish community. We have already noted that in traditional religious culture, the collective body of Israel is regarded as the carrier of the Torah, and every Jewish community is recognized as the Jewish people writ small. We now add that, by virtue of Sinaitic revelation, the collective body of Israel bears religious authority,[28] which is delegated to every community.[29]

The RKF assumed the authority of the community from its early years. For the communal framework of the kibbutz heightened the close-knit affinity of kibbutz members to the point where they felt that they were operating as one personality, so to speak, infused with primary religious power, i.e., as a charismatic community. As stated retrospectively in 1951:

> We assumed the authority to determine ... practices even though they were not always in accord with what is written in the *Shulḥan Arukh* ... We did this ... because of our religious feeling ... that a community is able to withstand the violation of an accepted religious practice. If an individual transgresses that which is written in the *Shulḥan Arukh*, his religious outlook may be utterly destroyed. However, a religious community that lives a communal life with collective responsibility can assume responsibility in this sphere too. Only thus can we explain to ourselves how we have dared to touch areas which, from the formal point of view, we were unqualified to touch.[30]

Probably the most significant area in which the religious kibbutzim have departed from the traditional religious norms on the basis of the autonomous authority of the Jewish community is in women's involvement in public life. Traditional religion, as expressed in the *Shulḥan Arukh*, aims at segregating the sexes and limiting the role of women to family and household. In entitling women to participate equally with men in public life, the RKF drew upon the legitimation of Torah-im-Derekh Eretz and ha-Po'el ha-Mizraḥi, but far outstripped them. Indeed, the very structure of kibbutz life severely curtails family roles to the point where most household functions are eliminated and most female roles are rendered public roles. The RKF went even further by lowering some of the traditional barriers, anchored in law and custom, designed to keep the sexes apart; for example, mixed dancing and swimming, which are not generally accepted within Orthodox Jewry, were accepted within the community framework. The RKF schools are co-educational even to the point that girls and boys learn Talmud together in the same classes. Furthermore, although the principle of a "mixed society" does not apply to religious ritual, the RKF has introduced the Bat Mitzvah (confirmation of girls), in which the father of the girl is called to the Torah and the celebrant herself delivers a Bat Mitzvah talk.[31]

THE STRUCTURE OF RELIGIOUS AUTHORITY IN THE RKF

The question of the religious authority of the kibbutz collective leads us to two related questions: (1) what is the authoritative institution within the RKF that draws the line between a "legitimate" and a "non-legitimate" deviation from established religious culture?; and (2) how does this institution accord with the institutions of kibbutz authority in general?

Like the secular kibbutz movement, as a democratic–egalitarian society, the RKF concentrates social authority in the collective. Formally this authority resides in the General Assembly of the individual religious kibbutz and in the diverse committees, especially the secretariat, to which the General Assembly delegates its authority. The General Assembly also expresses the religious voice of the kibbutz community authority. In practice, however, the General Assembly delegates its authority to an elected Committee for Guiding Religious Life.

The model of the Committee for Guiding Religious Life was the Central Religious Committee of the RKF, which was established for the first time in 1937 and renewed several times afterwards. The core of this committee consisted of members from both the ideological and the religious elites of the movement, the latter comprising former students of *yeshivot* and rabbinical seminaries, including some who were ordained.[32] The Committees for Guiding Religious Life of the individual kibbutzim were not formally established until 1947.

While the Committee for Guiding Religious Life constituted the formal religious authority of each kibbutz, the authority of its constituent members was informal. In other words, the authoritative roles of the members of this committee were barely differentiated from their primary economic roles on the kibbutz. Even those members who had been ordained as rabbis eschewed official religious roles, opting for the pioneer role. Indeed, the two spheres of authority – that of the collective in all matters pertaining to the kibbutz community and that of the members of the Committee for Guiding Religious Life – were two sides of the same coin. For, while the Committee members might determine the religious life-manner of their kibbutz community, their decisions were subject to the direct control of the General Assembly. In that they were closely involved in the ideological–social reality of their community, and formally shared equal rights and obligations with all other members, they were able to operate within the framework of the social consensus.[33]

This general structure of religious authority, which pertained for more than the first twenty years of the RKF, did not, however, ever gain complete internal legitimation. According to the ideal of the RKF founders, the religious kibbutz should constitute a "pre-eminent Torah community" whose members are imbued with knowledge of Torah. Such a quality would have strengthened its charismatic standing in taking independent positions on religious questions. But the fact is that many members of RKF kibbutzim were not well-versed in the sources of Judaism. Indeed, from the thirties onward a recurring theme in kibbutz literature was the need for each kibbutz to have a rabbi who would devote himself to teaching Torah and exerting influence on the "waverers" and "deviants" in matters of religion. However, although the history of the RKF until the late sixties includes many accounts of attempts by individual settlements to hire outside rabbis, there was only one case where such a rabbi was successfully absorbed within the kibbutz fabric; he served for five years.[34]

The important point for our discussion – in terms of the relationship between the RKF and the rest of the Jewish religious world – is that it was the Torah scholars among the members, especially those in the various Religious Committees, who directed the process of finding solutions to problematic situations involving *halakhah*. Capable of formulating halakhic problems within the symbolic framework of Torah erudition, these Torah scholars were intermediaries between the RKF and the Rabbinate. It was they who distinguished between those problems involving *halakhah* that did and did not demand a rabbinical ruling. The fact that many of these members had academic backgrounds enabled them to adopt a critical–historical approach to the relationship between the Rabbinate and *halakhah*, and gave them confidence in the correctness of their decisions. Moreover, since these members saw themselves as representatives of a religious movement referring to the whole Jewish people, and not only to their own communities, they felt justified in relying on rabbis to whom they felt close, both in Eretz Israel and in the Jewish world at large, either because of their religious–national outlook, or because of their sensitivity to the problems posed by modernity. If these scholars may have directed the RKF toward positions which did not always co-ordinate with those of the

Rabbinate, it is also they who ensured that the RKF remained within the Orthodox framework.

THE RKF AS A RELIGIOUS CENTER: AN ASSESSMENT

By creating a new religious social reality that integrates traditional and national values at the practical level, the RKF created a new cultural subcenter within Orthodox Jewry. Indeed, through the pioneering roles and institutions that it cultivated, it created new channels for religious salvation.

The RKF did not intend these channels to displace the study of Torah, the traditional channel of salvation in Jewish life. However, pitting "pioneering missions in terms of the practice of sacred Torah precepts" against Torah study, the RKF awarded the former religious priority.[35] Indeed, in the 1930s and 1940s, and even in the 1950s, many of the Orthodox youth that were organized in pioneering religious movements in both the Diaspora and Eretz Israel were committed to the religious culture promoted by the RKF and viewed kibbutz life as "a life of Torah." While only a relatively small part of this youth actually joined the RKF, the latter continued to constitute for them – as well as for others, such as the small academic religious intelligentsia of the period – a cultural center within Orthodox Jewry, as well as a positive reference-group. The outstanding defense record of the religious kibbutzim,[36] the high level of their economic performance and – especially – their blend of universal and traditional elements within the national reality, encouraged national religious youth to identify strongly with the RKF in the process of its adaptation to, and integration within, Jewish national society.

Within Religious Zionist circles in general, however, the RKF did not enjoy high esteem as an innovative religious center offering a new life-style for serving God. Indeed, the attitude of Religious Zionist leadership toward the RKF in the period of its rationalizing thrust was ambivalent. Highly appreciated for its pioneering achievement under a religious nimbus, the RKF was also suspect because of its clear-cut socialist identity and especially because of its independent religious position on *halakhah*-related problems.

And insofar as the RKF constituting a new religious subcenter for Orthodox Jewry in general is concerned, the latter has largely been oblivious of the RKF. As noted above, this Jewry has never given the

RKF the type of recognition as a religious elite that the secular kibbutz movement has received within national Jewry. Self-labor, social equality, commitment to national defense and economic roles, agricultural settlement – these were values of national Jewish society but not of traditional Jewish society. If we add to these values the strong solidarity displayed by the RKF with secular nationalist Jewry, and its independent religious thrust, it is no wonder that Orthodox Jewry regarded the RKF as located on its margin.

On the other hand, if, in the course of its development, the RKF has remained within the boundaries of Orthodox Jewry, it has done so because of the halakhic discipline that it has maintained. Deviating from the essential elements of *halakhah* would have impaired the RKF's traditional religious legitimacy and disrupted its essential identity.

> It sometimes happens ... that the halakhic solution propounded does not meet our needs ... In such cases, we have no alternative but to accept it, though we do so reluctantly. And we accept it in order not to infringe discipline.[37]

It would seem that the resolve of the RKF to accept the authority of the Rabbinate in matters of *halakhah* derived particularly from a social factor: the fear of breaking away from Orthodox Jewry. For it is mainly through this Jewry, and through *halakhah*, though not necessarily through the Rabbinate,[38] that the RKF has maintained its link to Sinai. But, inasmuch as the Rabbinate constitutes a central social institution for the consolidation of Orthodox Jewry, disobeying it would have been tantamount to undermining the very structure of Orthodox Jewry.

Thus, in the meeting of innovative–ideological forces embodied in secular nationalism, and conservative–religious forces embodied in Orthodox Jewry, in the social framework of the RKF, the latter has exerted a stronger pull than the former. As stated in 1942,

> Seeing the great danger of a diminishing of the stature of *halakhah*, we are forced against our will into a position of defense and protection of the framework of *halakhah* ... into an alliance with the conservative elements within the [Jewish] people, although we feel closer in spirit to the innovative and revolutionary elements.[39]

And as relations between the RKF and Orthodox Jewry became more institutionalized within the context of the national community, the conservative component of religion tended to gain strength. Thus, by 1958 it could be stated that:

> We have not made progress towards the goal to which we aspire, regeneration of our Torah, and finding solutions for the questions that come up again and again... We even adhere strictly to customs sanctified by previous generations, without knowing how to sanctify our own life-patterns.[40]

BETWEEN RELIGION AND IDEOLOGY

We have noted at several points in this book that *halakhah* is the focal point of the major confrontations between religion and ideology in the context of modern Jewish religious life. The affirmation of *halakhah* by the innovative religious movements that arose within Orthodox Jewry in modern times determined the ascendancy of the past over the present in their cultures. The RKF acted in a similar fashion. It might have reversed the standing of the two time-dimensions if, in the face of the imperviousness of the established religious authority to national revival, it had given in to the temptation to displace halakhic with ideological norms in all problematic situations, under the inspiration of a religious mission and imbued with charismatic authority. But, if the RKF is presented first and foremost as a religious rather than an ideological movement, the reason lies in its acceptance of the yoke of *halakhah* in these situations:

> *Halakhah*... as that... objective revelation that came from above, from the mountaintop, in the sound of the ram's horn, which announced the heteronomous "I" [Exodus 20:2], in contrast to the autonomous "I" within us, with all its religiosity...[41]

The new cultural elements created under the influence of national reality were integrated into the RKF cultural system around the "backbone" of traditional culture, anchored in the vital transcendent center of the past – Sinai.

Afterword

What is the nature of the religious impulses and thought that prevail within the Religious Kibbutz Federation at the outset of the 1990s, a generation or so after its original effervescent period? And what is the relationship between the RKF's innovative religious culture and its commitment, as part of Orthodox Judaism, to the mainstream religious tradition? Against the backdrop of the dimming of revolutionary ideology in Israel society at large, the attenuation of partisan boundaries within Israel's Orthodox Jewry, and the formation of a second and third generation within the RKF – the modulation of the RKF original religious ferment calls for separate study. Here I can no more than sketch the change in broad structural lines.

I indicated at the end of the last chapter that since the late 1950s the conservative component appears to prevail within the religious consciousness of the RKF and that the latter's bonds with Orthodox Jewry have tightened. The institutionalization of the role of rabbi in the Orthodox kibbutz – a process that began in the mid-1960s – is the salient expression of this development. In 1990 most RKF kibbutzim have their own rabbis, usually graduates of both Torah va-Avodah youth movements and Zionist *yeshivot*, who perform defined tasks such as the teaching of Torah. However, the RKF's communal life-pattern continues to stimulate its innovative religious thrust. In 1978 the RKF took a significant step in grounding its meaningful world in traditional culture, when it established Yeshivat ha-Kibbutz ha-Dati to serve as a Torah center in the spirit of its religious ideology. In 1988 the *yeshivah* moved to its permanent home in Kibbutz Ein Tzurim.

Since the late 1950s, the RKF has shifted the focus of its religious pioneering effort from the mastery of natural and social reality, to the socio–cultural integration of Israel's Jewish society. The awareness of this mission that crystallized, as we noted in the last chapter, in the 1950s and 1960s, intensified in the 1980s in reaction to the growing political strength of Israel's ultra-Orthodox sector and the consequent sharpening of the secular–religious polarization. The growing appreciation within the secular sector of the RKF's intermediary position between the poles of tradition and modernity heightened consciousness of this mission. In 1987, the Twentieth Council of the RKF expressed the movement's sense of obligation to constitute a bridge between Israel's religious and secular camps. This religious–pioneering task was institutionalized with the founding of the Jacob Herzog Center for Jewish Studies, also in 1988 at Kibbutz Ein Tzurim.

A relatively recent question that has exercised the RKF relates to the territory of Eretz Israel occupied by the Israel army in the Six Day War in 1967, that is, the "West Bank" and Gaza strip. In the wake of this war, a new ideological stream emerged from Religious Zionism, which regards the territorial integrity of Eretz Israel as a religious value. The RKF split on this value: while one group, in the name of "integral Eretz Israel," opposes the relinquishment of the occupied territory, the other is willing to subordinate this value to political considerations that might moderate the Israeli–Palestinian conflict. To preserve the consensus among its members, the RKF has sidetracked the territorial issue; those new settlements that it has created beyond the 1967 borders were established only in areas where religious kibbutzim existed before 1948. The relative strength of the opposing political views within the RKF may be gauged by the elections to the Twelfth Knesset in 1989. Two Religious Zionist parties, each representing an opposite view on the territorial question, took part in these elections – "Mafdal" (territorial integrity) and "Meimad" (accommodation) – and each received about a third of the votes in the RKF. However, 60 percent of the total vote in the Religious Kibbutz Federation went to parties (including Mafdal) that champion territorial integrity. The fact that this deep difference on a cardinal issue in Israeli life has not undermined the RKF's stability seems to attest to the quality of its unique religious culture.

APPENDIX A

The Religious Kibbutz Federation settlements (1989)
(in order of settlement)

Settlement	Settlement date	Founders' origin	Population
Tirat Tzvi	1937	Germany, Poland, Romania	740
Sdei Eliyahu	1939	Germany	700
Yavne	1940	Germany	910
Be'erot Yitzhak	1943	Germany, Czechoslovakia	525
Kfar Etzion(1)[1]	1943	Poland	—
Massu'ot Yitzhak[2]	1945	Hungary, Czechoslovakia	—
Ein Ha-Natziv	1946	Germany	680
Ein Tzurim	1946	Eretz Israel	560
Kfar Darom[3]	1946	Germany	—
Saad	1947	Eretz Israel	770
Shluhot	1948	Germany, Austria	590
Lavi	1949	Germany, England	600
Alumim	1966	Israel	410
Kfar Etzion (2)[4]	1967	Israel	460
Maale Ha-Gilboah	1968	Israel, United States	320
Rosh Tzurim	1969	Israel	290
Migdal Oz	1977	Israel	170
Beit Rimon	1979	England, Israel	150
Meirav	1982	Israel	130
Netzarim	1984	Israel	60

1 Kibbutz destroyed in the Israel War of Independence, 1948.
2 Converted to a *moshav shitufi* (combining features of kibbutz and moshav) in 1950.
3 Converted to a *moshav shitufi* in 1961.
4 Resettled by children of first Kfar Etzion.

APPENDIX B

About the religious kibbutz movement members quoted in this book

Admanit, Tzuri'el (1915–73) was born in Berlin, Germany, where he completed secondary school. He also studied at the Montreux Yeshiva in Switzerland. A member of the Ezra youth movement and Bachad, the Religious Zionist pioneering movement, he immigrated to Eretz Israel in 1937, joined Kibbutz Rodges (later Kibbutz Yavne), and lived on the kibbutz until his death, working mostly in its dairy barn and as a youth group educator. A posthumous collection of his articles, *Within the Stream and Against It* (Hebrew), was published in 1977.

Ahiman (Chmelnik), Hanokh (1917–) was born in Bialystok, Poland, and completed secondary school there. He studied at the Tahkemony Rabbinical Seminary in Warsaw and was ordained as rabbi. A leader of ha-Shomer ha-Dati youth movement, he immigrated to Eretz Israel in 1940 and joined Kvuzat Avraham (later Kfar Etzion). He worked mostly as a vegetable gardener, and also edited *Alonim* (1944–6). He is one of the few male survivors of his kibbutz, that was destroyed in the Israel War of Independence of 1948, and lives today in the town of Efrat.

Friedman, Simha (1911–90) was born in Stryj, Poland. He studied at the University of Berlin and graduated from the Hildesheimer Rabbinical Seminary. Immigrating to Eretz Israel in 1939, he joined Kibbutz Tirat Tzvi in 1943, where he lived until his death, working mostly as a teacher. He was a member of the Israeli Knesset, 1969–77.

Goldman, Eliezer (1918–) was born in Brooklyn, New York. He graduated from Yeshiva College and the Rabbi Isaac Elhanan Rabbinical Seminary in New York. Immigrating to Eretz Israel in 1938, he joined Kibbutz Sdei Eliyahu in 1941, where he has lived since, working mostly as a vegetable gardener and teacher. He began to teach philosophy at Bar-Ilan University in 1964, and eventually became a professor at that institution.

Herz, Avraham (Rudi) (1905–   ) was born in Aachen, Germany. He was a member of Jung-Juedischer Wanderbund and Ezra youth movements, as well as a founding member of Bachad. A graduate agronomist from the Munich Technological Institute, he joined Kibbutz Rodges (later Kibbutz Yavne) upon his immigration to Eretz Israel in 1933. He has been a member of that kibbutz ever since, working mostly as its farm manager.

Karni'el (Treller), Shalom (1912–48) was born in Cracow, Poland, and completed secondary school in that city. A leader of ha-Shomer ha-Dati youth movement, he joined Kvuzat Avraham (later Kfar Etzion) upon immigrating to Eretz Israel in 1939, and worked mostly as a youth group educator. He also edited *Alonim* in 1947. He was killed in the Israel War of Independence.

Lutvak, Yosef (1910–82) was born in Kuty, Poland, and brought up in Czernowitz, Romania. He studied electrical engineering at the University of Brno, Czechoslovakia. Immigrating to Eretz Israel in 1931, he joined Kvuzat Shaḥal (later Kibbutz Tirat Tzvi). He was a member of his kibbutz until 1947, and worked there mostly as a vegetable gardener.

Naḥlon (Nusbecher), Aharon (1911–   ) was born in Nasaud, Hungary. He studied at the Rabbi Hoffman Yeshiva in Frankfort am Main and was a member of Mizraḥi Youth. He joined Kibbutz Rodges after his immigration to Eretz Israel in 1933. Moving to Krutzat Aryei (later Kibbutz Sdei Eliyahu) in 1937, he has worked mostly in the grain-growing and poultry branches of the kibbutz. He has an LL. M. from the Hebrew University in Jerusalem.

Or (Orlian), Me'ir (1911–75) was born in Riga, Latvia. A member of Mizraḥi Youth, he immigrated to Eretz Israel in 1932, joined Kvuzat Shaḥal (later Kibbutz Tirat Tzvi) and, until his death, worked mostly as the bookkeeper of his kibbutz. He also edited *Alonim*, 1948–9. A posthumous collection of his articles, *The Light That Shines* (Hebrew), was published in 1987.

Rappel, Dov (1917–   ) was born in Warsaw, Poland where he completed secondary school. He was a member of ha-Shomer ha-Dati youth movement. After receiving ordination at the Taḥkemoni Rabbinical Seminary, he immigrated to Eretz Israel in 1936. He joined the Religious Kibbutz Federation in 1942, and has been a member of Kibbutz Yavne since 1947, where he has worked mostly as a teacher. He began to teach in the School of Education of Bar-Ilan University in 1967, where he eventually became a professor.

Rosenblueth, Pinḥas (Eric) (1906–85) was born in Berlin, Germany. He studied at the Hildesheimer Rabbinical Seminary and the University of Berlin, from which he received a Ph.D. The leader of the Ezra youth movement group that joined Bachad, he immigrated to Eretz Israel in 1934 and joined Kibbutz Rodges. He was one of the foremost educators in the Religious Youth Aliyah program, and remained within the religious kibbutz framework, as a member of Kibbutz Yavne, until 1947.

Rosenthal, Eliezer Shimshon (1915–80) was born in Strassburg, Germany. A member of Ezra, he immigrated to Eretz Israel in 1934, where he studied and was ordained at the Merkaz ha-Rav Yeshiva of Chief Rabbi Abraham Kuk. He served as the rabbi of Kibbutz Rodges (later Kibbutz Yavne) from 1937 to 1942. He later studied at The Hebrew University in Jerusalem and eventually became professor of Talmud at that institution.

Shilo'aḥ (Slokhovoy), Me'ir (1911–   ) was born in Kishinev, Romania. A member of the Bnei Akivah youth movement and the Mizraḥi Pioneer, he studied at the Kishinev Yeshiva and was ordained as rabbi. He immigrated to Eretz Israel in 1938 and joined Kibbutz Rodges (later Kibbutz Yavne), where he has been living ever since, working mostly as the cobbler of his kibbutz.

Unna, Gedaliah (1901–38) was born in Mannheim, Germany. He belonged to the Blau Weiss youth movement. After studying at the University of Berlin, where he received a Ph.D. in physics, and at the Hildesheimer Rabbinical Seminary, where he was ordained as rabbi, he immigrated to Eretz Israel in 1930. He joined Kibbutz Rodges four years later, and worked as a vegetable gardener. One of the founders of Tirat Tzvi, he died of complications secondary to malaria a year after his kibbutz settled on the land.

Unna, Moshe (1902–89) was born in Mannheim, Germany. A graduate agronomist from the University of Berlin, he also studied at the Hildesheimer Rabbinical Seminary. He headed the first religious pioneering farms in Germany, immigrated to Eretz Israel in 1927, and became a founding member of Kibbutz Rodges in 1931. In 1940 he moved to Kibbutz Sdei Eliyahu, where he lived until his death. He was a member of the Israeli Knesset, 1949–69, and Deputy Minister of Education of the Israeli Government, 1956–8. Regarded as the leading ideologue of the Religious Kibbutz Movement since its inception, his major ideological work is *A Partnership of Truth* (Hebrew).

Ya'ir, Efrayim (1916–   ) was born in Luebeck, Germany, and brought up in Berlin. A member of the Brit ha-No'ar ha-Dati and Bachad, he immigrated to Eretz Israel in 1936 and joined Kibbutz Tirat Tzvi in 1938, where he has lived ever since. He has worked mostly in the dairy barn and poultry branches of his kibbutz. He has also been an editor of *Amudim* 1958–61, 1966–8.

APPENDIX C

Ideological periodicals referred to in book
(Individual kibbutz publications are not included in this list)

Alonim – a Religious Kibbutz Federation organ. Appeared irregularly, 1938–49, Tel Aviv.
Alonim Le-Informatziyah Pnimit – a Religious Kibbutz Federation publication. Appeared irregularly in stencil, 1938–42, Tel Aviv.
Amudim – the Religious Kibbutz Federation monthly that succeeded *Yedi'ot Ha-Kibbutz Ha-Dati*. Began publication in 1956, Tel Aviv.
Ba-Mishot – a national religious weekly, 1940–6, Jerusalem.
Choser Bachad (Bachad Informationsrundschreiben) – organ of Brit Chalutzim Datiim in Germany. Appeared irregularly, 1929–36, Rodges and Geringshof.
Ha-Hed – a Religious Zionist monthly, Religious Department of the Jewish National Fund, 1926–53, Jerusalem.
Ha-Mizraḥ – a World Mizraḥi Organization monthly, 1903–4, Cracow.
Ha-O'helah – the "left wing ha-Po'el ha-Mizraḥi" organ. Published irregularly, 1925–6, Jerusalem.
Ha-Po'el Ha-Mizraḥi – ha-Po'el ha-Mizraḥi monthly, 1923–5, Jerusalem.
Ha-Tor – World Mizraḥi Organization weekly, 1921–34, Jerusalem.
Netivah – World Torah va-Avodah Movement periodical, 1926–53, Jerusalem.
Ohaleinu – the central publication of the ha-Shomer ha-Dati and Bnei Akivah youth movements in Poland, 1934–9, Warsaw.
Shdemot – the organ of the Youth Division of the Iḥud ha-Kvutzot ve-ha-Kibbutzim Federation. Began publication in 1960, Tel Aviv.
Tikvah – bulletin of the East Galicia (Poland) Bnei Akivah youth movement, ca. 1933–5, Lwow.
Yedi'ot Ha-Kibbutz Ha-Dati – an organ of the Religious Kibbutz Federation, 1942–55, Tel Aviv.
Zera'im – Eretz Israel Bnei Akivah youth movement monthly. Began publication in 1935, Jerusalem.
Zion – German Mizraḥi Organization monthly, 1929–38, Berlin.

Notes

INTRODUCTION

1. Cf. W. Schluchter, "The paradox of rationalization," in G. Roth and W. Schluchter, *Max Weber's Vision of History* (1979), p. 15.
2. T. Parsons, *The Structure of Social Action* (1937), p. 567.
3. As Max Wiener put it, secularization amongst western European Jews took fewer decades than it took centuries for the Christian societies in which the Jews lived. See his *Die Juedische Religion in Zeitalter der Emanzipation* (1933), p. 7.
4. See Chap. 1.
5. On the relationship between a charismatic breakthrough and rationalization in Max Weber's thought, see Parsons (note 2 above), and Wolfgang Mommsen, "Towards a reconstruction of Max Weber's concept of history," in Sam Whimster and Scott Lash, eds., *Max Weber's Rationality and Modernity* (1987).
6. Max Weber, *The Protestant Ethic and the Spirit of Capitalism* (1958).
7. See, for example, Robert N. Bellah, ed., *Religion and Progress in Modern Asia* (1965); Clifford Geertz, ed., *Old Societies and New States* (1963). On the Protestant ethic as a yardstick for examining the modernizing potential of traditional cultures, see S. N. Eisenstadt, ed., *The Protestant Ethic and Modernization* (1968).
8. Eisenstadt *ibid.*, p. 10ff.
9. Bellah (note 7 above), pp. 215–22.
10. On socialism and progress, see S. N. Eisenstadt, "Socialism and tradition," in S. N. Eisenstadt and Y. Azmon, eds., *Socialism and Tradition* (1975), pp. 1–18; on liberalism and progress, see S. N. Bellah, *Beyond Belief* (1970), pp. 66–8.
11. Werner Sombart, *The Jews and Modern Capitalism* (1951). Sombart also sought to adduce historical evidence to prove the key role of the Jews in developing capitalism, but later research has refuted this evidence. See Bert F. Hoselitz, "Introduction to the American edition [of 1951]," and David S. Landes, "The Jewish merchant – typology and Stereotypology in Germany," *Leo Baeck Year Book* 19 (1974), pp. 21–2.
12. Max Weber, *Ancient Judaism* (1952).

13. Max Weber, *Economy and Society* (1968) II, pp. 611ff.
14. For these levels of rationalization, see T. Parsons, "Introduction," to Max Weber, *The Sociology of Religion* (1964), pp. xxxii–xxxiii.
15. See, for example, C. J. H. Hayes, *Nationalism and Religion* (1960); Raymond Aron, *The Opium of the Intellectuals* (1959).
16. For this method, which draws upon Husserl's phenomenology, and existentialism, especially Heidegger's system, see A. Schutz, *Collected Papers* I, *The Problem of Social Reality* (1962); E. A. Tiryakian, "Structural sociology," in J. C. McKinney and E. A. Tiryakian, eds., *Theoretical Sociology* (1970), pp. 112–35.

1. CONCEPTUAL AND HISTORICAL BACKGROUND

1. Eliezer S. Rosenthal, *Towards the Third Council* [of the Religious Kibbutz Federation] (Hebrew) (1945), p. 62. On the grappling between the two components of the religious consciousness, the conservative and the innovative, cf. H. Hoeffding, *The Philosophy of Religion* (1906), pp. 148–9.
2. On this conceptual system, see Edward Shils, "Center and Periphery," and "Charisma, Order and Status," in his *Center and Periphery* (1975).
3. On Weber's conception of charisma as developed by Shils and Eisenstadt, see E. Shils *ibid.*, pp. 127–34, and S. N. Eisenstadt, "Introduction" to *Max Weber on Charisma and Institution Building* (1968).
4. See Peter L. Berger and Thomas Luckmann, *The Social Construction of Reality* (1966).
5. *Ibid.*, pp. 104–28.
6. Cf. Shils (note 2 above), pp. 197–201.
7. *Ibid.*, pp. 3–4.
8. Eisenstadt (note 3 above), p. ix.
9. See Menahem Elon, *The Principles of Jewish Law* (1975), p. 16.
10. For these hermeneutical rules, see L. Jacobs, "Hermeneutics," *Encyclopedia Judaica* 8:366–72.
11. Yitzhak Heinemann, *The Rationales for the Mitzvot in Jewish Literature* (Hebrew), 2 vols. (1953).
12. Leon Roth, *Judaism, a Portrait* (1960), pp. 75–80.
13. See Gershom Scholem, "The meaning of Torah in Jewish mysticism," in *On the Kabbalah and its Symbolism* (1965), pp. 32–86.
14. *Midrash Rabbah*, vol. I (1961), p. 1; Judah ben Bezalel Loew, *Glory of Israel* (Hebrew) (1955), chap. 17.
15. Fifteenth-century philosopher Joseph Albo expressed the dynamic relationship between Torah and changing reality as follows: "... the

law of God cannot be perfect so as to be adequate for all times, because the ever new details of human relations, their customs and their acts, are too numerous to be embraced in a book. Therefore Moses was given orally certain general principles, only briefly alluded to in the Torah, by means of which the wise men in every generation may work out the details as they appear." *Book of Principles* (Hebrew) (1930), vol. III, chap. 23. See also Elon (note 9 above), p. 53.

16. Tractate *Menahot* 99 a-b.
17. For these expressions, see Elon (note 9 above), pp. 76–7ff. Elon refers to the commentary of Rashi, the pre-eminent eleventh-century exegete, on the verse "It is time to act for the Lord," in Tractate *Yomah* 69a: "When one comes to perform a service for the sake of the Lord, it is permissible to transgress the Torah."
18. See, for example, J. Leibowitz, *Zion* (Berlin) 2, May 1930, p. 62.
19. See Henri Bergson, *The Two Sources of Morality and Religion (1935)*; M. Buber, *On Judaism* (1967), pp. 79–81.
20. See R. J. Z. Werblowsky, "Hanouca et Noël, ou Judaïsme et Christianisme," *Revue de l'Histoire des Religions* 145 (1954), p. 64. Compare with the perception of the RKF, as expressed by one of its leading ideological figures: "The basic conception of the Jewish people as we understand it is the following: This is a people ... that was formed by a spiritual act (the giving of the Torah), and whose existence is linked to the fact that it is the carrier of 'Torah,' which shapes its spiritual image and imposes upon it life-orders. Beyond this incumbent framework of 'immediate life' ... a purpose has been set for the people towards which it ... lives and works: the messianic era." M. Unna, *Amudim* 131 (June 1957), p. 27.
21. See Jacob Katz, *Tradition and Crisis* (1958).
22. Max Wiener, *Die Juedische Religion in Zeitalter der Emanzipation* (1933), p. 28.
23. We see this in the formula "The custom of Israel is Torah"; see Shlomo ben Aderet, *The Torah of the Long House* (Hebrew) (1608), p. 34a. We also see it in a slightly different formulation that expresses an independent religious identification with former generations, "Our fathers' custom is Torah"; see Tosefot annotation to Tractate *Menahot* 20a.
24. E. Nottingham, *Religion and Society* (1954), pp. 42–50.
25. See Ze'ev Falk, *Law and Religion* (1981), pp. 146–7. In the words of fifteenth-century Rabbi Moshe Mintz, "For every rabbi and expert has been authorized as master from the mouth of a master, up to our teacher Moses, peace be with him." Adduced by M. Breuer, *The Ashkenazi Rabbinate in the Middle Ages* (Hebrew) (1976), p. 109. For rabbinical traditional authority in an historical perspective, see J. Katz, "Rabbinical authority and authorization in the Middle Ages,"

in I. Twersky, ed., *Studies in Medieval Jewish History and Literature* (1979), pp. 41–56.
26. G. Scholem, *Sabbatai Sevi: the Mystical Messiah 1626–1676* (1973).
27. See E. A. Tiryakian, "Structural sociology," in J. C. McKinney and E. A. Tiryakian, eds., *Theoretical Sociology* (1970), pp. 112–35, and S. N. Eisenstadt, *Tradition, Change and Modernity* (1973), pp. 143–6.
28. D. Biale, *Gershom Scholem: Kabbalah and Counter-History* (1979), pp. 159–65.
29. Yitzhak Baer, "Origins of the Jewish communal organization in the Middle Ages" (Hebrew), *Zion*, 15 (1950), pp. 11–12.
30. See J. Katz, "Even though he sinned he is still a Jew," *The Gershom Scholem Anniversary Volume* (Hebrew) (1958), pp. 71–91.
31. See J. Katz, *Out of the Ghetto* (1973).
32. Wiener (note 22 above), p. 19.
33. S. N. Eisenstadt, *Israel Society* (1967), pp. 2–3.
34. On Ahad Ha-Am's and Ha'im Nahman Bialik's perception of the Jewish people as a supreme entity that imparts sanctity, see Eliezer Schweid, *Judaism and Secular Culture* (Hebrew) (1961), chap. 1, especially pp. 29, 36, 58–9. Other expressions that allude to components of the transcendent center of secular Zionism are related to the concept of "history" and also to the concept of "God," but in a non-traditional sense (see Yaari on this page and notes 36, 37 below).
35. In E. Margalit, *Ha-Shomer Ha-Tza'ir from a Youth Community to Revolutionary Marxism* (Hebrew) (1971), p. 148. Ya'ari was the leader of the extreme left-wing ha-Shomer ha-Tza'ir kibbutz federation.
36. A leading figure in the kibbutz movement states in 1946: "[We] who were condemned as violators of the Sabbath possessed a deep religious feeling for [our] endeavor and faith. [We] did not violate the Sabbath, for after six days of arduous labor [we] went to work on the seventh day in order to fulfill the mission with which the sovereign of history charged [us]: to create the dawn of the working people returning to its ancestral land." Kaddish Luzinsky (Luz), in *On the Social Image of the Hebrew Village in Eretz Israel* (Hebrew) (1946), p. 73.

On the perception of the pioneering endeavor through the motif of the sacred in the writings of Y. H. Brenner, A. D. Gordon, and B. Katzenelson, leading ideologues of the socialist Zionist movement, see Y. Ben-Aharon, "On three stages in the way of the Jewish people" (Hebrew), *Shdemot* 76 (September 1980), pp. 22–7.

On socialist Zionist ideology as "civil religion," see Charles S. Liebman and Eliezer Don-Yihye, *Civil Religion in Israel* (1983), pp. 25–58.
37. On the charismatic power of Jewish nationalism within the kibbutz movement, see S. Landshut, *The Kvutzah* (Hebrew) (1944), pp. 163–4. For an exposition of the charismatic experience as informed by "history," see B. Katzenelson, *The Pioneer Book* (Hebrew), ed. M. Bassok,

(1940), pp. 61–2: "When history, as it were, proceeds to effect upheavals and transformations in a people's life, it secretly chooses its emissaries, its volunteers, to perform its will... Pioneering and voluntarism signify the commencement of a celebration in a people's life. Through them a people's soul is elevated and its divine inspiration is revealed, and without them a new period cannot be sanctified."

38. Luzinsky (note 36 above), p. 147.
39. For these value-orientations in the context of kibbutz life, see H. Barkai, *The Kibbutz: an Experiment in Microsocialism* (1971), pp. 12–14. See also Yonina Talmon, *Family and Community in the Kibbutz* (1970), pp. 203ff.
40. The dialectical nature of the sacred in the kibbutz context is clearly expressed by a member of the second kibbutz generation in his analysis of the experience of the secular founding fathers: "You have deposed God from the summit of his seat and with reverent trepidation placed the kibbutz values on his empty throne." *Shdemot* 17 (April 1965), p. 6.
41. See K. Wilhelm, "The Jewish community in the post-emancipation period," *Leo Baeck Year Book* 2 (1957), pp. 47–75.
42. On the difficulties in defining religion, see Eric J. Sharpe, *Understanding Religion* (1983), chap. 3; on the sharp variance in definitions of ideology, see Daniel Bell, "Afterword, 1988," *The End of Ideology Debate* (1988), pp. 433ff.
43. T. Parsons, *The Social System* (1951), p. 350.
44. On the "strain" theory for explaining the formation of new ideologies, see, for example, Erik H. Erikson, *Young Man Luther: a Study of Psychoanalysis and History* (1958); C. Geertz, "Ideology as a cultural system," in his *The Interpretation of Cultures* (1973), pp. 48–76.
45. Victor W. Turner, *The Ritual Process: Structure and anti-Structure* (1969), chap. 3.
46. Cf. A. Swidler, "Culture in action: symbols and strategies," *American Sociological Review* 51 (1986), pp. 273–86.
47. Rabbi Moses Sofer (1762–1839), who coined this slogan, was the most influential rabbi in the Orthodox Jewish world in the first half of the nineteenth century. A native of Frankfort am Main, Sofer moved to Pressburg, Hungary, at the turn of the century, and established a voluntarily secluded, traditionalistic community. The conservative religious ideology that he cultivated was designed to entrench traditionalistic Judaism in the modern world. See Katz, (note 31 above), pp. 157–60.
48. Shils seems to address such a center when he poses the question: "Does a traditional reception of belief embrace in an inarticulate form some elementary image of a connection with the beginning of the universe, the origin of time, the point at which mankind was more in contact with the sacred source which set it into motion and provides the scheme for its right ordering?," *Center and Periphery*, p. 191.

49. For the revelation at Sinai as a center of time, see Werblowsky (note 20 above), especially p. 60.
50. See Wiener (note 22 above), p. 28.
51. G. Scholem, *The Messianic Idea in Judaism* (1971), p. 289.
52. See P. Berger, *The Sacred Canopy* (1969), p. 6; E. H. Erikson, "Ontogeny of ritualization," *Philosophical Transactions of the Royal Society of London*, series B, vol. 251 (772) (1966), pp. 337–49.
53. See, for example, G. Van der Leeuw, *Religion in Essence and Manifestation* (1948), p. 462.

2. TORAH-IM-DEREKH ERETZ

1. See the discussion in I. Grunfeld, *Judaism Eternal: Selected Essays from the Writings of Rabbi Samson Raphael Hirsch* (1956), pp. xv–xvii.
2. A. Altmann, *Moses Mendelssohn* (1973).
3. See J. Katz, *Out of the Ghetto* (1973), pp. 66–8.
4. For the beginnings of the concept of "Derekh Eretz" in Scripture, and its evolution in rabbinic Judaism, see J. Carlebach, "The foundations of German–Jewish Orthodoxy: an interpretation," *Leo Baeck Year Book* 33 (1988), pp. 70ff.
5. For the terminological similarities in the thought of Wessely and Hirsch, see Carlebach, *ibid.*, pp. 82–3.
6. For Bernays' influence on Hirsch, see especially Y. Heinemann, "The relationship between S. R. Hirsch and his teacher Yitzhak Bernays" (Hebrew), *Zion* 16 (1951), pp. 44–90.
7. Of particular importance for understanding Hirsch's educational influence is his *Commentary to the Pentateuch*, which incorporated his major ideas. This commentary was studied widely and regularly by Orthodox German Jews.
8. For Hirsch's biography, see Noah H. Rosenbloom, *Tradition in an Age of Reform* (1976).
9. M. Meyer, *Response to Modernity* (1988), chap. 1.
10. *Ibid.*, p. 74.
11. In presenting the worldview and ethos of Torah-im-Derekh Eretz, I have drawn upon the following of Hirsch's works: (a) *Neunzehn Briefe ueber Judentum* (published 1836; edn. referred to here 1889). The English translation of this work, by Bernard Drachman, *The Nineteen Letters of Ben Uziel* (1899) is not always adequate, and references to this work are to the German original; (b) *Judaism Eternal* (see note 1), two volumes, consisting of essays translated from Hirsch's *Gesammelte Schriften*, (1902–10), six volumes; (c) *Commentary to the Pentateuch* (1971); (d) *Commentary to Psalms* (1960); (e) *Commentary to Chapters of the Fathers* (1967).
12. *Gesammelte Schriften* II, p. 422.
13. M. Kalvary, *Between Seed and Harvest* (Hebrew) (1947), p. 114. See also

A. Barth, *Our Generation Faces Eternal Problems* (1954), chap. 1. We note that Kalvary and Barth were grandchildren of Rabbi Esriel Hildesheimer, who founded the Orthodox Rabbinical Seminary in Berlin and headed it for many years (see page 44).
14. *Commentary to Genesis* 1:11.
15. *Commentary to Exodus* 19:6, and *Neunzehn Briefe*, pp. 88, 38.
16. "Introduction" to *Commentary to Psalms*.
17. *Gesammelte Schriften*, V, p. 566.
18. See S. W. Baron, "The revolution of 1848 and Jewish scholarship," *Proceedings of the Academy for Jewish Research* 20 (1951), p. 35.
19. *Neunzehn Briefe*, pp. 55, 90.
20. *Ibid.*, pp. 101, 105, 110–11, 114. Victor Turner termed this type of situation a "liminal" state. See Turner, *The Ritual Process: Structure and anti-Structure* (1969), chap. 3. This charismatic drive may have been induced in Hirsch by the religious experience that he describes in the last letter of his *Neunzehn Briefe:* "I have climbed alone to a height from which a new view displays itself to me. On that account it devolves on me ... to descend ... and begin again the journey with friends who will join me." For Hirsch's solitary religious experience, see R. Liberles, "Champion of orthodoxy: the emergence of Samson Raphael Hirsch as religious leader," *AJS Review* 5 (1981), pp. 43–60.
21. *Neunzehn Briefe*, pp. 109, 110. See also p. 106: "We shall contemplate nature in the spirit of David and listen to history with the ear of Isaiah."
22. *Ibid.*, pp. 90, 106, 110.
23. From Hirsch's manifesto in reaction to the reform-oriented rabbinical synod that convened in Braunschweig in 1844. Published in Y. Emmanuel, ed., *Rabbi Samson Raphel Hirsch: His Teachings and Method* (Hebrew) (1962), p. 335. I am grateful to Professor Mordechai Breuer for bringing this source to my attention.
24. *Judaism Eternal* II, p. 106. In the English version, divine sacredness is inaccurately translated as "divine teaching."
25. In the words of Heinemann, Hirsch "adapted the past to the ideal of the present." (See note 6 above, p. 85).
26. I. Heinemann, "Supplementary remarks on the secession from the Frankfurt Jewish community under Samson Raphael Hirsch," *Historia Judaica* 10 (1948), pp. 126–7; "Samson Raphael Hirsch, the formative years of the leader of modern Orthodoxy," *ibid.*, 13 (1951), pp. 46–7.
27. *Commentary to Chapters of the Fathers*, 2:2.
28. Although Hirsch took a stand against Kabbalah – the major source for this conception of Torah – he was familiar with its literature and seems to have been influenced by its concepts. See J. Katz, "S. R. Hirsch, the rightwinger and leftwinger," in M. Breuer, ed., *Torah-im-Derekh Eretz; the Movement, its Personages, its Thoughts* (Hebrew) (1987), pp. 19–21.
29. *Judaism Eternal* II, pp. 118–20.
30. *Commentary to Psalms* 19:8. Italics added.

31. *Ibid.*, 119:99.
32. *Judaism Eternal* II, p. 149.
33. *Ibid.*, p. 26.
34. *Commentary to Chapters of the Fathers* 6:10.
35. See *Commentary to Genesis* 18:17–19. Hirsch perceived man's partnership with God in completing Creation as fulfilled principally in the perfecting of social life. For the same partnership at the level of nature, see Barth (note 13 above), the chapter "The Partnership."
36. *Neunzehn Briefe*, pp. 15, 19, 21, 26, 27, 38.
37. *Commentary to Psalms* 8:6.
38. *Commentary to Genesis* 9:27.
39. *Neunzehn Briefe*, p. 79.
40. *Ibid.*, pp. 104–5, note.
41. *Ibid.*, p. 79.
42. *Ibid.*, pp. 97ff.
43. *Commentary to Genesis* 1:26.
44. *Ibid.*, 1:28.
45. Y. Breuer, *Moriah* (Hebrew) (1954), pp. 58–9.
46. "The world submits to man, for him to submit himself and the world to God, and for him to transform this earthly world into the home for the Kingdom of God." *Commentary to Exodus* 35:1.
47. It is of interest that, although Hirsch discredited socialism because, *inter alia*, it abuses individualism (*Judaism Eternal* I, p. 41), his collective orientation is compatible with that of socialism. Indeed, as we shall see in chap. 6, this orientation stood the Religious Kibbutz Federation in good stead when it set about forming its socialistic communities. In fact, Moses Hess, a contemporary of Hirsch who also marked off halakhic Judaism's value-orientations, grasped them in a socialistic context. See A. Fishman, "Moses Hess on Judaism and its aptness for a socialist civilization," *The Journal of Religion* 63:2 (April 1983), pp. 143–58.
48. *Judaism Eternal* II, p. 98.
49. *Ibid.*, p. 103.
50. See J. Rosenheim, "The historical significance of the struggle for secession from the Frankfort Jewish community," *Historia Judaica* 10 (1948), pp. 135–46, as well as the articles by S. Japhet and I. Heinemann in that issue. For the historical background for Hirsch's secession, see R. Liberles, *Religious Conflict in Social Context: the Resurgence of Orthodox Judaism in Frankfort am Main 1838–1877* (1985).
51. *Judaism Eternal* II, pp. 236–7.
52. See, on this subject, M. Breuer, *Juedische Orthodoxie im Deutschen Reich 1871–1918* (1986).
53. *Judaism Eternal* II, p. 95.
54. See Marion A. Kaplan, *The Jewish Feminist Movement in Germany: The Campaigns of the Juedischer Frauenbund 1904–1938* (1979).

55. See Katz (note 28 above), pp. 16–19.
56. On Hildesheimer and his role in institutionalizing Torah-im-Derekh Eretz, see Carlebach (note 4 above), pp. 85–8.
57. See M. Breuer, *The "Torah-im-Derekh Eretz" of Samson Raphael Hirsch* (1970), p. 43.
58. Thus Hirsch repudiated the Jewish national movement that was getting under way in his last years in Eastern Europe.
59. J. Leibowitz, "Zur Tarbuth Frage," *Choser Bachad* 2 (Neue Folge), Geringshof, Av 5692 (1932).

3. RELIGIOUS ZIONISM

1. The term "Eastern Europe" refers to the Russian Empire, which included Poland and the Baltic states. The rise and consolidation of Religious Zionism, first as a system of thought and later as a political movement, against the socio-cultural background of the disintegrating east European Jewish order, is extensively portrayed in Ehud Luz, *Parallels Meet: Religion and Nationalism in the Early Zionist Movement (1882–1904)* (1988).
2. See Howard M. Sachar, *The Course of Modern Jewish History* (1957), p. 208. For explicit Religious Zionist sensitivity to the lack of integration between "man" and Jew in the Orthodox Jew, see Rabbi Shmuel Y. Rabinowitz, *Religion and Nationalism* (Hebrew) (1900), pp. 94ff: "To be sure, religious Jews have a great deal to draw upon in defending their [religious] positions ... in a way that 'the man and Jew' in them can exist together, without being at loggerheads."
3. Rabbi Tzvi Hirsch Kalischer first expounded his religious national thinking in a letter to the German–Jewish financier Amschel Rothschild, in 1836, the same year in which S. R. Hirsch's first work, *Neunzehn Briefe ueber Judentum* was published. For the text of Kalischer's letter, see Y. Klausner, ed., *The Zionist Writings of Rabbi Kalischer* (Hebrew) (1946), pp. 2–14.
4. The foremost exposition of the thought of these two rabbis is to be found in Jacob Katz, "The historical image of Rabbi Tzvi Hirsch Kalischer," and "Messianism and nationalism in the thought of Rabbi Yehuda Alkalai," in his *Jewish Nationalism* (Hebrew) (1979). See also Shlomo Avineri, *The Making of Modern Zionism* (1981), chap. 4. Selected writings of these two rabbinic figures in English translation are included in Arthur Hertzberg, *The Zionist Idea* (1973), pp. 105–7, 111–14.
5. Yehiel M. Pines, *The Children of My Spirit* (Hebrew) (1872), I, p. 2.
6. *Ha-Mizraḥ* (1903), p. 2.
7. Luz (note 1 above), pp. 46ff.
8. In 1912, the anti-Zionist traditionalistic Orthodox leaders in Eastern Europe joined forces with the anti-Zionist modern Orthodox leaders in

Germany – the Hirschian secessionist component of the Torah-im-Derekh Eretz movement – and founded Agudat Israel (Union of Israel), whose central idea was the exclusive sovereignty of the Torah in Jewish existence.

9. East European Jewry did not produce a religious reform movement to which Religious Zionism would have had to relate in terms of Jewish solidarity.

10. See J. Katz, "The Jewish national movement: a sociological analysis," in his *Jewish Emancipation and Self-Emancipation* (1986).

11. See, especially, Ze'ev Yaavetz, "The unity" and "Education and the Jewish national community" (Hebrew), *Ha-Mizrah* (1903), pp. 10–17, 67–75.

12. See Pines (note 5 above), II, pp. 62–4: "All wisdom and knowledge that are useful in the light of truth and orderly social life smack of Torah study. We cannot remain content with making the Enlightenment religion's sister; sisters tend to quarrel. The Enlightenment must become religion's daughter, and then religion will heap its affection on the world and society, on knowledge and the crafts. In short, religion will integrate with the new life, as it was wont with the life of every past generation."

13. Zionist settlement in Eretz Israel began in 1882. The first major problem involving *halakhah* and national needs that the settlers had to face was the observance of the sabbatical year of 5649 (1888–9); by then eleven Jewish settlements had been established. According to *halakhah*, Jewish-owned land in Eretz Israel is to remain fallow in the sabbatical year, a practice which the settlements could not afford to follow. The solution offered by leading rabbis in the Diaspora was the fictitious sale of the land to a Gentile and the working of the land by Gentiles during the sabbatical year. However, the Eretz Israel rabbis opposed this solution and insisted that working the land cease throughout the year. For the controversy that this issue aroused, see Luz (note 1 above), pp. 33–7. In Chap. 7 below, we shall discuss the treatment of the sabbatical year problem by the Religious Kibbutz Federation. We shall shortly return to the problems stemming from the conflict between *halakhah* and certain national needs.

14. See, for example, Yaavetz (note 11 above), pp. 11–13, 331.

15. Adapted, with slight changes, from the English translation in Hertzberg (note 4 above), p. 102. While institutionalized *mitzvot* are recognized by all halakhic authorities as strictly binding, non-institutionalized *mitzvot* express rules of conduct in Jewish religious life whose normative cogency is less stringent. Thirteenth-century philosopher and biblical exegete, Nahmanides, defined *yishuv Eretz Israel* as a binding *mitzvah*, but this view has not been accepted by the consensus of halakhic authorities. For Nahmanides' view, see his gloss to Maimonides' *The Book of Precepts* (Hebrew), *mitzvah* 4.

16. Reprinted in S. Z. Shragai, *Vision and Realization* (Hebrew) (1957), p. 109.
17. See Katz (note 4 above), p. 337.
18. For the employment of this talmudic phrase by Rabbis Kalischer and Alkalai to designate the post-Emancipation period, see Katz (note 4 above), pp. 293, 328.
19. In Y. A. Slutzky, ed., *Return to Zion* (Hebrew) (1892), pp. 70–1. See also the editorial of *Ha-Ivri* (New York), of November 16 1917, two weeks after the issue of the Balfour Declaration, in reaction to the conquest of Jerusalem by the British Army: "We do not know whether the current transformation already marks the final moment of our redemption and revival, but there is no doubt that this conquest [of Jerusalem] is to be considered one of the significant steps in this process." The editor of *Ha-Ivri* was Rabbi Me'ir Berlin, who later headed the World Mizraḥi Organization.
20. See Yaavetz (note 11 above), p. 16, and Slutzky (note 19 above), p. 83.
21. Rabbi Yitzhak Nissenbaum, *National Judaism* (Hebrew) (1920), pp. 28–9. Rabbi Nissenbaum (1868–1942) was the central figure in the Religious Zionist movement in Poland between the two World Wars. And in a manifesto published in 1902 by a group of *yeshivah* students in Minsk, Belorussia, who identified with Mizraḥi, the following phrase appears: "A Torah of life from a God of life, that encompasses the entire life of man on earth." See Rabbi Y. Berman, "The beginnings of Mizraḥi's educational course" (Hebrew), *Ha-Hed*, Iyar-Tammuz 5702 (1942), p. 11.
22. Yaavetz (note 11 above), p. 73.
23. *Ibid.*, pp. 16–17,
24. See, for example, the protocol of the meeting between representatives of ha-Po'el ha-Mizraḥi agricultural groups and the Chief Rabbis of Tel Aviv, dealing with milking and security maintenance on the Sabbath, published in *Ha-Hed*, Tammuz 5696 (1936).
25. The Sanhedrin was the supreme legislative and judicial assembly that existed in Eretz Israel for the interpretation of the Law, before and after the destruction of the Second Temple.
26. See especially Rabbi Y. L. Maimon, "On the history of the Sanhedrin renewal idea" (Hebrew), *Sinai* 30 (1952), pp. 6–8.
27. Yaavetz (note 11 above), p. 327.
28. Mizraḥi is an acronym for *Merkaz Ruḥani* (spiritual center).
29. On Mizraḥi ideology and activities until the mid-1930s, see P. Churgin and L. Gellman, eds., *Mizrachi Jubilee Publication of the Mizrachi Organization of America 1911–1936* (1936).
30. One notable exception where Rabbi Kuk took an independent stand on a halakhic question *vis-à-vis* the traditionalistic rabbinate of Eretz Israel was his endorsement of the dispensation to sell the land of Eretz

Israel fictitiously to a Gentile for the duration of the sabbatical year (see note 13 above).

31. See, for example, the statement of Rabbi Y. L. Kowalsky at the second convention of the Mizraḥi organization in Poland (1919): "We must give our youth the chance to develop in the spirit of our Torah, in the spirit of God, and also in the spirit of modernity. We are obliged to create a modern Jewish cultural life based on a true foundation of the Jewish tradition." Cited in E. Mendelsohn, *Zionism in Poland* (1981), p. 173.

32. The Religious Zionist thinker Yeshayahu Wolfsberg (Aviad) attributes the practicality of the Mizraḥi founders to their religiously exoteric Lithuanian–Jewish background. See his *Ha-Mizraḥi – Ha-Po'el Ha-Mizraḥi* (Hebrew) (1946), pp. 45–6.

33. The sole exception was Rabbi Yeshayahu Shapiro, a scion of a Hassidic dynasty who, however, never actually served as a rabbi.

34. See S. H. Landau, "Torah and Israel," *The Writings of Shmu'el Ha'im Landau* (Hebrew) (1938), pp. 7–16.

35. Hirsch wrote: "Unlike other nations where the Law is created for the nation, in Israel the nation is created for the Law." S. R. Hirsch, *Horev*, section 714.

36. Landau (note 34 above), p. 38. Both Hirsch's and Landau's phrases are taken from *Kohelet Rabbah* 1:4: "For who was created for the sake of whom: Torah for Israel or Israel for Torah?"

37. In the Balfour Declaration of November 1917, the British Government pledged itself to facilitate the creation of a national home for the Jewish people in Palestine. The San Remo Conference of the Entente Powers, in April 1920, assigned the Mandate for Palestine to Great Britain, and included the Balfour Declaration within the terms of the Mandate.

38. In the elections to the First Elected Assembly of the Jewish community in Eretz Israel in 1920, the Socialist Zionist parties received 37% of the vote, Mizraḥi 3.5%, and the anti-Zionist Orthodox 17%. (This was the only election held during the Mandatory period in which the anti-Zionist Orthodox took part.)

39. From the "Founding Proclamation" of ha-Po'el ha-Mizraḥi, published in *Ha-Po'el Ha-Mizraḥi*, Tammuz-Av 5685 (1925), p. 179.

40. The original association of *Torah* and *avodah* is in *Chapters of the Fathers* 1:2, where *avodah* connotes Temple worship. However, *avodah* also connotes labor, and it is in this sense that ha-Po'el ha-Mizraḥi modified the original meaning of the Talmudic term in its association with Torah.

41. See note 39 above.

42. M. S. Geshuri, *From Road Paving Until Building the Workers' House* (Hebrew) (1927), pp. 12–13.

43. *Ha-Po'el Ha-Mizraḥi*, Tevet-Shvat 5685 (1925), p. 29.

44. N. Gardi, "Our essence" (Hebrew), *Ha-Po'el Ha-Mizrahi*, Nisan 5683 (1923), p. 28.
45. See Y. Bernstein, *Ha-Po'el Ha-Mizrahi*, Av 5684 (1924), p. 18: "In our desire to upbuild the Land, we wish first to solve what is known in kabbalistic language as 'the exile of the Divine Presence' . . . to give our people once again the opportunity to restore the Divine Presence, as in the days of old."
46. Y. Bernstein in Y. Aminoah and Y. Bernstein, eds., *A Compilation* (Hebrew) (1931), p. 16.
47. Bar-bei-Rav (S. H. Landau), "Rabbis, heed your deeds" (Hebrew), *Ha-Mizrahi*, 6 Nisan 5684 (1924), p. 3.
48. Rabbi Y. Shapiro, *Netivah*, 2 Nisan 5689 (1929), pp. 224–5. The English translation is taken from *Forum* 23 (spring 1975), pp. 97–9.
49. A. Rothstein, "Our return to the source" (Hebrew), *Ha-Po'el Ha-Mizrahi*, Av 5684 (1924), p. 28.
50. Y. Gur-Aryei, "The aspiration of the generations" (Hebrew), in *A Compilation* (see note 46), pp. 45–6.
51. S. Z. Shragai, "The holy rebellion doctrine" (Hebrew), *Netivah*, 1 Tammuz 5704 (1944), p. 2.
52. Landau (note 34 above), pp. 32–3.
53. In 1924 ha-Po'el ha-Mizrahi split into a left wing, which joined the Histadrut as a "ha-Po'el ha-Mizrahi" faction, and a right wing, which continued to exist independently, but maintained close ties with Mizrahi. In 1927 the left wing left the Histadrut and rejoined the independent ha-Po'el ha-Mizrahi.
54. Y. Bernstein, "On the unification" (Hebrew), *Ha-'Ohelah* 2–3 (c. 1925), pp. 40–1.
55. Landau (note 34 above), pp. 36–43. The English translation of these passages and subsequent excerpts from Landau's article, "Toward an explanation of our ideology," are adapted from A. Hertzberg, *The Zionist Idea* (1973), pp. 434–9.
56. Thus, "a life of labor . . . is actually Torah, the spirit of the Torah as it is carried out." S. Barukhuni in *A Compilation* (note 46 above), p. 36.
57. "Rachel Berkman, of blessed memory" (Hebrew), *Netivah*, 13 Heshvan 5796 (1936), p. 3.
58. A federation of Mizrahi and the World Torah va-Avodah movement. The latter, formed in 1925, consisted of ha-Po'el ha-Mizrahi in Eretz Israel and Tze'irei Mizrahi (Mizrahi Youth) and he-Halutz ha-Mizrahi (the Mizrahi pioneer) in the Diaspora.
59. In 1956, when ha-Po'el ha-Mizrahi and Mizrahi united into one political party, Mafdal, (an acronym for Miflagah Datit Le'umit [National Religious Party]), ha-Po'el ha-Mizrahi had nine representatives in Israel's Knesset and Mizrahi two. After 1956 ha-Po'el ha-Mizrahi continued its independent existence as a labor organization.
60. S. Z. Shragai, "Within the private domain" (Hebrew), *Netivah*, 13 Av

5694 (1934), p. 2. Cf. the statement of Shlomo Lavi, a leading ideologue of the secular kibbutz movement: "We need a living God; indeed, He dwells in our midst. He is the God of Israel who charges us with living justly, with laboring, with ... a communal life. It is this God and His [social] *mitzvot* that we seek to hand down to our children." Shlomo Lavi, *Selected Writings* (Hebrew), II (1944), p. 88.
61. Landau (note 34 above), pp. 38, 31.
62. Rabbi Y. Shapiro (note 48 above).
63. See A. Fishman, "Religion and communal life in an evolutionary-functional perspective: the Orthodox kibbutzim," *Comparative Studies in Society and History* 29 (1987), pp. 763–86. I intend to return to this theme in a forthcoming work.
64. S. Z. Shragai, "The role and work of Mizraḥi" (Hebrew), *Ha-Tor*, 30 Nisan 5689 (1929), p. 8; "The work in the camp" (Hebrew), *Netivah* 5690 (1930), pp. 69–70; and his serial "In the camp" (Hebrew), beginning in *Netivah*, 15 Shvat 5694 (1934).
65. Shragai, *Netivah*, 30 Sivan 5694 (1934), p. 2.

4. THE FOUNDATIONS OF THE RELIGIOUS KIBBUTZ MOVEMENT

1. N. Amino'aḥ, *A Religious Labor Movement* (Hebrew) (1931), pp. 40–1.
2. Rodges was named after a religious pioneering training-farm in Germany. Shaḥal is an acronym for Shmu'el Ḥa'im Landau.
3. The largest component of the East European pioneering movement emerged from Poland, but there were also components from Czechoslovakia, Romania, and Hungary.
4. A recurring theme in Religious Zionist literature of the 1920s and part of the 1930s is the need "to remove the shame" of Orthodox Jewry's meager role in the Zionist endeavor. See, for example, *Ha-Po'el Ha-Mizraḥi*, Av 5683 (1923), p. 4 and *Netivah*, 26 Tammuz 5697 (1937), p. 1.
5. See Tzurie'l Admanit, *The Bnei Akivah Book* (Hebrew), ed. Y. Lev (c. 1960), p. 105.
6. The sensitivity of the East European Orthodox youth, that was emerging from traditional Jewish society, to the gap between their Jewish religious and their human identities is concisely expressed by a graduate of the Bnei Akivah youth movement in Eastern Galicia: "The creation of a type of whole person is the task of kibbutz life. If this is difficult for others, for us it is far more difficult. For despite our heavy emphasis on 'man,' the task of creating a religious person in whom humanity and religion go hand in hand and blend into one, will always confront us." B. Imber, *Tikvah* (c. 1935), pp. 1–2.
7. In 1941, the distribution of RKF members and candidates for membership according to countries of origin was as follows: Germany, 55

percent; Poland, 17 percent; Czechoslovakia, 11 percent; Austria, 6 percent; Romania, 3 percent; other countries, approximately 7 percent. See *Alonim*, Tammuz 5701 (1941), p. 70.
8. In Germany, as we shall see below, the influence of the German youth movement was direct. In Eastern Europe, Orthodox youth adopted the youth movement pattern from the secular Zionist pioneering movements, which, in turn, were directly influenced by the German model.
9. B. Z. Grodzhensky in *Pathways* (Hebrew), ed. M. Krone (1938), p. 120. And the writer adds: "One feels an upheaval of the spirit ... the stirring of the blood for action and deeds. I am being born again."
10. *Ibid.*, p. 52. See also the quotation from Leibowitz (p. 75).
11. J. Leibowitz, "Zur Tarbuth Frage," *Choser Bachad* 1–2 (Neue Folge), Adar II and Av, 5692 (1932).
12. Yeshayahu Leibowitz was later to become a professor of organic chemistry at The Hebrew University of Jerusalem, and an eminent public figure in Israel.
13. These quoted words form a chapter title in W. Z. Laqueur, *Young Germany* (1962). For the Orthodox Jewish segment in the German youth movement, see p. 155.
14. A. Feilchenfeld, "The direction of our work," in *Aryei Lutz Feilchenfeld, of Blessed Memory* (Hebrew) (c. 1935), pp. 11–2.
15. E. Ya'ir, "42 Grenadier Street in Berlin" (Hebrew), *Ba-Mishor*, November 11 1944, p. 7.
16. For the religious experiences of German Orthodox youth as related by Moshe Unna, see p. 97. Unna himself had such experiences when he encountered a Hassidic ambience in Germany, at a Jewish-owned farm where he was undergoing agricultural training. See his *Archetype: Religious Zionism's Training Project in Germany in its Initial Steps* (Hebrew) (January 1989), p. 39.
17. G. Unna, "Ein neuer Weg," *Zion* 1 (April 1929), p. 49.
18. M. Unna, "Die juedische Form des religioesen Sozialismus," *Zion* 6 (1934), p. 5.
19. Mizraḥi Youth, which was founded on a national basis in 1927, was affiliated ideologically and organizationally to the World Torah va-Avodah movement (see Y. Walk, "The Torah va-Avodah Movement in Germany," *Leo Baeck Yearbook* 6 [1961], pp. 243–4); Ezra, founded in 1919, was a non-political youth movement associated with the secessionist communities inspired by S. R. Hirsch (see H. Abt, "Juedische Jugendbewegung," in *Nachlat Z'wi*, beginning with the June–July 1932 issue). Although Ezra did not regard itself as either Zionist or socialist, it included a defined group that identified strongly with Eretz Israel and also with socialist values. For a comprehensive overview of the religious pioneering movement in Germany in its formative period, see Walk's article.
20. Sch. Bombach, *Die Tnuath Torah va-Awoda* (ms.) (1934), p. 22. Central

Archives of ha-Kibbutz ha-Dati, Kvutzat Yavne. For the atmosphere at the Betzenrod training-farm, see also Walk (note 19 above), pp. 246–7.
21. *Choser Bachad* 2, January 1929.
22. Leibowitz (note 11 above).
23. E. Simon, "Zum Jubilaeum von Rodges," *Zion* 6 (1934), p. 46. Ernst Simon was later to become professor of education at The Hebrew University of Jerusalem, and a highly regarded figure in Israeli life.
24. J. Leibowitz, *Zion* 2 (1930), p. 64.
25. E. Rosenblueth, *Zion* 2 (1930), p. 60.
26. Leibowitz (note 11 above).
27. E. Rosenblueth, *Methodik der Eretz Israel-Arbeit* (1932), p. 7.
28. *Grundriss eines Erziehungsprogramms* (c. 1933), p. 12.
29. The declaration for kibbutz had been made in Germany. See Walk (note 19 above), pp. 255–6.
30. Sch. B., *Bachad Rundschreiben* 5 (December 1929).
31. A graduate of the Eastern Galician Bnei Akivah youth movement writes in retrospect: "We, the sons of religious homes, who frequented the *kloyz* (Hassidic place of worship) ... were ashamed of the quiet around us and of the opposition of most of our spokesmen and teachers to the national revival. But it was hard for us to cut ourselves off from our original environment." D. Knohl, *Netivah*, Adar-Nisan 5707 (1947). A 1940 entry from the diary of the Bnei Akivah youth movement in Romania states: "We see how life is astir in other movements... Why do not we have anything?... Religious youth, having no direction, is degenerating." (Quoted in the bulletin of the Bnei Akivah youth group in Kfar Etzion, September 1944.) And one brought up in the Carpathian mountains writes in his kibbutz's bulletin: "We could not reconcile ourselves to the degeneracy and rot of the life of idleness about us, notwithstanding all the values that we held dear, that we grieved were expiring." Ephraim Gottlieb, *Massu'ot* (Kibbutz Massu'ot Yitzḥak), 15 Shvat 5705 (1945).
32. *Pathways* (note 9 above), p. 14.
33. Particularly the Slavkov training-farm in western Galicia.
34. The first branches of ha-Shomer ha-Dati and Bnei Akivah in Poland were founded in 1929–30. The former embraced Congress Poland and western Galicia, and the latter eastern Galicia.
35. Y. Yefet, *Leaves of Torah va-Avodah Thought* (Hebrew), ed. S. Z. Cahana and M. Krone (1937), pp. 17–18.
36. Thus M. Krone writes in 1937: "We are beginning to become accustomed to the idea that the interweaving of religious life with universal–cultural progress ... is not a sign of hypocrisy or naïveté, but of a worldview that has attained synthesis." *Leaves* (note 35 above), p. 30.

37. H. Chmelnik (Aḥiman), *The Group Expression of the Incipient-Kibbutz Members of Ha-Shomer Ha-Dati* (Hebrew) (Warsaw) (1938), pp. 14–15.
38. S. Treller (Karni'el), *Pathways* (note 9 above), p. 148.
39. *Ohaleinu*, Tevet-Shvat 5696 (1936), p. 11.
40. The term *kvutzah* denoted a relatively small communal group.

5. CHARISMA AND RATIONALIZATION

1. For the relationship between charisma and rationalization at the specific levels of meaning and behavior in Max Weber's thought, which will be discussed in this chapter, see S. N. Eisenstadt, "Introduction," *Max Weber on Charisma and Institution Building* (1968), pp. liiff.
2. H. Chmelnik (Aḥiman), "On the character of the religious kibbutz and its problems" (Hebrew), *Alonim* 21, Iyar 5706 (1946), pp. 2–3.
3. A. Nusbecher (Naḥlon), "On creating a religious cultural ambience" (Hebrew), *Dappim* (Rodges), 15 Tammuz 5698 (1938), p. 2. A "complete and unified life" is presented "in contrast to the torn life of the Jew in the *galut*."
4. Y. Friedman, "Religiosity" (Hebrew), *Ba-Alot Ha-No'ar* (Rodges Youth Aliyah Group) 4 (1935), p. 14.
5. Y. Lutvak, "The kibbutz theme in our camp," *Report of the Fifth Conference of ha-Po'el ha-Mizraḥi* (Hebrew) (1935), p. 48.
6. M. Slokhovoy (Shilo'aḥ), "Let's take stock" (Hebrew), *Yoman Ha-Meshek* (Kibbutz Rodges), 22 Sivan 5699 (1939), p. 3.
7. For the concept of "mythical time" as a transcendent reality and as a prototype for realization in empirical reality, see M. Eliade, *Cosmos and History* (1938), pp. 3ff.
8. A. Feilchenfeld, "The direction of our work," *Ba-Alot Ha-No'ar* 4, (note 4 above), p. 2.
9. A Polish youth movement leader adduces this notion from the fifteenth-century biblical commentator, Abarbanel, in the Introduction to his commentary on Isaiah: "In the messianic era there will no longer be kings and princes, but all will be as equal as they were at the beginning of creation." Y. Yefet, "The vision of the future and the task of the present," in *Leaves of Torah va-Avodah Thought* (Hebrew), S. Z. Cahana and M. Krone, eds., (1937), p. 19. And the writer adds: "So long as people will be divided into classes and strata, absolute justice cannot prevail... Your neighbor, like you, was created in God's image, and all are equal before Him. Uproot egoism and your heart will be free to love" (pp. 19–20).
10. A member of a religious pioneering movement in Poland described his experience on the training-farm: "Among the comrades I am filled with a strange feeling... of family closeness, a closeness of blood and psyche." B. Z. Grodzhensky, *Pathways* (Hebrew), ed. M. Krone (1938), p. 121.

11. Lutvak (note 5 above).
12. M. Orlian (Or), "Regular days" in *On the First Anniversary of Tirat Tzvi* (Hebrew) ed. M. Krone (1938), p. 48. Cf. Eliade (note 7 above), p. 10, who characterizes the first plowing as an act that transforms cosmic chaos into a meaningful order.
13. R. Herz, "Kibbutz Rodges," *Zion* (Berlin) 6 (1934), p. 51.
14. M. Scheinbach, "On the question of the religiousness in our midst" (Hebrew), *Niveinu* (Sdei Eliyahau), Erev Pessaḥ 5701 (1941), p. 1.
15. M. Krone, "On the agendas" (Hebrew), *Dappim* (Rodges), 3 Sivan 5698 (1938), p. 1.
16. E. Ya'ir, "What names shall we give our children?" (Hebrew), *Ba-Tirah* (Tirat Tzvi), 26 Iyar 5698 (1938), p. 7. Cf. Van der Leeuw, *Religion in Essence and Manifestation* (1938), pp. 197–8.
17. From a letter from Yaakov Yisrael to Reuven Me'iri, 1943, in the Sons of the Etzion Bloc Association archives.
18. H. Chmelnik (Aḥiman), "On the character of the religious kibbutz and its problems" (Hebrew), *Alonim* 19, Adar I 5706 (1946), p. 22.
19. Yefet (note 9 above), p. 22.
20. H. Gvaryahu, "As the evening of the third day approached – from the notes of a Tirat Tzvi settler" (Hebrew), *Zra'im*, Adar I 5698 (1938), p. 5.
21. *Shalom Karni'el: His Life and Thought* (Hebrew), Sha'ul Raz, ed. (1967), p. 285.
22. M. Orlian (Or), "A Passover Haggadah" (Hebrew), *Ba-Tirah* (Tirat Tzvi), Erev Pessaḥ 5698 (1938), p. 2.
23. M. Perlman, "The synagogue and prayer service," in A. Fishman, ed., *The Religious Kibbutz Movement* (1957), p. 66.
24. E. Goldman, "The religious significance of Independence Day" (Hebrew), *Amudim* 119, Iyar 5717 (1957), p. 4.
25. Tzuri'el Admanit writes in this vein in 1960: "The very perception of the State of Israel as a stage in the messianic redemption entitles us to search for the special here-and-now contents of Torah observance." *The Bnei Akivah Book* (Hebrew), ed. Y. Lev (c. 1960), p. 107.
26. E. Goldman, (note 24 above).
27. F.A.M., *Kol Be-Ramah* (Rammat ha-Shomron – Be'erot Yitzhak) 6 Sivan 5698 (1938), p. 11.
28. H. Heinemann, *Torah and the Social Order* (c. 1942), p. 11. Rabbi Hans Yosef Heinemann was a leading figure in Bachad in Germany in the mid-1930s, and afterwards in England. He was later to become a professor of Midrash literature at The Hebrew University in Jerusalem.
29. S. B. Feldman, "Religion and social-mindedness" (Hebrew), *Ha-Hed*, Adar 5698 (1938), p. 17. Emphasis added.
30. A. Nusbecher (Naḥlon), "The way of religious youth" (Hebrew), *Ha-Hed*, Iyar-Sivan 5698 (1938), p. 8.
31. These expressions are taken from Heinemann (note 28 above).

32. M. Or, "A clarification of matters" (Hebrew), *Ba-Tirah* (Tirat Tzvi), 14 Shvat 5699 (1939), p. 13.
33. For the concepts of Bund and Commune, see Yonina Talmon, *Family and Community in the Kibbutz* (1972), pp. 2–3; Erik Cohen, "The structural transformation of the kibbutz," in G. K. Zolschan and W. Hirsch, eds., *Social Change* (1973), pp. 703–42. For these concepts in the context of the RKF experience, see A. Fishman, "Religion and communal life in an evolutionary–functional perspective; the Orthodox kibbutzim," *Comparative Studies in Society and History*, 29 (4) (October 1987), pp. 763–86.
34. Hermann Schmalenbach used the term "Bund" to categorize the highly affective relations that characterized the German youth movement. See his "Communion – a sociological category," in G. Lueschen and G. P. Stone, eds., *Schmalenbach on Society and Experience* (1977).
35. From the protocol of the Second Council of the RKF (1941), cited in the Bnei Akivah publication, *An Introduction to the Kibbutz Question* (Hebrew) (1943), p. 20.
36. "Kibbutz Rodges" (Hebrew), *Netivah*, 13 Kislev 5697 (1937), p. 3.
37. This point is well clarified by S. Haimowitz in his article "Towards new stages," in *Alonim Le-Informatziyah Pnimit*, Tevet 5701 (1941), p. 9: "In the youth movement and training-farm, social and ideological filaments become woven into a unified fabric; the dream's distance from reality enhances its image, which, in turn, widens the conceptual horizon and strengthens the desire to create and improve. In the kibbutz, on the other hand, there is a 'reality' that works against the ideal. If the ideal is cultivated, reality retouches and purifies it, and makes it a guiding light. Those groups which did not undergo such a [visionary] period are condemned to a life without horizons and purpose; they then lack creative drive without which they cannot exist."
38. A. Herz, "How did centralizing the farm economy affect kibbutz development?" (Hebrew), *Amudim* 181, Tammuz 5721 (1961), p. 20.
39. M. Unna, "Law and ordinance in the kibbutz" (Hebrew), *Alonim* 19, Adar II 5706 (1946), p. 4.
40. D. Rappel, "A constitution or by-laws?" (Hebrew), *Alonim* 21, Iyar 5706 (1946), p. 5.
41. R. Herz (note 13 above), p. 76.
42. M. Unna, "The nature of the religious kibbutz" (Hebrew), *Netivah*, 9 Adar 5696 (1936), p. 4.
43. D. Fogel, *Protocol of the Meeting in Rammat ha-Shomron* (Hebrew), Heshvan 5698 (1937), p. 13.
44. Y. Kali, *Ba-Tirah* (Tirat Tzvi), 16 Iyar 5699 (1939), pp. 10–11.
45. From the protocol of the committee meeting, in the Central Archives of the Religious Kibbutz Federation, Kibbutz Yavne.
46. S. Karni'el, "The cultural element in the religious kibbutz" (Hebrew), *Nevatim* (Kfar Etzion – Alumim), 1 Kislev 5705 (1945), p. 2.

47. Yefet, *Leaves* (note 9 above), p. 17.
48. E. Rosenblueth, "The path of religious youth in the land," in *In the Paths of Youth* (Hebrew), ed. G. Ḥanokh (1938), p. 72.
49. *Ibid.*, pp. 72–3.
50. M. Unna, "The elements and tasks of the religious kibbutz" (Hebrew), *Alonim*, Sivan, 5702 (1942), p. 6. Emphasis added.
51. Y. Lutvak, "On the direction of the religious farm economy" (Hebrew), *Kvutzateinu* (Kibbutz Rodges), 18 Shvat 5697 (1937), p. 2.
52. Marduk, "On clarifying the religious question," *Shvu'on Sdei Eliyahu*, 16 Shvat 5700 (1940), p. 2.
53. N. Bar-Giora, *Sdei Eliyahu* (Hebrew) (2nd edition, 1956), p. 64.
54. Cf. A. Swidler, "The concept of rationality in the work of Max Weber," *Sociological Inquiry* 43 (1973), pp. 35–42.
55. This passage and the following lengthy quotation are parts of an address that Unna delivered at an RKF conference at the end of 1939. The text of the address was published in 1942, under the title "The elements and tasks of the religious kibbutz" (note 50 above).
56. *Ibid.*
57. *Dappim* (Rodges), 3 Elul 5699 (1939), p. 1. This conception of the relationship between the sacred and secular reflects the religious philosophy of Rabbi Abraham Kuk (See N. Rotenstreich, *Jewish Philosophy in Modern Times* [1968], chap. 7, especially pp. 221–2.) For a later reference in RKF literature to this conception in Rabbi Kuk's teachings, see A. Paltiel, "On contemporary problems" (Hebrew), *Yedi'ot Ha-Shavu'ah* (Kibbutz Ein ha-Natziv), 15 Shvat 5711 (1951), p. 3: "People of harmony see secularism as a function of the sacred; the difference is gradual."
58. S. Shechter, "On our religious condition" (Hebrew), *Alonim*, Shvat 5702 (1942), p. 4.
59. *Ibid.*
60. E. Goldman, "Traditional or scientific education for our children?" (Hebrew), *Alonim*, Tishrei, 5704 (1943), p. 4.
61. This statement by Gedaliah Unna is paraphrased in *Miscellany in Memory of Gedaliah Unna, of Blessed Memory* (Hebrew), ed. E. S. Rosenthal (1940), p. 13.
62. N. Bar-Giora, *Sdei Eliyahu* (Hebrew) (1947), pp. 81–2.
63. S. Aḥituv, "How does one educate towards the kibbutz?" (Hebrew), *Amudim* 147, Tishrei 5719 (1958), p. 11.

6. THE HALAKHIC–SOCIALIST COLLECTIVE

1. *Miscellany in Memory of Gedaliah Unna of Blessed Memory* (Hebrew), ed. E. S. Rosenthal (1940), p. 13.
2. For self-rationalization as a means of divine worship, see Maimonides, *The Eight Chapters of Maimonides on Ethics* (1966), chap. 4–5; for the perception of the *mitzvot* as a means for self-rationalization, see *Guide for*

the Perplexed (1963), part II, chap. 33; for reason binding man to God, see *Guide*, part II, chap. 51; for the religious–political ethic, see *Guide*, part II, chap. 40; on the thrust toward the perfection of society as a means for divine worship, see *Guide*, part III, chap. 27.
3. E. S. Rosenthal, "Clarification summaries" (Hebrew), *Dappim* (Rodges), 7 Menahem Av 5698 (1938), p. 2.
4. E. Rosenblueth, "The problems of religion" (Hebrew), *Alonim*, Nisan 5702 (1942), p. 9.
5. For this concept, see Max Weber, *The Methodology of the Social Sciences* (1949), p. 90.
6. E. Ya'ir, "The influence of Hassidism on the religious kibbutz" (Hebrew), *Amudim* 170, Tammuz 5720 (1960), p. 10.
7. E. Goldman, "On the religious personality in the religious kvutza," in A. Fishman, ed., *The Religious Kibbutz Movement* (1957), p. 54.
8. A. Nusbecher (Nahlon), "On creating a religious cultural ambience" (Hebrew), *Dappim* (Rodges), 15 Tammuz 5698 (1938), p. 2.
9. M. Unna, "The orientation of education and learning in Judaism" (Hebrew) in *In the Paths of Thought and Deed* (1955), p. 17.
10. Y. Drori, from the unpublished protocol of the Fourth Council of the Religious Kibbutz Federation, 1951. Located in the RKF Central Archives, Kibbutz Yavne.
11. E. Goldman, "Co-operative consumption" (Hebrew), *Yedi'ot Ha-Kibbutz Ha-Dati* 100, Sivan 5714 (1954), p. 51.
12. Adduced by E. S. Rosenthal (note 3 above); also by Y. Cohen, *Amudim* 182, Av 5721 (1961), p. 28.
13. A. Nahlon, "The religious experience and Hassidism" (Hebrew), *Amudim* 164, Tevet 5720 (1960), p. 8.
14. See M. Breuer, "Pilpul," *Encyclopedia Judaica* 8:366–72.
15. M. Ben-Yitzhak and E. Ya'ir, "Between the religious kibbutz and the *yeshivot*" (Hebrew), *Amudim* 190, Adar II 5722 (1962), pp. 163–4.
16. Quoted in Bar-Giora, *Sdei Eliyahu* (2nd edition, 1957), p. 24.
17. Y. Ascher, "The harvest celebration" (Hebrew), *Yedi'ot Yavne* (Kibbutz Yavne), 6 Tammuz 5710 (1950), p. 1.
18. A. Nahlon, "The mission of the Religious Kibbutz Federation" (Hebrew), *Amudim* 132, Tammuz 5716 (1956), p. 24.
19. M. Or, "Moshe Unna's web of creation" (Hebrew), *Yedi'ot Ha-Kibbutz Ha-Dati* 106, Shvat 5715 (1955), p. 4.
20. "We must get to know the special factors that operate in the contemporary social regime – in the economic sphere as well as in other spheres – that determine one's social class and relation to society. These iron laws are more decisive than one's personal [character] in determining behavior – whether one is righteous or evil." E. Rosenblueth, "The problems of religion" (Hebrew), *Alonim*, Nisan 5702 (1942), p. 9.
21. S. Schechter, "On our religious condition" (Hebrew), *Alonim*, Shvat 5702 (1942), p. 3.

22. *Ibid.*
23. *Ibid.*
24. E. S. Rosenthal, [no title] *Alonim*, Shvat 5702 (1942), pp. 8–9.
25. Schechter (note 21 above).
26. Naḥlon (note 18 above).
27. The term *shli'aḥ tzibbur* is ordinarily employed for the leader of the communal prayer service.
28. *Ha-Kibbutz Ha-Dati* [no author] (1949), p. 7.
29. M. Unna, "The elements and tasks of the religious kibbutz" (Hebrew), *Alonim*, Sivan 5702 (1942), p. 5.
30. M. Bolleh, "On the improvement of the prayer form" (Hebrew), *Niv Ha-Kvutza* (Kibbutz Yavne), Erev Sukkot 5706 (1945), p. 2. The writer adduces Maimonides' notion in *Guide for the Perplexed*, part II, chap. 27.
31. Relating to the thought of Maimonides, Moshe Unna states in 1959: "We are enjoined to establish the perfected society, in which the individual will find his place by his adjustment thereto. That is to say, by subordinating individual will to the needs of the public and working for its welfare. For that purpose one must acquire the ethic that is useful for society; on this basis one can advance towards inner perfection." *Protocol of the Tenth Council of the Religious Kibbutz Federation* (Hebrew), Rosh ha-Shana 5720 (1959), p. 15.
32. "If we are to rely only on our reason we shall surely err . . . It is for this reason that we are in need of divine law for delineating the absolute boundary for human behavior, and for the definite constitution of the perfected society." Rosenblueth (note 20 above), p. 14.
33. Unna (note 29 above), p. 7.
34. E. Simon, *Talmid Chacham und Chalutz* (1934).
35. *Ibid.*, pp. 2–8.
36. T. Admanit, *The Bnei Akivah Book* (Hebrew), ed. Y. Lev (c. 1960), p. 109.
37. M. Unna, *The Third Council of the Religious Kibbutz Federation* (Hebrew) (1946), p. 51.
38. See Dov Rappel, "Aspects of Education," in A. Fishman, ed., *The Religious Kibbutz Movement* (1957), pp. 75–6.
39. *Protocol of the Tenth Council* (see note 31), p. 78.
40. E. Ya'ir, "The culture of entertainment" (Hebrew), *Amudim* 205, Sivan 5723 (1963), pp. 237–8.
41. See the discussion in T. Parsons, *The Structure of Social Action* (1937), pp. 482ff.

7. THE CONFRONTATION BETWEEN *HALAKHAH* AND EXTERNAL REALITY

1. The socialist institution of shared property clashed with a number of halakhic norms whose observance is predicated on private property; for

example, a wedding-ring by which a man takes a woman in marriage. The RKF ruled that in such cases of conflict, the halakhic norm would prevail.
2. M. Unna, "Prophetic mission and religious socialism," in *In the Paths of Thought and Deed* (Hebrew) (1955), p. 54.
3. See above, chap. 6, pp. 102–3. See also S. Friedman, "The extension of the scope of *halakhah*," in A. Fishman, ed., *The Religious Kibbutz Movement* (1957), pp. 38–9.
4. "On the settling of Kfar Etzion" (Hebrew), *Alonim*, Sivan 5703 (1943), p. 3.
5. M. Unna, *Drawing Hearts to Torah and Mitzvot; Protocol of an RKF Seminar* (Hebrew) (1967), p. 11.
6. "An account of the meeting of the Committee for Clarifying Religious Problems" (Hebrew), *Ha-Hed*, Tammuz 5638 (1938), p. 12.
7. Note 4 above, p. 1.
8. E. S. Rosenthal, "In anticipation of the settlement of mountainous regions" (Hebrew), *Alonim*, Sivan 5703 (1943), p. 3.
9. See the discussion in T. Parsons, *The Structure of Social Action* (1937), pp. 256ff.
10. T. Admanit, "On the religious significance of the community," in Fishman (note 3 above), pp. 31–2.
11. Y. Lutvak, "On the direction of the religious farm economy" (Hebrew), *Kvutzateinu* (Rodges), 18 Shvat 5697 (1937), p. 2.
12. E. Goldman, *Halakhah and the State* (Hebrew) (1952), p. 39.
13. Y. Schlesinger, "The observance of the *mitzvot*" (Hebrew), *Alon Ein Tzurim* (Kibbutz Ein Tzurim), Hanukka 5713 (1952), p. 7.
14. M. Livne, "On the problem of hybrids" (Hebrew), *Alon Massu'ot Yitzḥak* (Kibbutz Massu'ot Yitzḥak), (c. 1945), p. 24.
15. Y. Lutvak (note 11 above).
16. See S. Friedman (note 3 above), pp. 42–5.
17. In 1990, Kibbutz Yavne had about 100,000 hens and incubated about fifteen million chicks.
18. This paragraph draws mostly upon an interview with Elimelekh Avital and David Hayisraeli of Kibbutz Yavne.
19. See S. Friedman in *The Celebration of Religious Holidays in the Kibbutz* (no editor) (1968), p. 17.
20. See Friedman (note 3 above), pp. 40–2.
21. *Ibid.*, p. 43.
22. See T. Admanit, "The observance of the agricultural *mitzvot* today," in Fishman (note 3 above), pp. 119–26.
23. See chap. 3, note 13.
24. For a review of the problems involving the observance of the sabbatical year from the beginnings of Zionist settlement, and for various approaches to their solution, see Rabbi Y. Heinemann, "Contempor-

ary observance of the sabbatical year," in Fishman (note 3 above), pp. 130–6.
25. See Z. Y. Kuk, *Ha-Hed*, Tammuz 5696 (1936) p. 16; A. Surky, *The Light of Elhanan* [Wasserman] (Hebrew) (1970), p. 75; Ḥa'im Ozer Grodzensky, *A Collection of Missives* (Hebrew) (1970), pp. 457–61.
26. Cf. S. Friedman's statement concerning the extinction of a field fire on the Sabbath: "While in such instances we obey the unequivocal injunction of *halakhah*, it would be true to say that we do so almost in a spirit of devoutness. This is not because we are so greatly concerned whether we save some straw from the fire, but rather because we feel that 'profanation of the Sabbath' in cases of this kind ensures the existence of the Jewish people in Eretz Israel." Friedman (note 3 above), p. 43.
27. *Ibid.*, pp. 41–2.
28. *Miscellany in Memory of Rabbi Gedaliah Unna of Blessed Memory* (Hebrew), ed. E. S. Rosenthal (1940), p. 13.
29. K. Davis, *Human Society* (1949), pp. 133–4.
30. E. Goldman, "Morality, religion and *halakhah*" (Hebrew), *De'ot* 22, winter 5723 (1963), p. 71.
31. See Rabbi Joseph B. Soloveitchik, *Halakhic Man* (1983), pp. 18–19, 83.
32. R. Herz, "Kibbutz Rodges," *Zion* 6 (1934), p. 54.
33. Reuven, "On current issues" (Hebrew), *Ba-Tirah* (Tirat Tzvi), 5 Av 5699 (1939), p. 6.
34. Thus an observer of Tirat Tzvi's life in the first year of settlement writes: "The members permit themselves to guard with arms on the Sabbath, and to light up the security spotlight; these actions involve 'saving an endangered life'. While they have arranged for the spotlight to automatically light up from time to time, they must also [perform labors prohibited on the Sabbath]: rotate it, activate its dynamo when it ceases working, add fuel, etc.," in "In Tirat Tzvi" (Hebrew), *Ha-Hed*, Marḥeshvan 5698 (1937), p. 9.
35. M. Or, "A letter to a young comrade" (Hebrew), *Amudim* 142, Sivan 5718 (1958), p. 19.
36. See A. Fishman and Y. Goldschmidt, "The Orthodox kibbutzim and economic success," *Journal for the Scientific Study of Religion* 29 (1990), pp. 505–11. From 1957 until 1979 there were three secular kibbutz groupings: ha-Kibbutz ha-Artzi, with 75 kibbutzim in 1979; Ḥever ha-Kvutzot ve-ha-Kibbutzim, with 82 kibbutzim; and ha-Kibbutz ha-Me'uḥad, with 60 kibbutzim. In 1979 the latter two federations united and formed the Takam (acronym for Tnuah Kibbutzit Me'uḥedet, the United Kibbutz Movement).
37. See A. Fishman, "Judaism and modernization: the case of the religious kibbutzim," *Social Forces* 62:1 (September 1983), pp. 9–31. The remainder of this chapter draws largely upon this article.
38. See H. Barkai, *Growth Patterns of the Kibbutz Economy* (1977), p. 264.

39. Y. Goldschmidt, "Adherence to values and economic success: the case of the Israeli communes," Working Paper, Faculty of Business, McMaster University, Ontario, Canada (1990).
40. In the 1972 study referred to above, the economic performances of the "German" kibbutzim of the RKF and the Ihud were compared. There are eight such kibbutzim in each federation. The comparison was enhanced by the fact that the two groups are similar in age and number of members. The findings indicate that the economic performance of the RKF group was higher than that of the Ihud. For details, see Fishman (note 37 above), pp. 21–2.
41. E. S. Rosenthal, (no title) *Alonim*, Shvat 5702 (1942), p. 9.
42. From unpublished data that I received from Professor Goldschmidt.
43. D. Rappel, "It is not quantity that counts, but purpose," *Self-Imposed Austerity; Protocol of an RKF Seminar* (Hebrew) (1968), p. 55.
44. E. Ya'ir, "The demand to restrain consumption" (Hebrew), *ibid.*, p. 51.
45. M. Ben-Tzvi, "Rabbis should be found for the young kibbutzim," *The Individual and the Public in the Religious Life of the Kibbutz; Protocol of an RKF Seminar* (Hebrew) (1970), p. 72.
46. Y. Levin, "The crown of the duty roster", *ibid.*, p. 90.

8. BETWEEN HETERONOMOUS AND AUTONOMOUS AUTHORITY

1. D. Knohl, "Speaking frankly" (Hebrew), *Netivah*, Adar-Nisan, 5707 (1947), p. 4.
2. E. Rosenblueth, "The path of religious youth in the Land," in *In the Paths of Youth* (Hebrew), ed. G. Ḥanokh (1938), p. 80.
3. In June 1948, when the ha-Po'el ha-Mizraḥi representative in the provisional socialist-centered government resigned over the Israel army's sinking of the right-wing sponsored, arms-carrying *Altalena*, the RKF, "regarding itself part of the working–pioneering camp in the state of Israel," issued a statement deploring the resignation. See *Yedi'ot Ha-Kibbutz Ha-Dati* 49, Menahem-Av 5708 (1948), p. 4.
4. The tension engendered by allegiance to the two conflicting reference-groups was well expressed in 1951, when the Religious Zionist parties joined hands with the non-Zionist religious parties in a "Religious Front" toward elections to the Second Knesset: "We wanted to see in our religious communal society not a random combination of elements that stem from contradicting sources, but we have to admit that we have not always been successful in this synthesis. We often swing from one position to another. We draw near the socialist camp, whose outlook is secular and even anti-religious, and on the other hand, we are tied politically to the 'Religious Front' that even speaks in our name. We are left forlorn and bewildered between these two camps...

We do not want to become a small degenerate sect." Y. Tzur, "On the fifth anniversary" (Hebrew), *Yedi'ot Ha-Kibbutz Ha-Dati* 62, 15 Adar I 5711 (1951), p. 5.

5. *Drawing Hearts to Torah and Mitzvot; Protocol of an RKF Seminar* (Hebrew) (1967), p. 5.
6. Cf. Tractate *Berakhot* 97a: "Even the empty-headed of Israel are as full of *mitzvot* as a pomegranate."
7. M. Unna, *A Proposal for the Party Program* (Hebrew) (1952), pp. 5–9.
8. See G. Schiff, *Tradition and Politics: the Religious Parties of Israel* (1977), p. 56.
9. An exchange of views regarding the participation of Orthodox kibbutzim in a regional Hanukka celebration held in a secular kibbutz that raised pigs illuminates the ambiguous position of the RKF toward the secular kibbutzim. A member of a religious kibbutz writes in the RKF organ: "If we have reached the sad situation whereby all the good relations with our [secular kibbutz] neighbors did not prevent them from turning our valley into a pre-eminent region for raising that impure animal, we must ask ourselves again: What is the limit to the price that we have to pay for good relations?" In reply, the editor of the periodical writes: "Our fundamental approach is to welcome joyfully the opportunity to meet with our neighbors... Unfortunately, there are Jews who raise pigs and violate the Sabbath, but they are still Jews! ... Only when we meet as brothers can our neighbors feel how proper are our ways." S. Samson, "How shall we celebrate?" (Hebrew), *Amudim* 152, Adar I 5719 (1959), pp. 6–8.
10. M. Shilo'aḥ, "Religion and tradition in the kibbutz" (Hebrew), *Amudim* 134, Elul 5717 (1957), pp. 16–17.
11. The structure of rabbinical authority is more complex, since this authority draws upon the other two elements that relate to Sinai: *halakhah*, and the Jewish people. On rabbinic authority in relation to these elements, see J. Katz, *Tradition and Crisis* (1958), pp. 86–90, 171.
12. M. Unna, "Kibbutz society and its law" (Hebrew), *Alonim* 30, Shvat 5707 (1947), p. 5.
13. The gap that existed in Eretz Israel between a considerable part of Orthodox Jewry and the institutions of the national community, at least in the 1920s and 1930s, is manifest in a statement of a kibbutz member of East European birth upon the occasion of the twenty-fifth anniversary of ha-Po'el ha-Mizraḥi: "How great is the accomplishment! The curse of 'ne'er-do-well' and the stigma of inaction has been removed from us; the feeling of inferiority and shame, the habit of walking on the sidelines, hesitation and lack of confidence in our practical ability, no longer exist. Instead, we have demonstrated that we are able to educate and create a type of a religious sportsman, a religious pioneer, a religious worker, a religious scientist, and a religious soldier." Knohl (note 1 above).

14. See, for example, the remarks of a leading member of ha-Po'el ha-Mizraḥi's *moshav* (small-holder co-operative) movement in 1936, regarding Kibbutz Rodges' refusal to hire a Gentile to milk on the Sabbath: "The argument that taking an Arab [to do the milking on the Sabbath] is no solution for the future Jewish state smacks of Reform. In Germany, too, the reformers argued that ... the *mitzvot* interfere with life, and one must therefore shake them off." N. Gardi, "Milking on the Sabbath" (Hebrew), *Netivah*, 1 Iyar 5696 (1936), p. 2.
15. E. Goldman, "On a certain booklet" (Hebrew), *Alonim*, Nisan 5702 (1942), p. 14.
16. E. Goldman, "In light of current events" (Hebrew), *Yedi'ot Ha-Kibbutz Ha-Dati* 91, Av 5713 (1953), p. 2.
17. M. Unna, "Settlement in blocs in theory and practice" (Hebrew), *Alonim* 33, Av-Elul 5707 (1947), p. 9.
18. M. Unna, "On the spiritual problems of the state" (Hebrew), *Alonim* 39, Kislev-Tevet 5710 (1950), p. 42.
19. Me'ir Or, "The Religious Kibbutz Federation Council in Yavne" (Hebrew), *Alonim* 38, Iyar-Sivan 5709 (1949), p. 2.
20. S. Friedman, *Protocol of the Meeting of the Central Religious Committee*, December 12 1946, p. 2. Located in the Central Archives of the RKF in Kibbutz Yavne.
21. T. Admanit, "Walking between the raindrops" (Hebrew), *Amudim* 312, Kislev 5732 (1972), p. 113.
22. T. Ilan, "Creative hermeneutics" (Hebrew), *The 1975 [Kibbutz] Lavi Conference*, p. 77. This statement was made in retrospect.
23. T. Admanit, "Rebellion and Orthodoxy" (Hebrew), *Amudim* 116, Kislev 5716 (1955), p. 9; M. Or, "Modern agriculture and *halakhah*" (Hebrew), *Netivah*, Shvat 5711 (1951), p. 7.
24. "A public statement on behalf of the Religious Kibbutz Federation Secretariat regarding drafting women" (Hebrew), *Yedi'ot Ha-Kibbutz Ha-Dati* 63, 30 Adar I 5711 (1951), pp. 3–4.
25. S. Friedman, "The extension of the scope of *halakhah*," in A. Fishman, ed., *The Religious Kibbutz Movement* (1957), p. 50, footnote.
26. See S. N. Eisenstadt, *Israel Society* (1967), pp. 318–19.
27. "The editor's reply" (Hebrew), *Yedi'ot Ha-Kibbutz Ha-Dati* 100, Sivan 5714 (1954), p. 18.
28. For a discussion of the authority that resides in the Jewish people, in the sense of "divine power that the very body of Israel possesses," see Rav Tza'ir, *In the Gates of Zion* (Hebrew) (1937), p. 191.
29. On communal religious authority, see M. Elon, *The Principles of Jewish Law* (1975), pp. 80–1.
30. From the protocol of the Fifth RKF Council, 1951, located in the Central Archives of the RKF in Kibbutz Yavne. And in a later formulation: "At the beginning of our historic path, we adopted a conception that we called 'the spirit of the Torah,' and we took on a

position of rebellion against traditional rabbinical authority *vis-à-vis* several central and essential questions. We believed that there are extra-halakhic criteria that prescribe our Torah and halakhic understanding." T. Ilan (note 22 above), pp. 76–7.

31. Traditionally, only boys are formally confirmed, through the Bar Mitzvah ceremony that is held within the framework of the prayer service. The highlight of this ceremony is the boy's reciting the Torah benedictions when he is called up to the Torah reading. It is also customary for him to deliver a talk based on the Torah portion read that week.

32. Of the four members of the first Central Religious Committee that was formed in 1938, two were ordained rabbis. In the second committee, chosen in 1946, two, or possibly three, of the seven members were ordained.

33. An interesting analysis of the RKF's reluctance to accept rabbinical spiritual leaders was published in the bulletin of the Office of the Chief Ashkenazi Rabbi in 1947. After extolling the RKF members for their sacrifice in overcoming the difficulties that religious pioneering involves, "Rabbi Y. Bar-Yo'el" (apparently a pseudonym of the Chief Rabbi himself, Isaac Herzog) finds it strange that this youth neglects such an important component of religious community life as a rabbi. He pins the blame mostly on the egalitarian premises of kibbutz life, and adds: "They need a rabbi to perform specific religious functions such as marriages and to [answer questions about] *kashrut*, but they are unwilling to accept a rabbi as a shepherd and as one who fashions the religious image [of the community]. Many kibbutz members also regard him as an unproductive individual." *Tzror Yedi'ot*, Elul 5707 (1947). When reprinted in the RKF organ, *Alonim*, this piece was followed by the editor's rebuttal. He denies that the religious kibbutzim are interested only in rabbinical functionaries and that they disqualify rabbis because they are unproductive. On the contrary, he states, the religious kibbutzim seek a "guide and teacher," but to fulfill such a role the rabbi must be "a partner in the [communal] endeavor..." See *Alonim* 34, Tishrei-Ḥeshvan 5708 (1947), pp. 29–30.

34. See the biographical sketch of Eliezer Shimshon Rosenthal in Appendix B.

35. A leading member of the RKF states in 1958: "Who will deny that the study of Torah precedes everything?... But there are times when it is incumbent upon the students and sages of Torah to go forth at the head of the people and to take upon themselves the burden of practice ... Let them not repeat the fatal error of the former generation, which left practice to non-religious youth and prevented *yeshiva* students from taking a direct, active part in the building endeavor." A. Herz, "This is not the way" (Hebrew), *Amudim* 143, Sivan 5718 (1958), p. 22.

36. See A. Fishman, "Ha-Kibbutz Ha-Dati," *Encyclopedia of Zionism* I (1971), p. 452.
37. S. Friedman (note 25 above), p. 49. The RKF's self-definition within the bounds of *halakhah* was pointedly demonstrated in 1952, when one of the movement's ideological leaders called for the abolition of the suspended *mitzvah* of sacrificing the first-born animal in the Temple. Arguing that in the formal accommodation of this *mitzvah* to the circumstances of a non-existing Temple – by the fictitious sale of the animal to a Gentile – even a minimal manifestation of the *mitzvah*'s symbolic meaning is lacking, he advocated substituting for the "sale" the recital of a specially composed prayer, "in memory of the *mitzvah*." This view, however, was emphatically rejected on the grounds that any rationale for the *mitzvah* is a matter of "religious speculation," which is extraneous to *halakhah*. See M. Or, "On the formal approach to the observance of the *mitzvot*" (Hebrew), *Yedi'ot Ha-Kibbutz Ha-Dati* 81 (August 1952), pp. 6–8, and the reply of E. Goldman, "Some remarks concerning the 'formal approach'" (Hebrew), *Yedi'ot Ha-Kibbutz Ha-Dati* 82 (September 1952), p. 7. See also the remarks of others who were close to the RKF that were published in *Yedi'ot Ha-Kibbutz Ha-Dati* 83 (October 1952).
38. Cf. the statement of Moshe Unna: "It is not the way of Judaism to create two types of people, rabbis and laymen ... The study of Torah is an obligation that falls upon all of Israel; it directly ties every member of the people to *halakhah*, even if one group is allowed to adjudicate and the other group is not allowed." M. Unna, "On the essence of the matter" (Hebrew), *Amudim* 155, Iyar 5719 (1959), p. 27.
39. S. Schechter, "On our religious condition" (Hebrew), *Alonim*, Shvat 5702 (1942), pp. 3–4.
40. S. Aptrot, "Opening address" (Hebrew), *Amudim* 159, Rosh ha-Shana 5720 (1959), p. 5.
41. E. S. Rosenthal, "Clarification summaries" (Hebrew), *Dappim* (Rodges), 22 Tammuz 5698 (1938), p. 5. The writer adds, "We have been influenced by many – I mention here only [Martin] Buber – who wanted to teach us that only the inner autonomous approval confirms the *mitzvot* ... instead of the singular revelation that came from above at Mount Sinai. According to that opinion, the sole ethos is the accentuation of man's self ... [However,] 'he who is commanded and observes a precept stands higher ...'" *ibid.*

Subject index

aggadah 12
Aggudat Israel 174 n.8
agricultural celebrations 99, 145
Altalena 189 n.3
Aryei, Kvutzat 80
authority, religious
  vested in
    Rabbinate 15, 118–19, 146
    single rabbi 132, 151
    community 151–2
  modes of
    charismatic 13, 23, 146
    see also Torah as primeval charisma
    traditional 12, 146

Bachad pioneering movement 72–6
  formation of 74
  ideology of 74–6
Bat Mitzvah 152
Balfour Declaration 56, 175 n.19
Betzenrod training farm 74
Bnei Akivah youth movement 78, 79
  founded by ha-Po'el dha-Mizrahi 62
Braunschweig, rabbinical synod in, 171 n.23
Brit ha-No'ar ha-Dati youth movement 74
Bund stage of kibbutz 88–9

charisma
  primeval mode of 10
    dialectical nature of 11
    in secular Zionism 18
    institutionalization 10
    in secular kibbutz 19
    sources of: *see* transcendent center; vital layers of reality; vital events
    see also rationalization; Torah as primeval charisma
  institutionalized mode of 10–11
    and tradition 11

    see also authority
charismatic community 152
Commune stage of kibbutz 89–91
  legitimation problem in religious kibbutz 91–3
cultural center 11
  Jewish Enlightenment as 17
  Zionism as 17
  see also Rabbinate, religious center; religious subcenters customs, as Torah 15
  Hirsch impugns validity of 37

daat Torah (opinion of Torah) 146, 151

Elected Assembly of Jewish national community 176 n.38
Emancipation, Jewish 16–17
  acclaimed by modern Orthodox movements 21–4, 36, 47–8
  in Eastern Europe 46, 56, 77
  in Germany 32
Enlightenment, Jewish 17
  in Germany 31–2
  in Eastern Europe 46, 48–9
existential–phenomenological method 6
Ezra youth movement 179 n.19

"full and complete life" ideal
  see universal identity

galut (exile), as perceived by
  Religious Kibbutz Movement 86, 95, 123, 181 n.3
Socialist Zionism 18
Torah va-Avodah 59, 60, 61
traditional society 15
Gemeinschaft
  in German Orthodox youth movements 72

basis for Torah renewal 74–5

halakhah 12
  determines ascendancy of past over present 26
  dynamics of 13, 53, 64–5, 116–19
  ethos of
    shared with that of science and socialism 101–9
    hard core of Judaism 24
    in systems of Mendelssohn and Hirsch 31, 34
  hermeneutics of 12, 41, 102–3, 117
  and history
    in Religious Kibbutz Movement's view 94–6
    lags behind new realities 134–6
    legal fictions in 123–4
    problems of, in national reality
      faced by Religious Zionism 52–3
      as experienced by religious kibbutzim
        involving the Sabbath 119, 129
        solutions to 124–7, 129–30
        involving agriculture 119
        solutions to 127–9
    rationalization of 122–30
      avenues for 130–3
      means and ends in 120–2
    restrains innovations 135
    served by technology 124
    see also metahalakhic principles
  halakhically-ordered community
    of religious kibbutz 96–9
    of Torah-im-Derekh Eretz 42
    of traditional society 14–15
    see also kehillah
Hassidism, influence on
  ha-Po'el ha-Mizrahi 55, 59, 64
  religious pioneering youth movements 73, 78
ḥidushei Torah (Torah innovations) 106, 118
Histadrut (General Federation of Labor) 57, 62, 144
history, approach towards, of
  Religious Zionism 57, 65–6
  Torah-im-Derekh Eretz 45
  Zionism 18
  see also halakhah
"holy rebellion"
  in ha-Po'el ha-Mizrahi 59–61
  in Religious Kibbutz Movement 87, 149

ideology
  in relation to religion 5–6, 20–7
  serves religion in religious kibbutz 97–9, 138–9
  see also religion; *mitzvot*; transcendent center

Jacob Herzog Center 159
Jewish people
  "pariah" state of, before Emancipation
    according to Hirsch 36, 40
    according to Weber 4
Jewish peoplehood
  supreme entity in secular Zionism 48–50
  religious value in Religious Zionism 18
Jewish society, traditional 14–15
Jewry, Orthodox
  East European 20, 46, 70–1
  in Eretz Israel 20, 54–5, 147
  German 20, 43–5, 70
  identity components of 146
Judaism
  Reform 17, 32, 33, 43
  Weber and Sombart on its modernizing capacity 3–4

Kabbalah, Lurianic 15–16, 48
kehillah (local religious community)
  embodies Jewish people 14, 42
  independent religious entity 14, 151–2
  see also halakhically-ordered community
kibbutz movement, secular 19, 144–5
  see also Religious Kibbutz Federation

Mafdal political party 159, 177 n.59
Marbek meat company 150
Meimad political party 152
messianic perspective, in
  traditional Jewish society 14
  Torah-im-Derekh Eretz 22, 45, 65
  Religious Zionism 22, 47–8, 65
  secular Zionism 18
metahalakhic principles 133–4
la-Mifne political faction 144
mitzvot 12
  ideological, in
    Religious Kibbutz Movement 91, 100, 116, 155
    Socialist Zionism 62
    Torah va-Avodah 58–64 *passim*
  non-institutionalized 51, 174 n.15
  see also halakhah
Mizrahi organization 53–4, 62
  Pioneer 78, 177 n.59
  Youth 74, 177 n.59, 179 n.19
  see women

Index

modernization, definition of 2

"Old Community" (of Eretz Israel) 54
Orthodox Jewry
  see Jewry

partnership of man with God 22
  in Religious Kibbutz Movement 108–9
  in Religious Zionism 47–8
  in Torah-im-Derekh Eretz 35, 41–2
pioneering movements, religious, in
  Eastern Europe 77–9
  Eretz Israel 79
  Germany 72–4
  "plausibility structure" 10
  in religious kibbutz 141
  ha-Po'el ha-Mizrahi 55–65, 147–8
    founding of 56–7
    "left wing" of 53
    as political party 62
    see also "holy rebellion"; Torah va-Avodah
  primary groups, new, in ha-Po'el ha-Mizrahi 57
  religious pioneering movements 70–2
"progress," ideology of, in
  liberalism and socialism 3
  Jewish Enlightenment and Zionism 17–18
  Torah-im-Derekh Eretz 41, 43
Protestantism, and modernization 2

Rabbinate, Orthodox
  enacts *halakhah* 118–19
  criticized by
    ha-Po'el ha-Mizrahi 65
    Religious Kibbutz Movement 149
  as a religious center 15
  traditionalistic 46, 54
    abides Torah-im-Derekh Eretz 44–5
    inimical to Zionism 50–1
  see also authority, traditional; *daat Torah*
rabbinical seminary, Orthodox (Berlin) 44
rationalization
  of charisma
    primeval 2, 81–3, 96–9
    institutionalized 100
  of life, in
    Protestantism 2
    secular kibbutz movement 19
    Torah-im-Derekh Eretz 40
    Religious Kibbutz Movement 111–12
  of religion, three modes of 5
    in ha-Po'el ha-Mizrahi 64
    in Protestantism 2

  in Religious Kibbutz Movement 104–9, 130–3
  see also rationalization of charisma
  in Torah-im-Derekh Eretz 41
  see also value-orientations
Reform Judaism see Judaism
religion,
  ascendent over ideology
    in Religious Kibbutz Movement 157
    in Torah va-Avodah 62
    in Torah-im-Derekh Eretz 43
  primacy of past over present 25–6
  and modernization 1–3
  rational, definition of 1
  ritual in 26
  see also ideology; transcendent center
religious consciousness 14, 24
  conservative component of, in
    traditional Jewish society 15
    Orthodox Jewry 146–7
    Religious Kibbutz Movement 156–7
  innovative component of
    see Torah as primeval charisma
religious kibbutz, legitimation of, in
  Bund stage 88
  Commune stage 96–9
Religious Kibbutz Federation
  celebrates May Day 144
  consolidation of 70–1
  challenges rabbinical authority 149–51
  charismatic religious experiences in 81–3
  criticizes religious political parties 147–8
  criticizes *Shulḥan Arukh* 147
  economic performance of 137–40
  educational principles of 113–14
  integrative mission of 142–3, 158–9
  and Orthodox Jewry 146–8, 155–6
  pragmatic approach to religious problems 135–6
  reference groups of 19–20, 141
  religious authority in 153–5
  religious–political ethic of 109–11
  and secular Zionism 143–5
  stand on "occupied territories" 159
  uniqueness among Orthodox
    modernizing movements 96–7, 135
  yeshivah of 158
  see also cultural center; *halakhah*;
    halakhically-ordered community;
    rationalization; salvation
religious subcenters
  kabbalistic groups 15–16
  Religious Kibbutz Movement 155–6
  Religious Zionism 54, 62
  Torah-im-Derekh Eretz 43–4

Religious Zionism 46–66
  as charismatic movement 48–9
  East European background of 46
  legitimation
    messianic perspective 47–8
    rational grounds 48–9
  uncohesiveness of ideological system 46
  see also cultural center; history; ha-Po'el ha-Mizraḥi Jewish peoplehood; Mizraḥi; partnership; solidarity; Torah; universal identity
Rodges
  training farm 74
  work camp and kibbutz 76–7

Sabbatean movement 15–16
sabbatical year 128, 174 n.13, 175 n.30
salvation
  in Bund stage 88
  in Commune stage 100
  world-rationalizing mode of, in
    biblical Judaism 4
    Protestantism 2
    Religious Kibbutz Movement 96–9, 104–9, 155
    secular kibbutz movement 19
    Torah-im-Derekh Eretz 39
Sanhedrin 53, 65, 149
San Remo Conference 56
science and technology
  conceived in religious terms, in
    Religious Kibbutz Movement 101–2, 107–8
    Torah-im-Derekh Eretz 40–1
  see also socialism
Shaḥal, Kvutzat 69, 79
ha-Shomer ha-Dati youth movement 78
Shulḥan Arukh (Code of Religious Law) 63, 147, 152
Sinaitic revelation,
  as charismatic event 13
  legitimates ideological values 25, 38, 63, 149
  and Orthodox Jewish identity 146
  recognizes historical change 84, 94–5
  as transcendent religious center 25, 157
shinuy (modification) 131–2
socialism, in
  secular kibbutz movement 19
  religious pioneering movements 70, 73, 76
  Religious Kibbutz Movement 101–12, 143–4
  see also halakhah, ethos of
solidarity, Jewish

religious, nature of 16
  in Religious Kibbutz Movement 142–3
  in Religious Zionism 49–50
  in Torah-im-Derekh Eretz 42

technology see science
Torah 11–13
  dialectical nature of 13
  "of God" and "of man" 32
  innovative potential of, in ideologies of
    Religious Kibbutz Movement 93–6
    Religious Zionism 50–2
    Torah-im-Derekh Eretz 37–9
  as institutionalized charisma
    in rabbinic role 15, 146
    in kehillah 14
    and rationalization in religious kibbutz 100
  "intention of," 14
    as social precepts 59, 64
    as pioneering reality 133
  meanings of 13–14
  as primeval charisma 12–13
    and institution building 61, 100
    in kabbalistic groups 15–16
    in Religious Kibbutz Movement 81–8
    in religious pioneering youth movements 71, 73, 78
    in Torah-im-Derekh Eretz 36–7
    in Torah va-Avodah 57–61
  written and oral modes of 12
  see also halakhah; mitzvot; ḥidushei Torah
"Torah scholar and pioneer" 112–13
Torah-im-Derekh Eretz 31–45
  its perception of Jewish mission 34–6
  as reaction to Reform Judaism 33–4
  relationship between its two components 37–9
  see also cultural center; halakhically-ordered community; messianic perspective; partnership; rationalization; religion; science; solidarity; Torah as primeval charisma; universal identity; value-orientations; women
Torah va-Avodah 57–61
  inspired by golden ages 57–9
  expresses original Hebrew socialism 58–9
  World Movement of 177 n.58
  see also ha-Po'el ha-Mizraḥi; "holy rebellion"; religion; Torah as primeval charisma
transcendent center of universe 9–10
  ideological 25
  religious 25

transformative capacities of cultures 3
  of Judaism 5

universal identity dimension, pursuit of, in
  Enlightenment and Zionism 17–18
  Religious Zionism 46, 50, 51
  Torah-im-Derekh Eretz 35–6, 37–9
  religious pioneering youth movements
    70–1, 75–6, 79

value-orientations
  of Hassidism, in
    ha-Po'el ha-Mizraḥi 64
  of halakhic Judaism, in
    Maimonides' system 102
    Religious Kibbutz Movement 104–7
    Torah-im-Derekh Eretz 40–1
  of Protestantism 2
  of secular kibbutz movement 19
vital events, charismatic 25, 36, 83, 85
vital layers of reality

historical 23, 52, 84
messianic 84
primordial 23, 38, 83

women
  status of, in
    ha-Po'el ha-Mizraḥi 61–2
    Religious Kibbutz Movement 152
    Torah-im-Derekh Eretz 43
  suffrage
    supported by Mizraḥi 55

yishuv (settlement of) *Eretz Israel* 51
  and halakhic adjudications 125–6, 133
Yom ha-Atzma'ut (Independence Day) 85–6,
    150–1

Zionism 17–18
  Socialist 18–19
  Religious *see* Religious Zionism

Index of names

(Figures in brackets indicate end numbers)

Abarbanel, Y. 181(9)
Abt, H. 179(19)
Admanit, T. 122, 178(5), 182(25), 186(36), 187(10), 191(21, 23)
Aḥad Ha-Am 168(34)
Aḥiman (Chmelnik), H. 81, 181(37), 182(18)
Aḥituv, S. 184(63)
Albo, J. 166(15)
Alkalai, Y.H., Rabbi 47, 175(18)
Altmann, A. 170(2)
Aminoʻaḥ, N. 178(1)
Aptrot, S. 193(40)
Aron, R. 166(15)
Aronson, S., Rabbi 129
Ascher, Y. 185(17)
Avineri, S. 173(4)
Avital, E. 187(18)
Azmon, Y. 165(10)

Baer, Y. 168(29)
Bar-Giora, N. 184(53, 62), 185(16)
Barkai, H. 169(39), 188(38)
Baron, S.W. 171(18)
Barth, A. 171(13), 172(35)
Barukhuni, S. 177(56)
Bassok, M. 168(38)
Bell, D. 169(42)
Bellah, R.N. 165(7, 10)
Ben-Aderet, S. 167(23)
Ben-Aharon, Y. 168(36)
Ben-Tzvi, M. 189(45)
Ben-Yitzhak, M. 185(15)
Berger, P.L. 10
Bergson, H. 167(19)
Berkman, R. 177(57)
Berlin, M., Rabbi 175(19)
Berman, Y., Rabbi 175(21)
Bernays, Y., Rabbi 33

Bernstein, Y. 177(45, 46, 54)
Biale, D. 168(28)
Bialik, Ḥ.N. 168(34)
Bolleh, M. 186(30)
Bombach, S. 179(120)
Brenner, Y.Ḥ. 168(36)
Breuer, M. 167(25), 171(23), 172(52), 173(57), 185(14)
Breuer, Y. 41
Buber, M. 167(19), 193(41)

Cahane, S.Z. 180(35)
Carlebach, J. 170(45), 173(56)
Churgin, P. 175(29)
Cohen, E. 183(33)
Cohen, Y. 185(12)

Davis, K. 133
Don-Yiḥye, E. 168(36)
Drachman, B. 170(11)
Drori, Y. 185(10)

Eisenstadt, S.N. 2–3, 11, 165(10), 181(1)
Eliade, M. 181(7), 182(12)
Elon, M. 166(9), 167(15, 17), 191(29)
Emmanuel, Y. 171(23)
Erikson, E. 169(44), 170(52)

Falk, Z. 167(25)
Feilchenfeld, A. 179(14), 181(8)
Feldman, S.B. 182(29)
Fishman, A. 172(47), 178(63), 182(23), 183(33), 188(36, 37), 193(36)
Fogel, D. 183(43)
Frank, T.P., Rabbi 130
Friedman, S. 149, 150, 187(3, 19), 188(26), 191(20, 25), 193(37)
Friedman, Y. 181(4)

200

Index

Gardi, N. 176(44), 191(14)
Geertz, C. 165(7), 169(44)
Gellman, L. 175(29)
Geshuri, M.S. 176(42)
Goldman, E. 99, 104, 147, 182(24), 184(60), 185(11), 187(12), 188(30), 191(15), 193(37)
Goldschmidt, Y. 138, 189(39)
Gordon, A.D. 168(36)
Gottlieb, E. 180(31)
Grodzensky, H.O., Rabbi 188(35)
Grodzhensky, B.Z. 179(9), 181(10)
Grunfeld, I. 170(1)
Gur-Aryei, Y. 173(50)
Gvaryahu, H. 182(20)

Haimowitz, S. 183(37)
Hanokh, G. 184(48)
Hayes, C.J.H. 166(15)
Hayisraeli, D. 187(18)
Heidegger, M. 166(16)
Heinemann, H.Y. 182(28), 187(24)
Heinemann, Y. 166(11), 170(6), 171(26)
Hertzberg, A. 173(4), 177(55)
Herz, A. 92, 182(13), 183(38), 188(32), 191(35)
Herzog, Y., Rabbi 192(33)
Hess, M. 172(47)
Hildesheimer, E., Rabbi 44, 171(13)
Hirsch, S.R. 31, 33–45 *passim*, 47, 56
Hirsch, W. 183(33)
Hoeffding, H. 166(1)
Hoselitz, B.F. 165(11)
Husserl, E. 166(16)

Ilan, T. 191(27), 192(30)
Imber, B. 178(6)

Jacobs, L. 166(10)
Jaffee, J., Rabbi 52
Japhet, S. 172(50)

Kali, Y. 183(44)
Kalischer, T.H., Rabbi 47, 48
Kalvary, M. 170(13)
Kaplan, M.A. 172(54)
Karni'el (Treller), S. 78, 84, 94, 183(46)
Katz, J. 167(21, 25), 168(30), 170(3), 173(4), 174(10)
Katzenelson, B. 168(36, 37)
Kirschbaum, M., Rabbi 129
Klausner, Y. 173(3)
Knohl, D. 180(31), 189(1), 190(13)
Kowalsky, Y.L., Rabbi 176(31)

Krone, M. 179(9), 180(35, 36), 173(30), 182(12, 15)
Kuk, A.Y., Rabbi 54, 55, 129, 184(57)
Kuk, Z.Y., Rabbi 188(25)

Landau, S.H. 55, 60, 61, 62, 177(47)
Landes, D.S. 165(11)
Landshut, Z. 168(37)
Laqueur, W.Z. 179(13)
Lash, S. 165(5)
Lavi, S. 178(60)
Leibowitz, Y. 72, 75, 167(18), 173(59), 179(11, 12)
Lev, Y. 6 178(5)
Levin, Y. 189(46)
Liberles, R. 171(20), 172(50)
Liebman, C. 168(36)
Livne, M. 187(14)
Loew, J., Rabbi 12
Luckman, T. 10
Lueschen, G. 183(34)
Lutvak, Y. 95, 181(5), 187(11)
Luz, E. 173(1)
Luz (Luzinsky), K. 19, 168(36)

McKinney, J.C. 166(16)
Maimon, Y.L., Rabbi 175(26)
Maimonides 102, 174(15), 186(30, 31)
Margalit, E. 168(35)
Me'iri, R. 182(17)
Mendelsohn, E. 176(31)
Mendelssohn, M. 31–2
Meyer, M. 170(9)
Mintz, M. Rabbi 167(25)
Mohlewer, S., Rabbi 51
Mommsen, W. 165(5)

Nahlon (Nusbecher), A. 87, 105, 181(3), 182(30), 185(8, 13, 18)
Nahmanides 173(15)
Nissenbaum, Y. Rabbi 175(21)
Nottingham, E. 167(24)

Or (Orlian), M. 85, 136, 182(12), 183(32), 185(19), 188(35), 191(19, 23), 193(37)

Palti'el, A. 184(57)
Parsons, T. 5, 21, 166(14), 186(41), 187(9)
Perlman, M. 182(23)
Pines, Y.M. 48, 174(12)

Rabinowitz, S.Y., Rabbi 173(2)
Rappel, D. 139, 183(40), 186(38), 189(43)
Rav Tza'ir 191(28)
Rashi 59, 167(17)

Raz, S. 182(21)
Reines, Y., Rabbi 49
Rosenbloom, N. 170(8)
Rosenblueth, P. 94, 180(25, 27), 184(48), 185(4, 20), 186(24) 189(2)
Rosenheim, J. 172(50)
Rosenthal, E.S. 103, 108, 130, 139, 166(1), 184(61), 185(12), 187(8), 192(34), 193(41)
Rotenstreich, N. 184(57)
Roth, G. 161(1)
Roth, L. 166(12)
Rothschild, A. 173(3)
Rothstein, A. 177(49)

Sachar, H.M. 173(2)
Samson, S. 190(9)
Schechter, S. 184(38), 185(21)
Scheinbach, M. 182(14)
Schiff, G. 190(8)
Schlesinger, Y. 187(13)
Schluchter, W. 165(1)
Schmalenbach, H. 183(34)
Scholem, G. 16, 166(13), 168(26), 170(5)
Schutz, A. 166(16)
Schweid, E. 168(34)
Shapiro, Y., Rabbi 63, 87, 176(33), 177(48)
Sharpe, E. 169(42)
Shiloʻaḥ (Slokhovoy), M. 145, 181(6)
Shils, E. 9, 169(48)
Shragai, S.Z. 51, 62, 65, 177(51, 60), 178(64)
Simon, E. 75, 112
Slutzky, Y.A. 175(19)
Sofer, M., Rabbi 169(47)
Soloveitchik, J.B., Rabbi 188(31)
Sombart, W. 4, 39

Stone, G.P. 183(34)
Surky, A. 188(25)
Swidler, A. 169(46), 184(54)

Talmon, Y. 169(39), 183(33)
Tillich, P. 70
Tiryakian, E.A. 166(16), 168(27)
Turner, V.W. 22, 171(20)
Twersky, I. 168(25)
Tzur, Y. 190(4)

Unna, G. 101, 107, 179(17), 184(61)
Unna, M. 91, 95, 96, 117, 143, 147, 148, 167(20), 179(16, 18), 183(39, 42), 184(50), 185(9), 196(31, 37), 187(25), 190(7, 12), 191(17, 18), 193(37)

Van der Leeuw, G. 170(53), 182(16)

Walk, Y. 179(19)
Wasserman, E., Rabbi 188(25)
Weber, M. 2, 3–4, 40, 109, 185(5)
Werblowsky, R.J.Z. 167(20), 170(49)
Wessely, H. 31–2
Whimster, S. 165(5)
Whitehead, A.N. 1, 81
Wiener, M. 165(3), 166(22)
Wilhelm, K. 169(41)
Wolfsberg, Y. 176(32)

Yaari, M. 18
Yaavetz, Z. 52, 53
Yaʻir, E. 140, 182(16), 185(6, 15), 186(40)
Yefet, Y. 180(35), 181(9), 184(47)
Yisrael, Y. 182(17)

Zolschan, G.K. 183(33)

SEP 1 1 1992